SO-BBC-604

DATE DUE

362.84 S   77752

Steeger, Henry.
AUTHOR
You can remake America.
TITLE

DATE LOANED	BORROWER'S NAME	DATE RETURNED
FEB 5 70	Mary Gueller	FEB 7 70

77752
Steeger

St. Procopius College Library
Maple Ave. and College Rd.
Lisle, Illinois

YOU CAN REMAKE AMERICA

You can REMAKE AMERICA

by Henry Steeger

Doubleday & Company, Inc.

Garden City, New York

To Shirley

362.84
S81y

Library of Congress Catalog Card Number 68–24833
Copyright © 1969 by Doubleday & Company, Inc.
All Rights Reserved
Printed in the United States of America

77752

Preface

I have written this book because I am an optimistic man and a hopeful one.

If I did not believe that the agony of our Negro citizens—which is the agony of our cities and our nation as well—can be and will be ended soon, I would not have written these pages.

If I did not believe that the voluntary action of individual Americans could speed this, I would not have bothered to set down these chapters.

And if I did not believe profoundly that there are tens of millions of my fellow citizens who are men of conscience and good will, men sufficiently concerned about the state of our society to do their best to bring about the American Dream, I would have used my time otherwise.

The business of America is not business, regardless of Calvin Coolidge's assertion. The business of this nation is fulfillment of the American Dream, to make this a land where each individual may find self-realization in freedom, dignity, and equality. We have made that Dream a reality for more people and for a greater proportion of our people than has any other nation in the history of the world. The exception, however, in such numbers as almost to make the Dream a mockery, is the American Negro.

Today the nation is gripped in a struggle to determine

whether the American Dream is available to Negroes as well as whites. The laws, the leaders, the teachers, the churches, economics, and simple justice say there is and that each Negro as well as each white is entitled to its privileges and fruits. Tradition, ignorance, superstition and fear, greed and emotion say *no*. Because it is right and because our survival as a nation depends on it, we must say *yes* in emphatic, unmistakable terms.

Negro Americans have, ever since the earliest days of the Republic, been telling us that the phrases "All men are created equal . . ." in the Declaration of Independence and "We the People . . ." in the Constitution include them. They have pointed to the soul-stirring revolutionary promises in those two documents and made their wholly justified claims to share them. The Negro has asserted these claims in different ways over the years—first in song, in prayer, in supplication, passively; then more actively, with writings, petitions, visitations to representatives of the power structure; then aggressively, through the demonstrations of the fifties and sixties; and now, with the gap between promise and practice, between whites and blacks widening rather than closing, the Negro has virtually shrieked in the last-resort outburst of the dispossessed, in riots in the cities.

Has he been heard? If greater police strength and repressive measures, the mobilization of instant-retaliatory and containing military power is the primary response, he has not. For, without fast, drastic, visible change, change that he actually experiences, this kind of response may be merely a prelude to genocide.

If we respond, as we must, honestly, sincerely, with emergency programs scaled to the needs and the people, this will indicate that we have heard. But these efforts will be nothing more than a stopgap and ultimately a waste if we do not go on, during the time purchased with the emergency measures, to launch and implement massive, prevasive programs that will truly bring down the "Walls of Jericho" that have sealed off our black citizens from their rightful places in our society.

I believe that individuals can and will play key roles in both the emergency responses and the even more demanding long-term programs that are called for now. I have seen what dedicated voluntary efforts by men—sometimes alone, others in small groups as well as in huge organizations—can do to revitalize people's lives. I have been fortunate enough to be closely associated with one group, the Urban League, that has pioneered in this vital field. It is because of the striking successes of the League and its enthusiastic staff and volunteers that I am confident that we will ultimately succeed.

Throughout more than half a century the League has steadily—and in recent years spectacularly—opened new vistas and achieved remarkably in advancing toward that eventual goal. It has spread to nearly a hundred cities, its methods have been widely adopted, its counsel has been sought and its results have been reassuring—but insufficient to the needs. This is not surprising, when even the federal government, with its exaggeratedly misnamed "War on Poverty" was insufficient to the needs.

But my experience with the League was extraordinary. It showed me that exceptional men and even ordinary men with exceptional strengths—dedication, determination, drive, articulateness, persuasiveness, and organizational ability—can literally move the world. These men and women, black and white, have done so. Others with the *will* to do so also can.

Oliver Wendell Holmes admonished: "A man should share the action and passion of his times at peril of being judged not to have lived." I endorse that wholeheartedly and submit that seldom in our history has there been such a compelling need for so many to share the central action of our times by participation.

Race relations today is not a spectator sport. It is an overriding concern. It affects us all vitally and requires and demands for our very national survival that we participate. It is the single most compelling business of this nation in a century. The assimilation of our Negro countrymen into the mainstream of American life has been deferred too long.

I have no single, sweeping program, no panacea for our current domestic troubles. Instead, I have some suggestions based on experience and observation of successful approaches to the problems that face us. Progress depends on people: you cannot computerize it. Only men of good will can make America live up to its finest ideals. It is my hope that concerned citizens will find in these pages examples that will help them to enlist in the effort and encouragement to do so *now*, while there is still time.

Acknowledgments

I owe to Lester J. Brooks a debt of gratitude for his essential involvement in the preparation of this book. He shouldered the major editorial responsibility with skill and unselfish determination to complete the task and he left no corner unexplored that might yield corroborative information.

And to Matthew J. Harris, my editor at Doubleday, the deepest appreciation and thanks for his almost unbelievable sensitivity to the racial situation. His suggestions and revisions pointed up and strengthened every aspect of the book.

Profound thanks go also to my associates at the National Urban League, both staff and Board, for the ideas generated during years of working together, as well as for reviewing the material in preparation.

Thanks also to Lester B. Granger, Whitney M. Young, Jr., Roy Wilkins, the late Martin Luther King, Jr., A. Philip Randolph, Edwin C. Berry, and a host of other great Civil Rights leaders who left deeply etched impressions, impossible to erase.

I'll be forever grateful to all the Executive Directors of the local Urban Leagues, who made my years as President and Board member of the League such a cherished experience.

And to my administrative assistant, Mrs. Lucile B. Tompkins, an orchid for all the typing, checking, and correcting.

Eternal thanks, of course, to my mother for her wisdom and wit, and to my wife, Shirley, who traveled all over the country with me in this work and who shared her remarkable and compassionate understanding of the myriad problems to be faced.

And to my children, Hal, Susi, and Nancy, my thanks for their constant cooperation. It was Nancy, together with Whitney Young's daughter Marcia, who conceived and started the Urban League Youth Community.

My thanks to the National Opinion Research Center, the Center for Urban Education, National Council of Churches, Opinion Research Corporation, National Committee Against Discrimination in Housing, Student Non-Violent Coordinating Committee, Southern Christian Leadership Conference, Congress of Racial Equality, National Council of Negro Women, Dr. John Morsell and his associates at the NAACP, the NAACP Legal Defense and Educational Fund, A. Philip Randolph Institute, for their cooperation and assistance in supplying material and suggestions for this book.

In addition, my good friends Ann E. Tanneyhill and Guichard Parris, of the National Urban League staff, were indispensable in gathering data and counseling about the manuscript. My warmest thanks are due them for their unstinting help.

Finally, thanks also for the contributions of my friends who gave me direct help: Mrs. Enid C. Baird, Nelson C. Jackson, Alexander J. Allen, William B. Harper, Sidney J. Harper, Dr. Jerome H. Holland, Dr. Rembert E. Stokes, John H. Johnson, Lindsley F. Kimball, Theodore W. Kheel, William R. Simms, Julius A. Thomas, Mahlon T. Puryear, Lloyd K. Garrison, Ivan C. McLeod, Ramon S. Scruggs, Daniel Davis, James R. Dumpson, and many others, Negro and white, dedicated to racial justice.

Contents

Introduction

Some years back, white citizens who styled themselves "liberal" were very smug and secure about racial problems. They were confident that progress was being made rapidly and that whites and blacks could march to Washington (as in 1963) and get laws allowing Negroes to eat at Southern lunch counters.

They made sure that each party they gave had at least one Negro, and they would talk far into the night about how awful the South was. They wrote occasional letters to newspapers and sent off small checks to civil rights organizations.

Each morning they looked into the mirror and silently thought that every day in every way, things were getting better.

But in the ghettos of America, often in homes a few blocks away from the complacent liberals, black men were angry about how things were getting worse—intolerably worse.

When the riots hit—in Watts, in Harlem, in Chicago, in a hundred cities since—white America was shocked out of its complacency and was forced to confront the deep divisions of our society. The problem was finally seen to be national, not regional. The relentless exploitation of the ghetto poor was at last seen to be taking place in the great liberal centers of the North, and not just in the backwoods counties of the South.

What the South was doing openly and brutally, the North

had been doing secretively and with subtlety. Those explosions were inevitable and when they came they should have surprised no one.

I tried to warn the nation before they hit. I pointed out that the poverty and unemployment of the ghetto were caused by discrimination; that Negroes lived in inferior, segregated housing, and that their children were being miseducated and pushed out of school by an unresponsive educational establishment.

And when, in those golden, complacent days of civil rights "victories," the National Urban League issued a call for adoption of a Domestic Marshall Plan, it evoked little response. People still thought that the right to eat at a lunch counter was what civil rights was all about.

But it is not. It is about the right all people have to achieve equally in life. It's about decent housing, good jobs, and quality education for all. It's about mobilizing the power of the poor so that the people of the ghetto are fully included in our society and in all of the benefits of the richest nation in the world's history.

That Domestic Marshall Plan was a blueprint to achieve those goals. It proposed that we do for America's poor what we so willingly did for our allies—and enemies—after World War II. Only such a massive, total approach can win the day.

Had the country listened to us in 1963, we would have been spared the crisis in which we now find ourselves. The Domestic Marshall Plan is still valid now, but a new element must be added to it.

That is the systematic eradication of white racism and white prejudice which is at the root of our problems. It took the Report of the National Advisory Commission on Civil Disorders to put the official stamp of approval on what Negroes have known for four hundred years. It was this commission, made up of respectable conservative or moderate individuals, who said that we are indeed a racist society.

The responsibility for ending this racism must lie with white citizens. Whites have always looked to Negroes for leadership in civil rights. Now they will have to supply that leadership themselves, for only white citizens can effectively counter the racism that is rending our society. The source of the problem lies in the white community, and that community will have to show that it has the moral stamina to cure itself.

White citizens must show that they don't have to ride on the moral coattails of Negroes. They will have to demonstrate to the three-fourths of the world which is nonwhite that they can eradicate the racism which oppresses Negroes and other minorities. And they will have to show that they will no longer allow the bigots and the backlashers, the Birchers and the Klan, to speak for them.

Changing attitudes is a lot easier than most people think. The experiences of soldiers in Vietnam who fought together in integrated units, and the experiences of people in the sports world offer examples of how whites and blacks can live, work, fight, and play together.

A good start in combating racism would be to challenge the code language which has come into general usage. What, for example, does "crime in the streets" mean to the people who use it so often? Does it mean the brutal murder of Dr. Martin Luther King, Jr.? Does it mean the white-collar crime and embezzlement which cost this nation enough each year to house thousands of the homeless? Does it mean the white loan sharks and crime syndicate bosses and cheating store owners who prey on the poor? I'm afraid it has just become a code phrase for Negro demonstrations and, lately, riots.

What does "neighborhood schools" mean when it is used by people who like to boast about how they traveled miles to get an education and who now bus their kids to private schools? Does it really mean the school around the corner or is it a code phrase for "Keep Negroes out of our schools"?

Our society is shot through with such contradictions and subtle racism. It's time for white people themselves to stand up and be counted in the fight to make ours a truly open society.

White people own the industries, the land, and the houses in America. They reap the benefits of our way of life, and theirs are the rewards of this society. It is their future which is at stake, perhaps more than that of Negroes, who, after all, have the least to lose.

White Americans must start changing our society. They must begin by making a visible, tangible witness to their intentions. The silent masses, the complacent individuals, must stand up for what is right. The respectable, decent people must publicly put themselves on record as being committed to equality. They have been silent for far too long, and now they must speak up and make this system work for all Americans. Because if we don't make it work for everybody, it won't work for anybody. The very survival of our country is at stake here.

Henry Steeger is uniquely qualified to help white citizens understand the crisis we are in and to help to change things. He was President of the National Urban League when I became its Executive Director in 1961, and he has continued as a member of our Board of Trustees and as a valued volunteer advisor and worker. His concern for our country and his deep commitment to equality enable him to interpret our racial crisis and the means needed to resolve it.

WHITNEY M. YOUNG, JR.

New York, New York
May 1968

Chapter 1

Civil Catastrophe or Survival?

That chapter heading may sound like the title for a Doomsday sermon by a fire-and-brimstone circuit preacher. Actually, it seems to me an appropriate description of the alternatives that face the cities of our nation today. But because I am an incurable optimist and because I have personal experience of whites and Negroes working together successfully, for me there is no question of whether we shall survive. The question is in what manner?

Before me on my desk are stacks of clippings from newspapers and magazines, news releases and reports about riots—American riots. Here, on these dry, clean, tidy bits of paper are the words that tell of the most incendiary internal calamity this nation has experienced since the Civil War. In these clippings are the reports of shots fired by brother at brother, the sickening *thwack* of nightstick against skull, of blood spurting, looters skittering and screaming in the night as the rattle of gunfire chases men gone berserk. In the clippings are the consuming crackle of fire, the shouts of defiance and sobs of uncomprehending pain. They are all there—and much more—in the tiny, desiccated bits of black ink on white paper.

What do they really tell, these alarming, melancholy reports on what we might call Civil War II? As the penetrating report of the National Advisory Commission on Civil Disorders (the so-called U. S. Riot Panel) graphically proved, they tell us too much and yet too little. They give us messages from the "underclass" in the slum, messages that often arrive at the wrong addresses with wrong emphases and are interpreted with maddening inaccuracy.

In the first place, the news reports did not tell how many ghetto dwellers stayed out of the riots or tried to stop them or how they suffered. It should be clearly understood that the overwhelming majority of those who are trapped in the slums did not riot. Less than 10 per cent participated actively, though practically all of them suffered from the destruction and violence. Many innocent people were caught in the whiplash of outbursts of violence and responses of law enforcement troopers. The lives of these people were disrupted, their homes were shattered and their safety and health seriously menaced. To tar all of them with the same brush by including them in references to "rioters" would be compounding injustice.

Urban Suicide

Essentially, in the riots in the cities the dwellers have spoken in the symbolic language of the man who "attempts" suicide. He leaves hints around that he is despondent, that he sees no point in living; he even "tries" to kill himself in such ways that he can be saved. He may telephone someone after taking an overdose of sleeping pills, for example, knowing that the person is concerned about him and will respond by sending medical aid to rescue him before the pills are fatal. He may slash his wrists at home, knowing that he will be found, perhaps unconscious and weak but still alive, by other members of the family. There are numerous other techniques used by the would-be "suicide."

Note the similarities to the ghetto dwellers' actions in

rioting: the suicide and the slum citizen have told their families and their friends their misery. Convinced that they are getting no help or are being misunderstood, they act to make unmistakably clear their anguish and dramatize their despair. They deliberately choose ways to destroy themselves that offer opportunities for rescue, and, so doing, place responsibility on the rescuer for survival. They say, in effect, "I don't care whether I live. or die. It's up to you." If the rescuer does not act in time or for some reason fails to save the "suicide," the guilt and blood, from the standpoint of the person destroying himself, are on the rescuer's hands.

This is one interpretation of the outbursts in our ghettos. It is an overriding one, beyond the specifics of retaliation against gouging, exploiting merchants; releasing pent-up anger against police brutality; striking back at slumlords by destroying their property; self-assertion as evidence of manhood; and others less significant but nonetheless real to the slum dweller.

Ghetto rioting is an inarticulate shriek for help from the drowning who, perhaps unlike our "suicide" above, are incapable of helping themselves. Liken the slums to newly emerged, desperately poor nations filled with unsophisticated young people (two-thirds or more under thirty years of age), lacking job skills but having plenty of health, education, and housing problems.

In some ways the slums are even worse off: there are, in the new nations, jobs for the citizens in the civil service and the businesses owned by nationals. In the slums, only a meager fraction of the businesses are home-owned and they are very small operations ($29 billion was spent by Negroes in 1967; less than 3 per cent of it in "black" businesses); and civil service jobs require literacy and skills not commonly found among ghetto dwellers.

For many new nations their geographic location, if not their natural resources, makes them strategically important to other nations in the world, and causes them to attract investment or financial aid. In the slums, despite their strategic locations, until recently we have ignored them and the people in them, generally condemning both as beyond hope. With urban renewal this has changed in specific localities and to a limited degree. But the usual, rather than the unusual, attitude has been concern for the potentially valuable real estate rather than the divinely valuable human lives in the ghetto.

The slum dwellers, having no capital and no claim on any, are unlike the new nations. They are unlike those hit hardest in the Great Depression of the Thirties, except that unemployment is devastatingly high: up to 26 per cent in the Thirties and about 34 per cent today among ghetto Negroes. During the Depression, farmers could dump their milk instead of marketing it and they attacked others who tried to run their blockades and get to market to sell milk. They could kill their pigs rather than sell them to the slaughterhouses. They did so to push prices on farm commodities up to at least a break-even point. When banks foreclosed mortgages on farms, armed farmers went to the sheriff's sales and brandished their weapons. Often they bought their neighbor's farm for one dollar, then resold it to the dispossessed for the same amount. No one disputed these "legal transactions."

Today we have more slum dwellers than farmers—the figures are 22,000,000 to 21,000,000. But the farmer has a historic equity of major proportions in America and there are vast mechanisms, developed over the centuries, to serve him and look out for his interests. The slum citizens are, for the most part, without a foothold in the society. They have no milk or pork to hold off the market to force prices on their livelihood up to a livable level. They possess little or nothing in the way of marketable goods or skills to bargain with.

Those we have locked in the slums, unlike the citizens of the new nations, hold no equity in the natural resources of the crumbling, confined corners of the earth they inhabit. That is, they have no claims if you overlook their rights by endurance and suffering subhuman conditions. But they are in possession of the terrain, and possession, as military strategists know, is frequently nine-tenths of the battle. Realization of this is rapidly changing the relationship of the ghetto dwellers to the larger society, and most of all, to the elements of society who have a stake in the central cities, whether it is ownership of property there, or investment in manufacturing operations located in the cities, or retail or service businesses that depend on the tranquility of the urban cores for their prosperity.

Economic Warfare

We are in the early stages of economic warfare between the dispossessed of the ghetto and their overlords, the society that sentences and confines them to penal servitude in these infested, stinking prisons without walls. The riots are a central thrust of this warfare and are the "hot" element of it, as contrasted with the "cool" elements, such as peaceful demonstrations, marches and picketing.

Warfare of any sort is neither tidy nor pretty. The economic warfare of the Thirties waged by the industrial unions against management, particularly in the auto industry, was a classic example. The CIO brought into play the innovation of the sit-down strike. It had to. If it had continued to limit its approach to conventional picketing it would have been outflanked by management. The auto companies could easily hire additional skilled labor to work the machines. But when the CIO workers occupied the factories and struck, remaining at their machines, management was helpless so long as the courts sustained the strikers, which they did.

In today's ghetto, there is no similar recourse visible to

those penned within it. Industry's personnel managers are
seeking sophisticated knowledge and ability, not rudimentary
muscle skills—the kinds all too abundant in the ghetto. The
great muscle-using industries are construction and building,
mining and services. But the ghetto is generally barren of such
industries. Those who somehow have been fortunate enough
to find jobs in these are exceedingly few and have to travel out
of the ghetto to work. It is impractical and impossible for
these few to exert any leverage by the sit-down strike technique where they work.

The point is that the slum dwellers are at last exercising
economic warfare against the power structure. They are no
longer sunk despondently, passively, glazed by incomprehen-
sion and paralyzed by inertia. They have been galvanized
to action by the realization that others have it so much better
(the message of TV and the other media) and that their condition doesn't improve just by sitting there. On the contrary,
it deteriorates.

The economic punch the ghetto can deliver is largely determined not by the ghetto but by the power structure.
Commodities can be withheld by farmers; slum dwellers have
nothing comparable. Labor can withhold its skills and prevent
management from using the tools of production; the poor,
having few skills, do not have such options. What pressure
can they apply? They can make the ghetto such a costly
luxury that society will recoil and say "this must cease."
Through decades of passivity alone, with precious little conscious effort in this direction, slum dwellers have all but
"achieved" this. Still, despite shock and grandiose promises
from society, little change has been noted by the "man on the
curb" in the ghetto.

If passivity and the plain, clearly visible raw wound of
slum life are not enough to stir aggressive, effective effort to
change conditions there, what can? The man on the curb
seems to have concluded—blindly but accurately—that raising

the cost of the ghetto to an intolerable level is the only way to stir the white power structure to action. The method, as we have seen, is through violence, arson, looting, assault, and destruction.

We have not had race riots—Negroes have not struck out at whites as such (in fact, interracial cooperation has been a "feature" of some of the riots)—we have had *economic* riots. No longer are the ghetto dwellers willing to squat on the curb and passively accept society's Marie Antoinette response: "Let them eat cake." They have become aware that they can hit whites where it hurts—in the pocketbook—by destroying the ghetto.

Sure, it hurts the slum dwellers more than it hurts those on the outside. The people in the slums are made homeless and their clothes and possessions are destroyed, not those of people living comfortably and securely in the suburbs. But a riot communicates desperation. And in the spill-over of rioting into the business areas of the major cities the power structure feels a hand clutching at its throat. This above all it cannot tolerate. The destruction of the viable areas of the city and the disruption of business are the ultimate threats. To these, business, society, the power structure, even you and I, whatever our color, must react to survive.

Responsible Action

I should like to think that the reaction will be swift and effective, not in suppression and oppression, but in liberation. What is responsible action in our cities today? In them the past really imprisons the future. And as we sit trapped in them we often ignore the voices that could lead us out of their dangerous stagnation. Even where the handwriting on the wall is vivid, men of intelligence too often sit mesmerized, without acting on the fateful signs that spell catastrophe if unheeded. Let me give you a specific.

In the spring of 1964 the National Urban League sent its housing expert, Paget Alves, to the ghetto of Rochester, a progressive, prosperous northern city. He found that the Negro population had quadrupled in the years between 1950 and 1960, that it was well on the way to doubling again by 1970. He found the ghetto seething with resentment at the impossible housing, the incredible crowding, the festering filth they were forced to live in because confined to the slums. They were practically up in arms about severe unemployment, *de facto* segregation in the schools, inadequate health services, miserably low incomes, and relatively few job opportunities.

As a result of Alves' fact-finding visit, Whitney Young, Executive Director of the Urban League, devoted an article to the situation in his weekly column *"To Be Equal."* On May 23, 1964, he wrote:

In our "middle-size cities," the racial kettle is heating to a boil. While a small fraction of their white citizenry are outspoken for or against the rights of Negroes, the vast majority of white Americans remain silent.

It is time for them to speak up.

The column then told of Paget Alves' trip to examine conditions in this city, and called it "a once placid community now rumbling with anger and frustration over segregation."

Yet Rochester's white citizens look the other way. The officials who make policy in that community have failed to do their utmost to make Negroes partners in shaping the destiny of their city.

However, unless they act, Rochester could become a small-scale Birmingham. So could Dayton, so could a hundred other sleeping cities.

Then Whitney Young gave a checklist of specific actions that could forestall trouble and hasten progress:

Make certain that independent-minded Negroes are appointed to all boards and public bodies.

The "power structure" of the community—the business, clergy, professional and civic leaders—must be mobilized in behalf of equal opportunities for Negroes.

Businessmen have an obligation not only to practice fair hiring, but to distribute scholarships to deserving Negro youngsters and to aid them through work-study programs.

Schools should be integrated; children must be brought up to prescribed levels of national scholastic performance.

Ghettos have to go. Public opinion must be mobilized in behalf of fair housing laws and realtors who discriminate must be brought to heel.

Housing needs of Negro poor must be met with public housing on integrated scatter sites throughout the metropolitan area. Human relations councils must be organized in suburbs to facilitate no-fuss integration of Negro families; and white home-sellers and Negro home-buyers must be brought together.

A vigorous war against poverty must be waged: training programs for unemployed; literacy programs; integrated hospitals and clinics, especially decent, comprehensive prenatal care.

Middle-size cities need some form of machinery, like the Urban League, to help open clogged channels of communications between the races and to aid Negro citizens to obtain their rights in housing, employment, labor unions, health and welfare programs and education.

"Many a middle-sized Rochester sleeps today," the Urban League executive concluded. "We must not allow them to become the Birminghams of tomorrow."

Now this, it seems to me, was an excellent example of speaking out responsibility with constructive suggestions to change a dangerous situation. As we all know, to our sorrow, the citizens who could effect these changes did not act swiftly enough, and Rochester's ghetto exploded exactly two months later.

Whitney Young's timely warning to Rochester and other middle-sized cities was in the pattern of his earlier action in developing and enunciating the League's call for a domestic Marshall Plan, to give Negro citizens a fair chance to achieve equality.

Have we learned from the warning of the riots? I should like to believe so, but the evidence is not reassuring. At the height of the riots, reported the New York *Times*, Buffalo's mayor went into the ghetto and promised to try to find thirty to thirty-five hundred jobs for Negro youths. The Chamber of Commerce agreed to manage the effort. However, only about four hundred jobs were forthcoming from local industry and all of them were temporary, summer jobs. The chairman of Buffalo's city planning board declared: "It is not and cannot be the responsibility of local government, business or industry to provide unnecessary jobs for unqualified people at any wage."

I believe that following the lead of this learned gentleman will only aggravate our problems and bring us new crises. He is not responsive to the threats or the magnitude of the needs. He uses the two reservations "unnecessary" and "unqualified." What he—and Buffalo—fail to see is that responsible action to prevent future outbreaks *must* include understanding that *jobs are necessary* and that the "unqualified" must be helped to qualify for them—in a hurry. This is just one example, but I fear that it is, unfortunately, all too typical.

Well, what must be done? The list of particulars is so long as to be virtually a reordering of American life (as the

"Riot Panel" report recommends, citing chapter and verse). In general, we must commit vastly more of our treasure to revolutionizing the lives and livelihood of our slum citizens. We must face the necessity of investing billions per year in this "inner space race" or, when we do put a man on the moon in our "outer space race," he may decide it's wiser to stay there than return to strife-torn America. There are many plausible suggestions for allocating the money required. The League's domestic Marshall Plan and its Operation Urban Survival are but two (discussed in later chapters).

Most such comprehensive plans agree that planning and cooperation between industry and government at all levels are absolutely imperative.

My own concern is that individuals, through their voluntary efforts, take the initiative now to move ahead in their communities. Grandiose schemes are notoriously difficult and slow to get off the ground. This is even more true when government is involved at various levels or when committees of businessmen are divvying up responsibility and organizing some nonprofit venture. Because the urgent need is for *immediate* action, this book is aimed at men and women of good will who are concerned about their nation, their heirs and their fellow men, people who are willing to make an effort today to insure a viable tomorrow.

In the pages that follow are suggested many ways that individuals acting on their own initiative or through established organizations may move their communities. If they cannot contribute time and effort, perhaps they can contribute money to agencies that work in the ghetto with the people who need help. I think automatically of the NAACP, the NAACP Legal Defense and Educational Fund, SCLC, CORE, the YWCA, Salvation Army, Urban League, and many others.

Because of my own close association with the League as

national trustee, committee member and president, I know best its virtuosity and drive, its effectiveness and startling results on minimum investment. The catalog of local Urban League efforts just in the summer of 1967 would be voluminous, but a few highlights will give an idea of its activities and its outreach to meet citizen needs. Here are briefs on what local Leagues accomplished in their cities:

WASHINGTON, D.C., *special summer employment effort placed 189 students in local retail and business positions . . . 70 trainees in a local department store chain . . . 41 young women in pre-vocational, remedial clerical program . . . 23 young men (some with police records) placed as street workers . . . "Future for Jimmy" program tutored 500 youngsters.*

WESTCHESTER, NEW YORK, *recruited 490 unskilled youths for job training . . . they received $60 weekly with higher pay later in factory, garage, and office jobs.*

HARTFORD, CONNECTICUT, *placed 200 teenagers from poverty areas in jobs as receptionists, office workers, machine operators, etc., with 60 local firms.*

PHILADELPHIA, PENNSYLVANIA, *trained 2500 hard-core unemployed.*

PEORIA, ILLINOIS, *placed 220 youths in jobs with nonprofit agencies.*

BATTLE CREEK, MICHIGAN, *helped develop Summer Youth Opportunity Program; drew up blueprint for "crisis intervention program" for street workers.*

CANTON, OHIO, *opened urban renewal social service center to solve relocation problems . . . with community leaders located 500 jobs for ghetto youths . . . expanded recreational facilities drawing 25,000.*

CINCINNATI, OHIO, *reached youths who rioted, placed more than 100 in special summer jobs . . . registered 300 for full-time jobs in joint community project.*

COLUMBUS, OHIO, *worked with employers, opened up 500 summer and part-time jobs during school year plus special "outreach" program that placed 100 more in full-time jobs . . . sparked project to improve police-community relations and set up "teen centers."*

FLINT, MICHIGAN, *nailed down commitments for 200 jobs after riots there; companies that had previously turned down League requests for on-the-job training spots began placing "orders."*

PONTIAC, MICHIGAN, *located summer jobs for 84 youths . . . organized community to demand changes in housing and welfare.*

WARREN, OHIO, *got jobs for 83 youths . . . opened up school swimming pools.*

CHICAGO, ILLINOIS, (*like other Leagues*) *intensified its "Operation Truth" activity, tracking down dangerous rumors, working with police and media in handling of tense situations . . . placed several hundred young people in jobs.*

ATLANTA, GEORGIA, *ran special summer cultural and recreational program for 500 youngsters . . . placed 300 people in on-the-job training . . . operated a family life program for 120 families.*

BIRMINGHAM, ALABAMA, *placed over 200 in jobs.*

NEW ORLEANS, LOUISIANA, *reached more than 2000 in on-the-job training programs.*

OKLAHOMA CITY, OKLAHOMA, *placed 800 young adults in summer jobs and training in special projects.*

TULSA, OKLAHOMA, *reached over 2500 with job placement programs.*

ELKHART, INDIANA, *found jobs for 50 youths.*

GARY, INDIANA, *placed more than 400 young adults in jobs or training situations.*

LOS ANGELES, CALIFORNIA, *recruited several hundred youths for jobs, including 100 to work in city government . . . brought 4000 youngsters into a summer camp program.*

PHOENIX, ARIZONA, *found 193 jobs for out of work young adults.*

ALBANY, NEW YORK, *helped form volunteer patrol of local citizens after rioting broke out . . . patrol was important in ending riots which stymied police.*

This sampling will give you some idea why I am so keen on the League and its achievements. But perhaps more than these citations you will appreciate this quotation that, to my mind, is a superb accolade. A Black Power leader in Dayton, Ohio, speaking to a public meeting said, "I can't give the League hell any more because it got fifteen jobs for my boys."

Riot Prevention

The chief way to prevent riots is for public and private sectors of American life to wipe out the prime riot causes—the miserably inadequate education, rotten housing, fumbling health and welfare services, unemployment and squalor that breed the philosophy "what have we got to lose?"

Corollary to this is proof of change. Those condemned to the ghetto must *see* evidence of change, must *experience* change for the better, or their attitude will continue to be contempt for society and themselves. Even today, Watts is still a backwater, though it has improved from the pre-riot time when it had 34 per cent unemployment, no movie theater, no hospital or ambulance service (babies actually died because they couldn't be rushed to hospitals in time), frustrating public transportation that was slow and inconvenient, expensive, and time-consuming for those lucky enough to have work.

The League has drafted a policy paper concerning riots. It breaks down into two sections—before a riot, i.e., prevention; after an outbreak, i.e., dampening and ending it.

Some of the prevention activities recommended include:

1. Identify conflict situations that could explode.
2. Draw up a schedule of specifics which public officials have power to grant immediately, actions that could mean tangible, feasible relief of slum grievances.
3. Maintain contact and communication with conservative as well as militant groups in the Negro community and particularly their leaders. Develop plans of collaboration to bring about important, widely recognized gains. Develop coordinated, concerted action capacity within and including all segments of the Negro community. Since each League includes on its board and committees white citizens who are influential in various segments of the larger community, it goes without saying that there will be continual Negro-white communication.
4. Spot and point out to all portions of the community the problems that will produce conflict if not resolved. Pinpoint direct and meaningful programming to reduce or eliminate these problems.

If a riot does break out, the League suggests the following:

1. Try to keep up communications between rioters and officials that will lead to negotiations.
2. Encourage city officials to go on "gripe tours" of the area so

that people can spill their grievances to men who can do something about them.

3. Police restraint is mandatory. The police must be encouraged to act firmly, but there is no place and this is no time for indiscriminate shooting, manhandling, false arrests, blasting people with firehoses, or any action that will increase sympathy for rioters.

4. "Peace teams" or patrols may be useful. However, there are definite limitations to their effectiveness and certain ground rules apply. For instance, the patrol should consist of people from the area, not whites or middle-class Negroes who live elsewhere. Rioters should be addressed as individuals, not as groups. Identify gang leaders of the riot; help them document and articulate specific grievances. Use all possible communication; do not insult nor offend rioters; try to see their gripes as legitimate and bring forth assurances that something will be done about them. Focus on self-defeating and destructive results of the riots, using residents of the area to make such statements. (One point stressed is "try to dominate the news with all the peace efforts being made rather than the killings, lootings, and burnings.")

5. The League details how a "coordinating headquarters" may be set up in the riot area to keep on top of the situation . . . everything from training staff and volunteers to use of bullhorns (to direct autos out of the area, to warn mothers and children to leave when shooting breaks out and/or to stay away from windows, doors, streets) to arranging food distribution. First-aid teams have to be organized, volunteers are needed for the hospital (if any) or dispensary, which immediately becomes jammed; legal teams are needed to protect the rights of those arrested and help in unraveling the legal problems after the riot. Emergency housing is a necessity, and a team to locate it is mandatory. Perhaps of lasting significance may be the effort to monitor the police, national guard, or other troops. Suggestions on this include a complaint form which can be made out by aggrieved citizens; volunteers to receive these; patrols to tour the riot area and photograph riot action to document mistreatment—

or help—by troopers; technical writers are needed to outline a domestic Marshall Plan for the area, scaled to get at the roots of the housing, education, training, health, welfare, and job shortcomings and to work up a plan to redevelop the riot-torn locations.

A National Urban League education department staff man prepared this working paper after close observation of riot conditions in several cities. He dressed "down" for his research, wore casual clothes, and mingled with street crowds in the Negro community. He checked closely with local League staff members in these cities and formulated the checklist above after difficult, dangerous, and detailed study, sifting, analysis, and counterchecking.

I believe it is a valuable set of guidelines for general use in our troubled cities. But even more, I believe it indicates the kind of professionalism that the League carries into the communities where it exists and serves to show why this agency is so necessary. You can understand why I urge people to pitch in and help such organizations as the League with all their might. Ways and means of doing so will be found in the chapters that follow.

Dignity of Man

The President's Budget Message to Congress in the crucial riot-ripped year of 1967 contained as one of its three main elements this introductory statement: "In our urgent domestic programs (for fiscal 1968) we will continue to press ahead, at a controlled and reasoned pace."

This "reasoned pace" turned out, in practice, to mean a slowdown in the antipoverty commitment. This fileting of the poverty program encouraged Congress to cut it still further. To an underclass led to believe, by the shrill publicity about a "War on Poverty," that emergency aid was on the way, it appeared that the rescue ship was running out of steam in the doldrums and would never make it to shore. This disillusionment undoubtedly contributed to the despair that erupted in the summer of 1967 in dozens of American cities.

As this is written, the insurance industry, in a widely trumpeted joint pledge, has said it would put up $1 billion to help finance ghetto rebuilding and renovation. The national business community's topmost leaders have met several times (with national TV coverage) and proclaimed an "Urban Coalition" to cope with the problems of the cities. This intensely reported series of conferences has yet to bear fruit, though it holds great promise. Promises, of course, are fine. But you can't live on them forever. It is to be hoped that the insurance industry and the Urban Coalition will not travel paths parallel to the federal slowdown, with similar disappointing, perhaps disastrous, results.

Still, let us suppose the maximum results are achieved by all-out effort on the part of government, industry, and private individuals and agencies. We may rebuild the physical, external aspects of the ghetto into fine examples of the most advanced twentieth-century architecture and still fail. We may place slum children in the finest educational facilities and still fall short. We may make available the latest health and welfare aids and find we've missed the mark.

I do not mean that we should hold up on any of the absolutely indispensable efforts noted above. Far from it. They should be rushed through under forced draft. I would, however, like to enter a plea that we not lose sight in these efforts of a fundamental component: human dignity.

In the case of our Negro citizens, particularly younger ones, this means incorporating in all our efforts the materials, attitudes, and treatment that will instill a positive sense of identity and self-esteem. For should we fail to do so, we may lose all. I agree with Dr. Kenneth B. Clark, the internationally known psychologist:

Probably the most difficult, nonrational manifestation of the new quest of Negro youth for an assertive and positive racial identity is to be found in the recent epidemic of riots or rebellions in Northern and some Southern urban ghettos . . . Beneath the random and clearly destructive and irrational behavior, there remains the pathetic logic of asserting self-esteem and searching for a positive identity by exposing oneself to danger and even inviting death. This is the quest for self-esteem of the truly desperate human being. This is the way those who have absolutely nothing to lose seek death. If this interpretation has any validity, all attempts at riot control in urban ghettos—running the gamut from antipoverty programs through more systematic and coercive police and militia action—will fail unless they have built within them the basis for the development of a positive self-esteem in Negro youth.[1]

I believe Dr. Clark's interpretation has great validity and I urge you who read this to keep it in mind when dealing with Negro fellow citizens in whatever way. To ignore it is to invite failure, a failure too costly to contemplate, too inhuman to countenance.

[1] Kenneth B. Clark, "The Search for Identity," in *Ebony* magazine, August 1967.

Chapter 2

Speak Out!

Men of good will and compassion need courage today. They need it to make the decisions and take action to bring about equality. They need guts and determination to create the climate where such action is possible.

For this, integrity that will not yield is necessary. In his *Profiles in Courage*, John Kennedy wisely observed "The courage of life is often a less dramatic spectacle than the courage of a final moment; but it is no less than a magnificent mixture of triumph and tragedy. A man does what he must— in spite of personal consequences, in spite of obstacles and dangers and pressures—and that is the basis of all human morality."

To see what we must do and *do* what we must is the true challenge. And seldom have right, justice, and morality been so clear-cut as they are in the case of our Negro fellow citizens. In our everyday lives each of us can help advance the Negro drive for equality. We have an inescapable responsibility to act and act positively. We need to speak up, to stand up and be counted in favor of civil rights. It is one of the painful paradoxes of our time that to uphold and defend the principles upon which America was established requires personal courage of a high order in these United States.

We have seen the advocates of equal opportunity and

status quo contend in city after city, north and south, east and west.

We have lived through the ordeal of Birmingham, the siege of Selma, the pain of Bogalusa. These and so many other confrontations have given proof of the intransigence and willful denial of rights by men in power in some of our cities. In many other cities the deprivation has been nearly as severe even if unplanned or unconscious. It has caused the Negro poor to strike out in ghetto uprisings in every section of the nation, from Boston to Watts, from St. Augustine and Atlanta to Omaha and even Seaside, Oregon, and all too many others.

We have had the nation's highest court, its chief executive and its highest lawmaking body put on the lawbooks one after another of the basic statutes on which a society of equal rights can be built. We have seen white Americans awaken at last to the inexcusable injustice of our treatment of colored Americans.

In this final third of the twentieth century there is only one way for Americans to prevent another full generation of civil strife, urban upheaval, and social turmoil. It is by recognizing that the contending forces are struggling over the central issues of American life and that each of us is a participant in that struggle. There is no such thing as non-involvement in this contest: it is as inescapable as the pollution in the air we breathe and the water we drink, the inadequacy of the streets we travel, the incidence of disease, the toll of crime and the bite of taxes.

As participants in the American experience each of us can and should play a positive role. We should have learned this much from recent history. And in spite of what some see as disinterest in civil rights at this point, I believe that there has been exceptional forward movement and that progress will accelerate. But it will not be automatic or rapid. Accomplishment depends on men. And, though the momentum of the civil rights struggle seems to some to be faltering, this is a superficial view. It is, in fact, changing its character.

Once major energy went into launching demonstrations which were highly publicized and galvanized hundreds of thousands across the nation to help the Negro. The greatest emphasis now is on helping individuals where they live. This is necessarily slower, less spectacular (but often even more dramatic, especially for the individual helped), even more necessary. But it isn't the kind of activity in which hundreds can march for a few hours, assuage their consciences, gain local fame and consider their "debt" to society and the Negro paid.

The nature of the civil rights movement has changed from the general to the particular.

One of the boys in the *Peanuts* comic strip says, "I love humanity—it's people I can't stand!" There was a good deal of this in the thousands who were so active during the large-scale demonstration phase of the movement. Now these dedicated souls have to look at the trees instead of the forest. The voices of the convinced men of compassion and good will are needed today as never before. They are needed in every kind and at every level of activity. Men of good will, I believe, outnumber those who would contain, confound, or curb the pace of equal rights.

It is important—more so than ever before—that we consciously speak up with the facts. The truth will set us all free. It will free Negro citizens from their economic, social, and political chains and free whites from the serious dangers of the incredible smugness and ignorance that have handicapped us for centuries. The logical starting point for speaking up is in the home. Each of us as parents has a responsibility to give our children insight into the world which will be his, not to hobble him with outmoded viewpoints suited only to conditions that existed in our day. We must instill respect for the worth of the individual.

Much of this we do by example, of course, and our children pick it up by "osmosis." However, who among us has not found his child coming home to repeat some nasty-mouthed rhyme or epithet. Speaking up begins at that point. Spiking the childish misinformation or thoughtless word requires not a flat prohibition: "Don't say that!" It takes an explanation for not saying it, a rationale that will stand up against the merciless incisiveness of juvenile logic. It may require considerable discussion, geared to the level of understanding of the youngster, of course.

Children today are television hounds, as every mother knows. I certainly have no quarrel with this. However, there are a couple of things I want to bring up.

First, I believe that youngsters should see on TV the news as well as the kiddie programs, adventure shows, and cartoons.

Second, there is a danger that youngsters will apply the same level of acceptance to dramatized events that they give to the news, and vice versa.

Children should witness the social revolution as it unfolds. They will see other children involved, some as participants, some as babes in arms in demonstrations for social justice. Our youngsters have a right to know why this goes on and what it means. The answers need not be in classical Fourth of July oratorical form. They should be specific. Why are there people blasted with fire hoses, beaten, run down by horses, galvanized by electric cattle prods? Can you explain it so that it carries a dimension other than some inverted seeking after "kicks"?

Can you tell your youngster, and make it believable, that Negro children and their parents who demonstrate seek here and now what for many Americans is simply taken for granted: decent homes, work, a share in the nation's wealth, a proper place in our cultural and social life?

Can you view TV newsclips of rioting in the ghettos of

the nation's cities and see behind the surface of the illegal fighting, looting, and destruction? Can you glimpse the frustration, the pent-up anger, the "dream denied" that surfaces in such paroxysms of blind outrage? Can you explain to your youngsters why ghetto dwellers distrust the police? Why sometimes insignificant incidents trigger magnum-scale holocausts? Can you make your child (who probably has never seen a real live rat) understand why some parents cannot prevent their children from being rat-bitten? Why they live cooped up seven or eight to a single room? How they exist without work or job? Why they don't move next door to *you* to escape it all?

Explaining the underlying causes of a riot is not easy. But letting the superficial, obviously destructive action "speak for itself" is perhaps even more dangerous in the long run.

Ours is a country which for the first time in the history of the world is coming to grips with genuine equality—economic, social, political—across racial and religious lines, for all its citizens.

As I said, there is a danger that the drama of reality will be confused by our TV-watching kids with the drama of illusion. If they apply the same principles observed in their cartoons and westerns to the real-life struggles shown in TV newscasts, the world will be a "good guys—bad guys" place. More than that, they will assume that the scenes on TV news are simply episodes in another piece of fiction in which the good guys inevitably wrap everything up in the final scene and the bad guys are mowed down or suitably punished.

For better or worse, the civil rights struggle cannot be so simply drawn, nor its solutions so neatly resolved. Some of the conditions protested may continue for years (look at the slow progress in school integration, for instance). Some of the bitter die-hards will continue to harass (look at the bombings, church burnings, and economic reprisals reported with depressing frequency). And it seems likely that outbursts such as the ghetto riots will occur from time to time. So this will be a continuing story that our children will not only see and hear for many years, but in which many of them will play important roles and by which all of them will be affected.

Which are the good guys? Let us try to see the participants in this struggle with understanding. Margaret Young (Mrs. Whitney Young, Jr.) tells of her youngest daughter watching on TV a southern Congressman denounce the March on Washington and vow that he would still not vote for the civil rights bill. "What's wrong with him that he has things, but he doesn't want other people to have them?" the child asked. Margaret's wonderful answer was, "Only insecure people are so threatened by sharing their rights, their jobs or their neighborhoods that they must deny others. Pity such people, don't hate them. Hatred is self-defeating." This response typifies the nonviolent approach, the Gandhian orientation of most of the civil rights struggle. Let us try to counsel our children as well, so that when they do reach the stage when they may participate they will act *for* rather than *against*.

Educating and training our youngsters to live in and appreciate a multiracial world is basic. We have to do our part in the home and see to it that the neighborhood, the schools and church do their part.

Respect for others usually comes from knowing them and understanding them. This is not easy when it comes to Negro citizens or to the Negro's heritage. In the first place, segregation has been so effective that few American youngsters go to school or church with Negro children. And because of housing segregation our neighborhoods are still, by and large, either white or Negro, rather than mixed. Because of this all too few of our children have the opportunity to play with boys and girls of other races.

There are many avenues to overcome these difficulties. There are nowadays more and more multiracial camps where youngsters of different backgrounds come together for summer work and play. In many suburbs around our largest cities there are well-supervised voluntary programs of bringing youngsters from the ghettos to spend summer vacation time in suburban homes and in day camp activities. The good old Fresh Air Fund in New York City pioneered this kind of thing decades ago and it has really caught on. If there is no such program in your area and you want to do something about it, check with your local YMCA-YWCA executives and write the National Recreation Association for information.

If your church has no Negro parishioners the reason may be quite legitimate—no Negroes in your area; none in your town; none interested in your religion. Or the reasons may be less apparent—even less defensible. You might speak out about this by questioning the lack, but more on this later. We were talking about positive experiences for our children and I would suggest that you look into the possibilities of your Sunday School reaching out to bring other youngsters into its program. I mean, of course, working out arrangements so that Negro and white children can get together, in or out of the Sunday School context, in exchange visits, in joint trips, picnics, projects, socials, pageants, theatricals, and so on.

The churches, schools, libraries, and the communications media—especially TV, the newspapers and magazines—are the chief agencies for educating our children and inculcating attitudes. Therefore, we have to use our influence to get these powerful mind-shapers to present undistorted, fair pictures of our fellow Americans. Too few of our countrymen know much about the Negro's heritage and his contribution to making Western civilization, as well as our nation, great.

In recent years the textbook publishers have begun to correct this oversight. More and more of them are publishing books about Negroes and including Negroes in the texts of teaching books from the "Bobby and Jane" first readers on up. (See Appendix A for more on this.) This is as it should be, and it should be extended.

Too few Americans know of the richness of the African background of our Negro citizens:

The greatness of the now-vanished cultures in Africa— Ghana, Mali, Oyo, Songhay—the contributions of the Negro to the heights of Egyptian civilization and to Moorish Spain.

The fact that Aesop was a slave, and St. Augustine, Alexandre Dumas, Aleksander Pushkin, James Audubon and many outstanding men in history were colored.

There were Negroes among the first Spanish and French explorers in America. Cortés and Pizarro and De Soto had Negroes among their troops.

Thirty Negroes were with Balboa in his discovery of the Pacific and the Negro explorer Estevanico made his way through what is now New Mexico and Arizona, carrying the flag of Spain, three hundred years before a wagon train rolled into the area.

The neglect of the Negro's role in world history as well as American history has crippled the self-image of Negro youngsters. It has also truncated the knowledge and understanding of all American youths. Few among them realize the role of Negroes, from Crispus Attucks to General Benjamin Davis, in defense of American liberty. Five thousand Negro troops served under George Washington in the revolutionary war; 187,000 fought during the Civil War and hundreds of thousands more during World Wars I and II and the Korean conflict. Today, of course, they are fighting heroically in Vietnam.

But the contributions of our Negro Americans have not been limited to warfare. There have been hundreds of scientists, educators, great men of medicine and the arts from colonial times to the present. That there could have been any at all, considering the odds against them, is amazing. And it holds promise for a flowering of Negro talent when the fruits of the current equal rights revolution are enjoyed by more of our colored citizens.

The point I am trying to make here is that TV stuffs our youngsters' heads with visions of an all-white world, with few exceptions. Now it is beyond the reach of all but a handful of us to change the content of the TV programs by a word or a wave of a contract. But we can make an effort to see that our children learn something about Negro contributions to civilization in general and to American culture in particular. Such efforts should not be confined to Negro History Week nor Brotherhood Week. They should be year-round. Little Black Sambo has held the stage for too long.

The time is long overdue for our youngsters to learn the heroic stories of Peter Sales, John Lawson, Dorie Miller, William Carney, Benjamin Banneker, Frederick Douglass, Phillis Wheatley, Harriet Tubman, and so many others. And the books with these stories are available. They have been in print for several years now. The concerned parent will make an effort to find them at the bookstore or the library. (See the list of titles in Appendix II.)

If you have influence with the library selection committee you can play an important role by seeing whether books have been bought with a view to breaking down the old stereotypes.

If you are on a library acquisition committee you have a fascinating and challenging opportunity to bring into the minds of readers the inspiring stories of Negroes who have achieved. Such stories are not only stimulating, but liberating, in freeing both whites and Negroes from their crippling stereotypes and lack of knowledge.

If you are on the school board in your town or the PTA of a local school you can dig in in a similar way. Find out about the curriculum and the reading material being used on your youngsters. And urge the school authorities to get the best available materials to counter the generations of callouses that racist literature has put on the minds of Americans.

You know, if anyone today was seeking a sure-fire conversational gambit he could scarcely choose a topic more likely to stir interest and reaction than race relations. Now obviously I am not recommending that this is a good reason for digging into the subject and bringing it up at the next cocktail party.

If I am any judge, it will come up anyway, whether you mention it or not.

I point this out because in our daily meetings with people there are all kinds of opportunities for giving insight and perspective to the undigested information that people too frequently repeat from a quick glance at headlines. The TV newscasts and the daily papers with their quickly written news stories—these are the great spawning beds of conclusion-jumping. All over the nation during the morning and evening TV news periods, one can practically hear judgments snapping. Too often they snap shut on the wrong mouse.

To spike the inflammable and unreliable talk about race relations and the civil rights struggle, concerned citizens should be prepared to speak out. I am not advocating any belligerent stance in which you offer to "put on the gloves" with all challengers on the subject because, first of all, no one has all the answers. The subject is just too large. But in talking with your neighbors and friends, you can keep informed on the most pertinent issues in your city, such as integration of the schools, and what has been done elsewhere with what results.

Where do you find the background information? It is as close as your nearest library. Here you should be able to find the recent books about developments in the social revolution and how and why they occurred. It seems that every week a dozen new books on the subject are printed. In addition you will find such "standard works" as Louis Lomax's *Negro Revolt*, Charles Silberman's *Crisis in Black and White*, Whitney Young's *To Be Equal*, and any number of others. You

may also find James Baldwin's books, but their greatest service
is to give you insight and empathy. There are government
publications from the Labor Department and the various
units of Health, Education, and Welfare, as well as Commerce and the Census. More and more of these are focusing
on problems of Negro citizens, are authoritative and well
done. (See Appendix II for a list of valuable books on race.)

You may want to check with reliable organizations for
information: the National Council of Churches, the Anti-
Defamation League of B'nai B'rith; American Friends Service
Committee; the Institute of Human Relations of the American
Jewish Committee; the local Urban League; the local chapter
of the NAACP; the various state human relations commissions;
the U. S. Commission on Civil Rights, the YWCA, etc. Talk
with your librarian, church leader, or the nearest school of
social work for specific recommendations on given subjects.

Today, in this period of transition when we all are
battered daily with a bombardment of information and misinformation on civil rights, there is a critical need for men
and women with guts to speak up. If they can speak with
knowledge and facts to counter the rolling fog of obfusca-
tion, cant, and fear-mongering, they are supremely needed.
Their voices should be raised. If the facts and figures are not
at hand but sound judgment is theirs, they can serve a high
purpose by exercising a *caveat* or two at the proper moments.

It can be a real service to inject into a murky discussion
a simple "it is too early to conclude . . ." or "the evidence on
that is incomplete," or "we have heard one side so far . . ."
And it can be an act of courage as well as conscience to
state, when the occasion demands, "I don't agree—I understand that . . ."

We owe to our business associates an attitude of candor on
this whole area of subject matter. At business lunches, meetings in social settings, and professional get-togethers we
should openly and frankly discuss our experiences in hiring,

training, and upgrading Negro workers, with all the pluses and minuses spelled out. We should do this with understanding and insight.

Likewise, we should sift the reports of others with care, suggesting, if our associates have not done so, some of the avenues that remain to be checked before reaching a conclusion. The National Association of Manufacturers, the National Industrial Conference Board, and the U. S. Chamber of Commerce have *solid* case histories and studies that can give you the required documentation.

We all have opportunities that cry out for a clear statement of fact or of our beliefs. I do not mean moments when one can ignite a debate that will last indefinitely, to the exclusion of business, socializing, or whatever was the original occasion for the meeting. But I do contend that a person can generally make his position understood gracefully, without causing an uproar. There are times when a man must speak out because it is right. This is such a time.

Chapter 3

Join Up and Join In

People working in the various civil rights organizations in the early 1950s often had the sensation that they had just awakened on an accelerating train. They didn't know quite how they got aboard, but they knew they were really going places!

In truth, activities in the whole civil rights field began to move so fast that it was difficult to keep up with them, let alone stand back and analyze or assess them adequately. I remember that my feeling in those early fifties was that more than ever before civil rights was nearing center stage of American life. The Republic was catching up with its unfinished business.

The fifties and early sixties was a period of protest. Segregation was an accepted fact in both north and south. It was the rule in all areas of the nation. Surveys showed that the north, while largely segregationist, was at least not as formally and legally opposed to integration as the south.

Negroes fought hard during those years for recognition. Real gains came slowly. White citizens in the north maintained a solid, though tacit wall of prejudice against the Negro, while at the same time regarding the Negro's problems as largely a southern concern.

During these years the NAACP was a rallying center for Negro protest. Cases were fought in the courts constantly, and in growing numbers. One of these was, of course, the historic Supreme Court hearing on segregation in the public schools.

CORE was staging more and more marches, picket lines, sit-ins, and Freedom Rides.

The Reverend Martin Luther King was organizing his Southern Christian Leadership Conference on an expanding basis.

SNCC had an enthusiastic group of well-trained college students and young people speeding from one trouble spot to another.

The Negro was raising his voice in agonized protest for the whole world to hear. He was reminding his white fellow citizens that it had been almost a hundred years since he had been promised freedom through the Emancipation Proclamation, but that he was still a second-class American, consigned to live for the most part in squalid ghettos.

By the sixties there was considerable confusion about the roles of the different civil rights agencies. Some people thought the NAACP was opposed to CORE, that CORE was fighting SNCC and that the National Urban League was jealous of all three.

I can remember being quizzed by reporters at the League's Annual Conference in Dayton in 1961 on this subject. One of them asked me with a glint in his eye: "What do you think about CORE?" It was meant as a baiting question, probably because there had been minor differences of opinion between the agencies at the local level in certain areas.

Actually, I have never heard serious criticism of the other agencies at any Urban League meetings. People may have been under the impression that there was conflict because each agency was working in the Civil Rights field. This would be a seemingly obvious cause for competition and jealousy.

What was not realized at the time, however, was that

while each organization at that time had the same overriding goal—integration—the methods of approach were different. It has always been so. And in these days of dozens of civil rights groups (most of them local, all of them vocal) attacking the status quo it might be useful to put the current action in perspective.

By now all whites have felt the sting of verbal attacks by such men as Malcolm X, Stokely Carmichael, Rap Brown, and James Baldwin. What makes them sting is the truth behind their whiplash. They cut to the core of our submerged guilt about generations of treatment of the Negro:

What does the American Negro think of the 4th of July?

"I answer: a day that reveals to him, more than all other days in the year, the gross injustice and cruelty to which he is the constant victim. To him your celebration is a sham; your boasted liberty, an unholy license; your national greatness, swelling vanity; your sounds of rejoicing are empty and heartless; . . . your prayers and hymns, your sermons and thanksgivings, with all your religious parade and solemnity, are, to him, more bombast, fraud, deception, impiety and hypocrisy—a thin veil to cover up crimes which would disgrace a nation of savages . . . You boast of your love of liberty, your superior civilization, and your pure Christianity, while the whole political power of the nation (as embodied in the two great political parties) is solemnly pledged to support and perpetuate the enslavement of . . . millions of your countrymen . . . You glory in your refinement and your universal education; yet you maintain a system as barbarous and dreadful as ever stained the character of a nation—a system begun in avarice, supported in pride, and perpetuated in cruelty . . ."

Who said it—Malcolm X? Rap Brown? Baldwin? No, the speaker was Frederick Douglass, the great Negro Abolitionist, in 1852. Some men are ahead of their times, but I find it sobering and saddening to note how pertinent, how contemporary Douglass' remarks are even today. They could easily be spoken with almost equal currency today by scores of Negro protest leaders.

There are differences, of course, and the major one is that in 1852 Douglass was the only Negro who was capable of uttering that outspoken condemnation and courageous enough to do so. Today, thousands of American Negroes are capable of uttering their most outspoken criticisms without fear and tens of thousands of their fellows (and many whites) are willing to demonstrate that they agree and demand changes. The other major difference today is that conditions are not anywhere near as bad as those that existed in Douglass' day, though, as examination of the ghettos shows, they are terribly, terribly bad.

Douglass was throughout his lifetime a rallying point for Negro aspirations, for full and complete civil rights for black Americans. But the high hopes of the Abolitionists and the "freedmen" were cynically sold out. The Supreme Court in 1875 and 1876 struck down the most important Reconstruction laws. Furthermore, the Compromise of 1876 made a political reality of the monumental indifference and the shrewd southern manipulation of white reaction against the ex-slaves. The Supreme Court's 1896 "separate but equal" decision froze into law a national system of segregation and took from all southern and most northern Negroes their major civil rights.

It was Booker T. Washington in this period who spoke for the Negro. He judged, correctly, that at that time only compromise and accommodation would pry out of the disinterested white majority jobs and educational opportunities. There were, by 1901, vociferous Negroes protesting that Washington was not speaking for them or for the majority of American black men. A leader of this movement was W. E. B. DuBois who squared away and opposed Washington forthrightly and absolutely, demanding full social and political equality for Negroes as the Constitution promised and calling

for complete assimilation rather than the segregation that
Washington endorsed.

In 1905 a group of twenty-nine Negro intellectuals decided the time was ripe to form a national protest organization
to fight segregation and discrimination. They envisioned
branches in each state that had a sizable Negro population.
They met that summer to launch their plans, but from the
first their efforts went awry. They planned to meet in
Buffalo, New York, but in that enlightened city and time,
the hotel chosen for the conference refused to accommodate
them. They moved across the border into Canada and held
their meetings in Niagara. They issued proclamations against
segregation and discrimination and took issue with Booker
T. Washington. His humble-pie approach, his gradualist
philosophy, and his acceptance of segregation was a sell-out
of Negro rights, they said. His approach destroyed the will
of Negroes to protest, they pointed out. They saw this
clearly in the following four years, as the Niagara Movement
foundered slowly, sinking even as the leaders fired salvos of
broadsides at the Establishment, at Washington (both Booker
T. and D.C.), and at fellow Negroes who did not rally to the
flag. The mass response they hoped for did not materialize.
The intellectual response was mild indeed even among their
fellows. Young, practical Negroes who had any ambition saw
that it was not judicious to associate with such "radicals" if
they expected to get ahead in a white-controlled society.

It was in 1908 that a race riot in Springfield, Illinois,
shocked the liberals out of their torpor. It was a gritty, bloody
three-day riot. It was savage, as riots usually are, and it was
notable for the unmasking of white bigotry in the city that
had prided itself on being the home of the Great Emancipator.
Scores of Negroes were killed or wounded and others were
driven out of Springfield as white mobs rampaged and destroyed the Negro section. The event hit the papers throughout the nation. A writer named William English Walling

challenged the country to revive the Abolitionist spirit to win justice for American Negroes.

There followed a series of conferences of white liberals and socialists who joined hands with the Niagara Movement Negro liberals to form, in 1910, the National Association for the Advancement of Colored People. DuBois became the director of publicity and research and was the only Negro on the staff. From the first the NAACP has been a membership organization, with branches in major cities where Negroes have settled. And from the first it has militantly clamored and fought for full equality for Negro citizens. Today the NAACP has some four hundred thousand members and is under the wise direction of Roy Wilkins.

Over the years the NAACP carried on the legal battles of the civil rights struggle from county courthouses to the Supreme Court. In 1939, with its tax status under attack, the organization spun off as a separate entity the NAACP Legal Defense and Educational Fund. Designed to centralize legal efforts and provide a tax-free agency to receive contributions, the NAACP Legal Defense Fund (as it is usually called) has spearheaded the struggle to secure full constitutional rights for Negroes through the courts.

Over the years, the efforts of the NAACP and the Defense Fund erased from the lawbooks the "grandfather" clauses and destroyed the white primary and racial segregation in state universities. Both agencies are responsible for stripping away many of the pillars of segregation, culminating in the 1954 presentation by the Fund's Special Counsel Thurgood Marshall (now Supreme Court Justice) of the case against public school segregation before the Supreme Court. Since then the Fund has brought hundreds of actions against police brutality, peonage, unlawful arrests—particularly of sit-in, Freedom Ride, and other demonstrators. In the last five years it defended twenty thousand peaceful protesters. Today it continues these activities and is the legal arm for pursuing in the courts the rights of Negroes and their allies against bigotry. Jack Greenberg, who happens to be white, is Director-Counsel of the Fund and heads a staff of twenty-eight full-time lawyers. They work with more than 250 cooperating attorneys stationed across the nation and at this writing have more than four hundred cases in progress, representing thirteen thousand persons.

The Urban League began in 1910 also, when trainloads and boatloads of Negroes were arriving in New York from the south. Some were brought in by unscrupulous employment agents who paid the boat or train fare for the immigrants and then exploited them unmercifully—hiring them out and giving them only a fraction of their earnings, charging exorbitantly for transportation and placement fees, shunting girls into prostitution, etc. Others came to the city on their own. Many found that decent housing was difficult, if not impossible to locate; most discovered their skills were not in demand in the marketplace. Most were either unskilled or used to kinds of work not found in the metropolis. All this has a familiar ring, does it not?

So, observing the need and noting also that these immigrant Negroes had no already-functioning assistance organizations as did immigrants from European countries, groups of concerned men and women in New York formed committees to aid the city's Negroes. Two of these organizations were the National League for Protection of Colored Women and the Committee on Industrial Conditions of Negroes in New York.

Responding to the Ph.D. thesis of a young Negro student at Columbia University, the leaders of these two committees agreed that the need was for basic social action including, but going beyond, measures to help find and equip Negroes for jobs and the protection of colored women from the "black slave" traffic. A third organization was therefore formed, called the Committee on Urban Conditions Among Negroes, and the young graduate student, Dr. George Edmund Haynes, was its staff member, to formulate its program, select young college-educated Negroes for social work training, and to organize local committees in other cities through these workers. Research and publicity were also to be the weapons to bring about equal opportunities.

The three committees decided to combine under the banner "the National League on Urban Conditions Among Negroes." Today we know it as the National Urban League. From the first it took pride in being interracial.

In that unforgettable phrase of the great sociologist Charles S. Johnson, the League's job was that of acting as midwife in the rebirth of the rural, southern Negro into the new life of the great industrial city.

Expanding into major cities of the north, the League tackled the problems of housing, jobs, vocational training, health, education, and welfare for Negro citizens. It still works on these problems, now with eight thousand volunteers and eight hundred professional staff members, white and Negro in 1968, in eighty-five cities, across the nation and throughout the south. It has a net of regional directors, a record of solid accomplishment in saving lives through finding work, housing, medical aid, welfare, and opportunities for literally hundreds of thousands of Negroes. (The League placed more than forty thousand Negroes in jobs in 1967 alone.)

Under Whitney Young, Jr., the National Urban League is perhaps the most vigorous and diverse of the civil rights organizations operating today. It has played an indispensable and exceptional role as continuing meeting ground for the races and the power structure in the cities where it operates. Since the League has time and again influenced the federal and state governments (as in the preparation of the War on Poverty legislation, largely outlined by League specialists) it is often referred to as the Negro "State Department," in the same sense that the NAACP is called the "Justice Department."

It was just as World War I began that the next significant development in the protest movement came along in the form of a West Indian Negro named Marcus Garvey. This extraordinary man was the prototype of today's Black Nationalist. He whipped up mass following for his Universal Negro Improvement Association. Its goals were separatism—economic, social, and cultural—and a return to Africa.

Building on the despair of the Negro masses, Garvey told his followers to abandon any hope that the whites would ever give the Negro a fair deal. The Negro leaders of the day he denounced for "selling-out." He extolled the beauty of blackness, declaring Christ and God to be black, and encouraged Negroes to turn their backs on the white world. This human dynamo organized cooperative grocery stores, cleaners, and a shipping company—all run by Negroes. Before long, however, most of these businesses failed; many ensnarled him in lawsuits. Finally, the federal authorities deported Garvey after convicting him of using the mails to defraud when he sold stock in his steamship company, which was to ferry American Negroes back to Africa. Thus ended, on a technicality, the career of the most effective, ebullient organizer of Negro discontent the country had yet seen. Echoes of Garvey are heard today in the rantings of the most outspoken Negro protesters as well as in the demands of some black extremists.

CORE—the Congress of Racial Equality—had its beginning in 1942 when it tried out Mahatma Gandhi's tactics and the technique pioneered by the CIO in the thirties—the sit-in. CORE used it in a Chicago restaurant with similar success. However, CORE did not really become a national force until the late fifties when it organized Freedom Rides, sit-ins, and demonstrations. Since the passage of much of the legislation CORE had demanded and agitated for, it has dwindled in effectiveness and importance. Since it had neither wide membership nor a network of professionals operating full-time, year-round on program activities, this decline was, perhaps, inevitable. Once aggressively interracial, CORE has been pushed increasingly into extreme positions, espousing "Black Power" and extremism in efforts to maintain grass roots backing. In 1968 CORE claimed forty-five chapters, some seventy-five staff and eighty thousand members.

It was 1956 when Mrs. Rosa Parks, like many thousands of American Negroes, got aboard a city bus after working all day at a downtown store. But this day was different. Mrs. Parks decided she was tired, too tired to walk to the back of the bus and sit in the Negro section. She just took the first seat she came to. The bus driver refused to move the bus until she moved and she was immovable.

From this incident grew the Montgomery, Alabama, bus boycott, coordinated by a young minister named Martin Luther King. To sustain Dr. King and his activities the Southern Christian Leadership Conference was organized. For more than a decade now the Reverend Dr. King and his followers have made history through their marches in Selma, Cicero, Atlanta, and dozens of other backwaters of bigotry. His wisdom and statesmanship were rewarded with the Nobel Peace Prize and the continuing devotion of the vast majority of American Negroes. It was clear, after his shameful, tragic assassination, that overwhelming numbers of whites considered Dr. King a saintly apostle of America's virtues. The Reverend Ralph Abernathy assumed leadership of SCLC after Dr. King's murder.

Curiously enough, it was Dr. King who was responsible for the formation of the Student Nonviolent Coordinating Committee ("Snick"). He called a conference of southern Negro college students in 1960 and the organization was a result. However, instead of becoming a docile auxiliary of

Dr. King's SCLC, SNCC almost immediately headed off on its own track.

Run by students and former students, SNCC with great enthusiasm and dedication and practically no money organized and sent into the field bands of volunteers to demonstrate, to protest, to help people register the vote, to educate and aid in housing, agriculture, and health and welfare activities. Hundreds of northern students, white and Negro, were drawn to SNCC's "service corps" and at the peak, in 1964, hundreds were serving in remote areas of the south.

In recent years, as SNCC leaders have been more and more outspoken about separatism, rejecting white aid, the organization has become more extreme and more isolated. Many of its former supporters have turned their backs in disillusionment as Stokely Carmichael and Rap Brown have shouted for "Black Power" and guns, for their pound of white flesh. Noisy and blatant, irresponsible and irreverent, SNCC now numbers less than a hundred members but its capacity to seize the headlines is perhaps unrivaled by the other civil rights organizations.

There are, in addition to these agencies, dozens of others with limited membership, circumscribed influence, and varying degrees of effectiveness. The black nationalist groups range from those that still favor return to Africa, through the ones demanding reparations now, to the Black Muslims with their goal of a separate black nation in the southern United States. At the other end of the spectrum are the Urban League and NAACP, whose goals are full participation and integration of Negroes in American life.

The Domestic Marshall Plan

As an example of the League's approach, let me tell you about the Domestic Marshall Plan. This was one of the most controversial issues ever faced by the League's Board of Trustees. The agency had always been interracial. It had many white staff members and the board was about evenly divided between whites and Negroes.

Board members adhered strictly to the doctrine of equality for Negro and white citizens. It was one of the fundamental principles of the organization. Even the League's symbol showed white and Negro workers striding forward together under the banner "American Teamwork Works."

The single-minded unity about this doctrine was rudely shattered one day when Whitney Young, Jr., the Executive Director, announced that the League should stand solidly behind a program of "special effort" for Negroes to help them catch up.

He did not ask that this effort should continue indefinitely into the future. He merely called for its application for a period of about ten years.

Quite a few of the white Board members came to me to discuss this "inflammatory" business. They felt that it would tarnish the image of the League as an interracial agency and that as president of the League I should do everything I could to influence Young to drop the matter. I must admit I had considerable concern about the validity of the doctrine myself. So we all had small conferences and tried to find answers which would bridge the gap. I had several conversations with Young on the subject. He clung tenaciously to the idea. He felt that his point of view was absolutely correct and would provide a much-needed answer to Negro poverty.

These talks convinced me beyond any question that he was right. If you examined his plan from the point of view of what was fair to the Negro, there was no conflict. The only difficulty I could foresee was that the press might twist the emphasis around to make it look as though we were demanding advantages for the Negro which would be denied to the white worker, a concept which would not be swallowed easily. There might be a tendency to forget that the request was merely for temporary relief.

My own doubts now removed, I joined Young in his efforts to promote the concept.

The announcement of the plan was made in May 1963. The basic theme of this proposal was simple: Negroes, having been denied their rights and discriminated against for so long, could not automatically step into the sunlight as equal citizens without special effort by their fellow Americans to make it possible.

The announcement was a bombshell. It immediately stirred tremendous controversy from coast to coast. Some critics misinterpreted the proposal to mean that Negroes were asking for a silver spoon for every mouth. Others opposed it with the argument that it would be undemocratic. Still others considered that it would make the Negro even more beholden to whites, and thereby tie his hands.

Of course, many backed the proposal from the first, seeing in it a sensible approach to overcoming severe handicaps. Its greatest contribution was, I believe, an almost instantaneous focusing of opinion-leader attention on the deprived status of American Negroes, for the first time. It has had profound effects on American thinking. And it has played a significant part in the development and shaping of antipoverty programs under the Office of Economic Opportunity, within the various federal departments and at state and city levels as well.

Basically, the domestic Marshall Plan program consisted of ten points. It called for:

1. Recognition of need for a *special effort* to overcome the serious handicaps afflicting Negro citizens.
2. Recognition of the potential and value of Negro citizens and moves to develop these.
3. Use of the best schools and teachers to instill in disadvantaged

youths a desire for excellence; to motivate them to achieve and prepare them to advance up the economic ladder.

4. A conscious, planned effort to bring qualified Negroes into "entrance jobs" in all types of employment; to upgrade them and aid them to qualify for advancement; to place them in responsible positions—including the full range of management positions.

5. Effective, positive action to destroy the ghetto and to open housing opportunities of all types on basis of need and ability to buy or rent.

6. The best services of health and welfare agencies, public and private, to the ghettoized population.

7. Naming qualified Negroes to all public and private boards and commissions, particularly those that shape policy in health, education, welfare, housing, and employment.

8. Fullest use by Negro citizens of every opportunity to acquire education and technical skills.

9. Reassessment of financial support of and cooperation with organizations committed to securing equal opportunity for Negro citizens, by government, foundations, labor, and business.

10. Negro citizens to carry their full share of responsibilities and participate in a meaningful way in every phase of community life.

The reporters immediately saw in the Plan meat for controversy. They picked up the story and played it with great relish. Some papers, like the New York *Times*, carried the story in favorable terms. Others ripped into Whitney Young and the League as advocating "indemnification," "compensatory activity," "special consideration," etc.

Some of the Board members must have shaken their heads in horror. This was just the type of language they feared, this was the interpretation they anticipated.

I was concerned myself with the twist some of the papers had placed on the plan. They accused us of advocating preferential treatment, but had not linked this up with the other half of the concept. They omitted the thought that the special effort was only to catch up with the white citizen and not to surpass him. They also overlooked the fact that the plan was made for a limited period only.

The Board members, however, took the jolt in good grace. I heard no adverse comment.

After all, the plan had gone through with a minimum of Board discussion.

The fortunate aspect of the situation which followed was that Whitney Young's advocacy of the doctrine proved to be dramatically successful.

Whatever doubts people may have had when they first heard the dreadful words "special effort" were apparently dissipated as they gave further thought to the justice of the proposal.

After all, as Young pointed out, the United States has always granted preferential treatment to those in distress. The people of this country committed some $17 billion to the shattered nations of the world in 1948. This was the Marshall Plan after which our Domestic Marshall Plan was named.

In more recent years the nation has contributed millions for employment, education, and welfare to Hungarian and Cuban refugees. Every year, in fact, we have provided emergency help to depressed and disaster areas, to people suffering from joblessness or devastation by hurricane, drought, flood, or other misfortunes.

Young said that the G.I. Bill of Rights after World War II was, in a sense, a recognition of the special need of our discharged veterans for education, housing, employment, and other benefits.

And we have the Antipoverty measures, the most recent— though limited—illustration of our national will to provide special treatment for those in distress.

I believe that the domestic Marshall Plan was a very tangible and prominent contribution by the League to the

Civil Rights program. It made headlines all over the United States, and it brought home the desperate plight of the Negro in more forceful terms than any other single statement of the times.

Today, at a distance of a few years from its announcement, the Domestic Marshall Plan proposal does not appear so revolutionary, so upsetting, so debatable as then. Perhaps it is a measure of both the distance we have come and the success of the proposal in shaping the nation's thinking since.

Two Leaders

Two of the most important personalities of this decade, by any historical reckoning but particularly in terms of civil rights progress, will be Presidents John F. Kennedy and Lyndon B. Johnson.

Relations between the National Urban League and President Kennedy were excellent. He was keenly interested in the work of the League and passed the word along through a mutual friend that he would like to have me correspond with him regularly on League activities.

Our first visit with President Kennedy back in 1962 was for me an awe-inspiring event. Whitney Young and I were ushered into the Oval Room opposite the entrance to the White House. We had spent the morning with Louis Martin, Vice Chairman of the Democratic Party, and with one of President Kennedy's secretaries. Our object was to become acquainted with some of the questions he might ask and to formulate properly some requests we were anxious to make.

President Kennedy had scheduled us for five o'clock, the last appointment period of the day, and the implication seemed to be that he might wish to speak with us a bit longer than he might have spent in the earlier periods.

At the White House no one seemed to be around to

conduct us to the President's quarters and there appeared to be no activity of any sort, so we began to wander around through the various rooms on the ground floor. We covered the Green Room, the Red Room, the State Dining Room, and the State Ballroom, walking around at leisure and being deeply impressed with the stately grandeur of these chambers. The historical paintings, books, and other treasures were arranged in excellent taste and filled me with awe.

We were back in the Oval Room again before anyone arrived to cut short our self-conducted tour and presently a secretary arrived to inform us that the President was ready to see us.

We climbed the stairs and President Kennedy came across the hallway on the second floor and partway down the staircase to greet us. He ushered us into the room with the famous rocking chair and I must say we had a very relaxed conversation, considering that we were speaking with the President of the United States, but John Kennedy was noted for his ability to put people at their ease and to bring the most out of them.

Whitney Young sat opposite the President on the sofa and I sat on a chair on his left, looking toward the doorway. I saw our old friend Andrew Hatcher standing there. He is a Negro and was one of President Kennedy's most effective assistants.

We presented the President with requests in each area of our four-point program. We asked for government backing to assure a better education for Negro children, equality of employment, better housing, and improvements in health and welfare.

When we finished he said, "I'll go for that." His attitude was sympathetic and we discussed these problems in a relaxed atmosphere.

Whitney Young asked the President whom he would designate to implement and carry out the program.

"Vice President Johnson," he answered immediately.

I was impressed with his practical manner. He was very interested in urban renewal and housing and got right down to the heart of the matter. He reeled off for us the names of all the Senators who would be for the measure and those who would be against it, and he asked us if we would be willing to speak with some of them. In each instance, when a measure was contemplated, he appeared to know instantly who would vote for it and who would vote against it.

There is no question that his years in the Senate were a boon to him in giving him the know-how to receive Congressional approval of his programs.

The National Urban League's association with the government in the implementation of antipoverty programs for education, employment, housing, and health and welfare stems from this visit to President Kennedy.

The purpose of this call was to offer to the federal government the resources of the Urban League in working with the administration's programs in the social welfare field. We suggested to the President that the executive heads of all the local Urban Leagues be brought to Washington for a two-day briefing on existing government programs and how these could be meshed into League concerns. Mr. Kennedy endorsed this plan heartily and even said it would be possible to cover some of the expenses from government funds. This meeting actually was held in 1964 and was addressed by President Johnson and his cabinet aides.

Mr. Johnson has been an enthusiastic friend of the League, and his interest in race relations is long-standing and deep. I will never forget our first Urban League official visit with him. It was in 1963 when he was still Vice President and was head of the President's Committee on Equal Employment Opportunity. This committee, we knew, had as its prime function the opening of new and better jobs for Negroes and other minority group Americans. So, of course, we were interested in talking with the man who headed it and seeing what could be done to speed up the painfully slow progress in this field.

About six of us from the League flew down to Washington to see Mr. Johnson. As we viewed the situation, the government had not extended itself sufficiently. Not enough Negroes were being placed in the building trades and we had a list of complaints specific to other fields.

Up to this point, I had no firsthand knowledge of the capabilities of Mr. Johnson, but any questions I may have had about his mental dexterity or his leadership abilities were quickly settled on this occasion. We sat around a large table in the Vice President's quarters in the Capitol and he called for his files on the subject of employment.

He then proceeded to pinpoint all of the jobs which had been placed and all of the industries which the government had opened up to Negroes under his administration of the President's Committee. It was most impressive. In fact, as he reviewed the figures, he seemed to become incensed with what appeared to be our unreasonable demands. So instead of our delegation holding him to account for a job not sufficiently well done, the situation was reversed and we found ourselves on the end of the scolding we had intended for him. It was all very skillfully handled and we parted on good terms. Vice President Johnson had been right about the efficient job he and his Committee had done. But we had also been right in the overall sense: not nearly enough Negroes had been hired, nor enough hired at upper grades. Even to this day we are still struggling with these problems.

As we left, the Vice President told us by way of explanation that the President did not as a rule give the Vice President many jobs to do, so that when he did pass them along it was very important for the Vice President to execute them to the utmost of his ability. It was a dramatic object lesson, one that we all should take to heart. Today, in race relations, there is no shortage of jobs to be done—far from it! In the chapters that follow, let's take a look at some of the pressing needs that call out for volunteers.

Chapter 4

Education

American Negroes are not getting the education they deserve. They are not getting the training they must have to land jobs.

This is true north and south, east and west, city and country. And it must change, or we can expect greater and greater welfare rolls, exploding ghettos and skyrocketing taxes to pay for the health, welfare, sanitation, fire, police, and other services required by dependent Americans. We want to put Negro citizens on their own two feet, prepared to make their own way in the world. A good education is the best way I know of to do this and education traditionally has been the springboard to success in America. The trouble has been—and still is—that for our Negro fellow citizens that springboard has been too short or too weak.

All of us have seen TV and newspaper coverage of frightened but determined Negro youngsters running the gauntlet of white hatred to enter once-segregated schools. But now that the glare of the spotlight is off we are only dimly aware that these acts of courage by Negro students and their parents continue and that the acts of hatred, unfortunately, continue also.

In many areas of the south Negro parents have received small cards with a picture of eyes peeking through a square in the center. The card says, "The eyes of the Klan are on you," and it is signed "United Klans of America, Inc." The message is meant to warn parents not to enroll their children in schools where whites are taught. The result, when the warning is ignored, varies.

Emerald Cunningham, fourteen, a crippled girl living in Grenada, Mississippi, reported her experience to the Southern Regional Council in 1966. As she went to enter the ninth grade, "We were walking down Poplar Street near Margin. I could see white people up ahead on the corner. Then a white man driving a blue Ford truck—he was wearing a black hat, trench coat, and sunglasses—drove by and parked across the street. I saw him pull a black pistol from his pocket and shoot it one time.

"It seemed like a signal to the whites to come, and they did. The Negroes (walking to school in a group) got scared. I had had polio and couldn't run, so I crossed to the other side of the street. He came right behind me and shoved me into a white lady's yard. He stuck the gun at my head. I couldn't do nothing but call the Lord.

"Fourteen more ran up and started beating me. I thought I was going to die. A man hit me with an iron pipe (pointing to a nasty bruise on her right leg). I tried to leave but the man with the gun said: 'Nigger, you move, I shoot your brain out.' I like to have shake like the wind blows. Then a white man pulled me up and said: 'Get away and don't come back.'"

This instance of an inhuman mob venting its spleen on a poor, maimed little girl who had the audacity to want a better education than was possible in the squalid, under-equipped, poorly staffed school she had previously attended is physically sickening. It **is** not so isolated a case as one might hope. In other situations different but no less outrageous methods have been used.

Joseph Hicks of Harrisville, Mississippi, welcomed the new civil rights laws so that his children could be better educated. He sent his youngsters to the formerly all-white school even though he was warned not to and repeatedly threatened if he did so. Once the children were enrolled, the bigots struck, though not at him or his children. They poisoned eleven of the cows in his small herd.

In the north we have for decades smugly clucked about such goings on, saying that these examples of "southern chivalry" were outrageous. We were comfortable and secure in the belief that we were so superior. But what we conveniently overlooked was the fact that we were simply using more "genteel" techniques to accomplish the same end—the continuance of segregated schooling.

Instead of force and intimidation, city fathers in the north simply gerrymandered school district lines so that blacks and whites would not mix in school. And we simply sloughed off the education of the youngsters in those segregated schools, giving them the poorest teachers, classrooms and equipment, the minimum library facilities and budgets. What did we get? Dropouts, pushouts, juvenile delinquents, and untrained youths unprepared for anything but a life of dependency. And, from this pool of mistreated manpower, we have reaped the whirlwind in crime and ghetto explosions from coast to coast.

North and south, east and west, quality education for *all* of our children is the paramount need today. There is no simple formula to bring this about. But let me offer a few suggestions, based on experience and observation.

Integration Without Tears

Is it possible to integrate the schools in a city without tears and tribulation? Contrary to what you might believe if you judged solely by the TV and newspaper headlines, it is. It has been done. And since Pittsburgh, Baltimore, Los Angeles,

St. Louis, Detroit, and Teaneck, New Jersey, have done it, your city should be able to also.

There is no set formula available, but there are a few observations that may be helpful. Judging from the experiences in cities where school integration has gone smoothly (relatively speaking), these are some of the helpful benchmarks found by the National Opinion Research Center:

School boards made up of business and community leaders rather than political party representatives have been more successful, whether appointed or elected. They are better able to reach agreement among themselves, they are better equipped to deal with the intricate, fuzzy, emotion-laden questions that come up.

The successful school boards cooled controversies rather than escalating them into ideological battles. They acted quickly and decisively and avoided drawn-out debates.

Although apprehensive of white parent opposition, the boards in the north have found that when the schools are actually desegregated the resistance has been timid and short-lived. Studies showed that most northern whites didn't object to school integration that occurred "naturally" but were dead set against "capitulation" to the "demands of the civil rights movement." The cities that began desegregating before strong civil rights demands were lodged openly, underwent minimal white opposition. The same was true when the school board clearly stated that it considered school integration to be a valuable goal. School boards that grudgingly announced gradual or limited programs and excused them by saying they were only launched in response to civil rights demands have drawn lightning to their heads and experienced considerable —and vociferous—white opposition.

The professional educators have taken integration to be a positive goal in the systems where the most progress has been made. Many of them may have done this on faith in the early days, but there now are many research studies that give them—and all interested citizens—scientific data to buttress the conclusion that the schools should be integrated. Perhaps the best single volume is *Equality of Educational Opportunity* by the U. S. Office of Education. It says flat out that one of the few factors within a school system's control that can improve pupil achievement is integration of the classroom. Many other tried-and-true factors—such as pupil-teacher ratio, per-pupil expenditure, or curriculum—were found to have little influence.

Unfortunately, with the central city becoming increasingly Negro and the public schools filling more and more with Negro children as the whites "escape" to the suburbs, integrated schooling becomes more and more elusive. Massive programs are needed and in some communities are employed —Baltimore buses 5000 and St. Louis 2600 pupils daily. In some areas integrated programs with suburban schools are under way. One is percolating along in Boston in cooperation with seven suburbs but only involves about 240 youngsters. Another such program in Hartford buses some 270 pupils from ghetto to first-rate suburban schools. And in Rochester, New York, a graduated plan places pupils in the school system of a suburb and will build to an estimated three hundred students participating.

Other factors in desegregating the schools successfully include:

Strong leadership by state and local officials.

Application of a plan to all *the community's schools.*

Sound planning to minimize possible racial friction in newly desegregated schools.

Maintaining or improvement of educational standards.

Desegregation of classrooms *in the schools as well as the schools themselves.*

Providing remedial and supportive services for students who lag.

All of these points and others are discussed succinctly in the 1967 Report of the U. S. Commission on Civil Rights, *Racial Isolation in the Public Schools.*

Start at the Top

Policy-making begins with the school board and unless your school board is representative of the entire community it probably will not serve the Negro community adequately. And if it shortchanges our Negro citizens it endangers our total community. Therefore, it is extremely important that your school board include Negro and other minority group representatives. It won't do to say that there just aren't any who are qualified or interested. This is not a time for lame excuses, but for action. It means seeking out, encouraging, and even building up interest, if need be, through contacts with the service organizations, unions, social and civic groups.

The next echelon is school administration. How many Negroes are in positions of significance? Skip the secretarial layer and the window-dressing. The question is whether the needs of your Negro citizens are being articulated in policy-making and policy-executing for your schools. If they are not represented it is imperative that they be brought in immediately. If you don't know the answer to this one, telephone or call on your superintendent of schools for the facts.

Now some may argue that the accident of a man's color does not necessarily qualify him to judge the educational needs of Negro citizens of your city as well as whites who have been specially trained in education. Though I would agree with this in general, I would point out that at this time and in these highly sensitive circumstances it is extremely

important that Negroes be represented on boards of education and in school administration. This is a working rule that
today can be ignored only at the peril of the whole community. The fact that school policy is of deep and consuming
concern to Negroes should not be news. That it can be the
fuse that ultimately blows the lid off your city may not be
quite as apparent, but it is equally true.

The third echelon that commands attention is the teacher
corps itself. Two questions are primary here: First, do you
have a proportion of Negro teachers that reflects the city
population picture and/or the school population proportions?
Second, do you have the Negro teachers teaching white children and white teachers teaching Negro children rather than
a segregated school situation in which the races are mutually
exclusive?

The second matter is one of policy and can be achieved by
the administrators and school board. The first matter, that
of staffing with Negro teachers, is one of policy, availability,
and determination.

Too often in the city schools of the north the lame excuse
is heard that "there just aren't qualified Negro teachers available." With all due respect, I tend to classify that as bologna,
appropriate to hang with the other salamis and sausages at
your local meat market. Let me tell you how volunteers in
Westchester County, New York, moved forty-seven of their
school districts to hire Negro teachers.

Teacher Recruitment

Back in 1954 there were only thirty-four Negro teachers in
eight school districts of Westchester, a county with a population of 809,000 in 1960. This was the finding of a survey of
county schools carried out under the direction of Walter

Ludwig, a teacher in the Mamaroneck schools. His committee of volunteers constituted the Education Committee of the Westchester Urban League. When the committee and the League saw the results they decided to do something and a small group of volunteers organized as the Teacher Recruitment Committee.

The committee's first step was a conference with the organization of school superintendents of the county. This resulted in the superintendents issuing an official nondiscrimination-in-hiring policy statement. However, the committee found that though the statement was printed and distributed widely, the policy itself was disregarded by most of those who had signed it.

The Committee decided that something more than words and waiting was necessary. So, in February of 1959 volunteers recruited by the Committee in each school district of the county went to call on their local schools. They went armed with copies of the Superintendents' official statement. Their purpose was to compile a roster of specific staff vacancies for the coming school year.

The information from all the school districts was assembled and the master list of county vacancies was mailed to Negro teachers who were registered with the Urban League; to various "contact" people who would be likely to hear of candidates in their areas; to college placement directors and the news media. Two Negro teachers were appointed as a direct result of the committee's efforts that year.

Bill Wolfe, executive director of the Westchester Urban League, reports that in four years, by continuing this fact-finding and disseminating project, these volunteers were responsible for placing eighty-five Negro teachers in the county's schools. Wolfe says that the Committee's placements not only increased the number of Negro teachers in the school systems, but also have created a new employment climate. A number of Negro teachers applied independently because of this new climate and some of them also found jobs.

The Teacher Recruitment Committee was interracial, of course. And the members learned about vacancies in various ways. Some school districts included the Committee on their mailing lists and automatically notified it about openings. In other districts, Committee members check their schools on a regular basis and report vacancies. In some, volunteers visit the school superintendents for preliminary lists, then turn these over to the Urban League which checks every two weeks to see how the picture changes.

To find qualified applicants, the Committee uses newspaper and magazine publicity—particularly the Negro press. The League screens applicants to see if they are qualified. They must hold the State Education Department certificate and be approved by the League's Teacher Panel.

This panel is composed of Negro teachers currently working in the county. Its fifteen members represent most of the large school districts. The panel meets one evening a month to interview applicants. It is a tough screening: in the 1963–64 year 450 teachers inquired about placement. Some 300 of these filled out registration forms and 162 notified the League they were certified. Of this group, 100 came from the Metropolitan area and 60 accepted the invitation to meet with the panel for an interview. Only 38 passed the screening.

The Committee sent more than 580 notices of vacancies to qualified registrants in 1964. Many of the teachers may have received notice of more than one opening. Each applicant also received a schedule of salaries for the entire county and a list of school superintendents. And the Committee sent to the hundreds of applicants who did not have teaching certificates information on New York State certification—the requirements and procedures for qualification. The Committee, says Bill Wolfe, helps other suburban communities to adapt its procedures. To assist them, the Committee has prepared a manual on its techniques and sends these upon request.

The Schools Themselves

What do you know about the schools that are teaching your children? So you've been to the PTA meetings and seen the fortress where your own child is taught. What about the other schools in your system? If you live in a city, chances are high that there are one or more predominantly Negro schools in your system. This is the case in most of our cities today.

At this stage I hope it is unnecessary to run through all the arguments favoring integrated schooling. Since 1954 they have been compelling. That year the Supreme Court in an eloquent decision said segregated schooling was illegal and harmful to Negro children.

As recently as 1967, the report of the U. S. Commission on Civil Rights focused on "Racial Isolation in the Public Schools" and pointed out the evils of segregated schooling— to whites as well as Negroes. In short, it found that the "Negro schools"—those with predominantly Negro enrollments—are considered inferior and treated as such by the community. Everyone connected with such schools—students, teachers, administrators—shares this view and is demoralized and paralyzed by it. "This stigma," said the Commission, "affects the achievement and attitudes of Negro students." The report showed—as just one out of scores of examples— that twelfth grade Negro students in segregated schools were performing at a level *more than two grades behind* their counterparts who went to integrated schools.

But the emphasis should be on the positive. For Negro student integration will bring the better facilities and teach-

ing that typically have been lacking—if not denied—to him
and will show him he is as good as any other child in the
city. Today, in his segregated classroom, he feels and believes he has been cut off from first class education and
shunted into an inferior school.

White children, says the report, are "deprived of something
of value when they grow up in isolation from children of
other races, when their self-assurance may rest in part upon
false notions of racial superiority, when they are not prepared by their school experience to participate fully in a
world rich in human diversity."

I hope that we can all agree that our children *all* deserve
the very best educations. Unfortunately, the disparities between the best and what most of our Negro youngsters receive are appalling. The reasons are many and varied, some
economic, some because of housing, some because of naked
prejudice. At any rate, if you, like the women in the Capitol
East section of Washington, D.C., want to do more than just
talk about this, why not follow their lead?

This group, composed of young wives of federal civil
servants who have moved into this once run-down area of
the Capitol, took a look at the schools and rose up in anger
and determination. This is what they did. They got together
and drew up a survey sheet covering the questions they considered important. Then they mimeographed the questions
and formed teams to call on the principals of each school
in their section of the city.

Their concern divided into three categories—physical
plant, personnel, and education. They did not get into curriculum questions, though they did ask about the availability
of teachers of art, music, science, etc., and asked the principals
how much more time of such specialized teachers they really
needed.

Take a look at their questionnaire. For your city some of
the questions may be unnecessary; others may be called for.

In any case, the technique is simple and effective. The results can give you the facts to evaluate the schooling your youngsters are getting. You may want to add questions about numbers of books in the school library, or numbers of teachers who are not certified and so on.

CAPITOL EAST QUESTIONNAIRE

SCHOOL _____ PRINCIPAL _____

Physical Plant
1. Size of fenced playground (square feet)_____.
2. Do children play anywhere other than playground (if so, please specify street, park, etc.)_____.
3. Does school have: falling plaster_____; rodents_____; broken windows_____; improper lighting_____; other facilities not in good repair (please explain)____

    _____.
4. Does school have adequate room for: nurse_____; counselors_____; art_____; music_____; science_____; foreign language_____; reading_____; remedial reading_____; special classes_____.
5. Does school have a slide projector?_____; motion picture equipment_____; other technological aids_____; What additional equipment is needed?_____

Educational Information
6. Average class size_____. Number in 3 largest classes _____ _____ _____. Number in 3 smallest regular classes_____ _____ _____.
7. Percentage absence on average day_____. Percentage truant on average day_____.
8. Number of dropouts in last academic year (high schools only)_____.
9. Do you have an adequate number of high quality, up-to-date textbooks? (if not, please explain subjects, grade levels lacking and estimate how many you need)____

    _____.
10. What percentage of textbooks may be taken home_____

    _____.
11. Are parents asked to pay for any special programs (please explain)_____. Are sub-

sidies available for those who cannot pay_____.

12. How much money do you get from PTA each year?
_____. What types of gifts do you get from
PTA?_____.

13. Is school open at night for adult education, clubs, etc.
(please specify)?_____.

14. Please list summer programs at school and how many
participate in each_____
_____.

15. What percentage of first grade students this year missed
kindergarten_____.

Personnel

16. Of the following, how many hours of service do you get
each month and how many do you need?

	HAVE	NEED
a. Art teachers		
b. Music teachers		
c. Science teachers		
d. Foreign lang. teachers		
e. Reading specialists		
f. Speech therapists		
g. Guidance counselors		
h. Social workers		
i. Librarians		
j. Nurses		
k. Health workers		
l. Secretaries		
m. Psychologists		

17. What other specialized personnel do you have and/or
need?_____.

18. In your judgment, how adequate is your personnel to
conduct an effective program under your present plan
of organization for instruction (excellent, good, fair, or
poor)? Please explain if you wish_____.

19. To what extent is present staff adequate to make effective changeover to team teaching, upgraded primary,
or other innovative programs?_____
_____.

20. What recommendations regarding personnel do you wish to offer to enable your school to do a better job in: your present plan of organization_____; innovative organization_____.

21. What recommendations would you make to enable your school to make a changeover to innovative methods regarding:
    a. Physical facilities_____.
    b. Equipment and supplies_____.
    c. Other resources_____.

22. Please explain what you would like to see a community organization concerned exclusively with public education do for your school. Also, please give us your additional comments and areas of concern. (Please feel free to use extra sheets for this or any other question).

In this survey in Washington the ladies discovered that 93 per cent of the public school pupils are Negroes, that 50 per cent of them drop out before graduation, that 52 per cent of the city's teachers are uncertified, and that youngsters in the area east of Rock Creek Park had half as many library books per pupil as those west of the Park in the upper-income, predominantly white section of the city. They also compiled impressive data for use in the hearings on education in the Capitol—data that helped change the system.

That, after all, is the only justification for going to the trouble of doing the time-consuming, thankless, information-gathering required. If you don't make use of it to change the conditions for the better, it has been a wasted exercise. Once you have the data, several avenues are open to you to use it. Your organization and others can discuss the data and take policy positions on it. You can present it to the PTA and get them to take a stand on it. It can be presented to the board of education with a petition or the resolutions approved by the various groups. And, of course, the press should receive full backgrounding on the project.

Integrating the Schools

Perhaps the knottiest of the knotty, this problem has generated more steam than Old Faithful. Three out of four Negro elementary school youngsters are in so-called Negro schools. And more than four out of five white youngsters are in all-white institutions. Not only that, the trend is increasingly seg-regationist. The reasons are not far to seek.

We all know that more and more the people in the suburbs are wealthier, better educated, hold better jobs and are white. The centers of our cities increasingly are becoming black prisons without walls. Within the city there are tight com-partments, ghettoes of blacks, whites, or nationality groups. *Zoning*, therefore, becomes a critically important matter.

In general, the U. S. Commission on Civil Rights recom-mends that school attendance areas be enlarged to encompass diverse groups, rather than just white or Negro families. *School-pairing* or the "Princeton Plan" has been effective only in small cities and towns. In these, where it is possible to cause the entire school population to go through one school, one building may be used for all kindergarten to grade three students, and a second for all grade four through grade six pupils. Thus the entire student population is mixed in the schools.

Bussing and *open enrollment*, the techniques that are most debated and hotly argued, have proven of limited success in most large cities. The reasons are several. Bussing and open enrollment are hampered when parents are required to initiate transfer requests and pay transportation costs and when there is limited space available in the white schools. Experience has shown, so far, that open enrollment does not appreciably desegregate the Negro schools.

Some of the new suggestions are for *"magnet"* schools—

a system of specialized school programs located in existing or new school buildings. New York has done this for decades, with its Bronx Science High School, Brooklyn Polytechnic, and the High School for the Performing Arts. Philadelphia is putting together such a program, with one high school specializing in commerce and business, another in space and aero science, and a third in government or human service. Naturally, these would draw from all races and parts of the city.

Still another scheme that has been proposed is one of *"educational complexes."* In this plan a "complex" would consist of up to eight elementary schools feeding as many as three middle or junior highs. The buildings would purposely be located so that the elementary schools would be within twenty minutes by bus of one another. The advantages would be accessibility of scarce resources such as psychologists, guidance counselors, special teachers, and research facilities and remedial programs with the specialists they require.

"Educational parks" are still another technique being widely discussed as a possible aid to quality education if not desegregation. As planned in Syracuse, New York, the parks would contain five buildings each, for four elementary classrooms and one central school for specialized services and facilities. These clusters would be located on the outskirts of the city, perhaps five clusters for this city of 216,000. For smaller cities one campus would encompass all the schools, elementary through senior high. Their locations would make possible integrating suburban students into the student body. And all the pupils in the town would mingle in this one kindergarten through fourth grade, a middle school, and a campus.

In East Orange, New Jersey, a small city of 77,000, an education plaza will serve all the youngsters of school age, including the nursery school tots. There will be a school with high school. In addition, a central building will contain offices, library, and curriculum center.

Now these are costly propositions, no question about it. But there are economies through consolidation of resources and improvements in quality of education. And the greatest boon of all, of course, decent schooling for all.

Our Stake in Integrated Education

That we all have a stake in integrated quality education for all children is shown by many studies by qualified researchers. Gerald S. Lesser and his associates at the Laboratory of Human Development, Graduate School of Education, Harvard, reported to the Massachusetts State Advisory Commission to the U. S. Commission on Civil Rights in 1964 about "some effects of segregation and desegregation in the schools."

Dr. Lesser found, as have other researchers, that "under segregated school conditions, Negro children are uniformly inferior in academic achievement to white children." But, interestingly, "the racial balancing of the schools contributes greatly to improving academic achievement of Negro children and, usually, of white children as well."

He reported on his five-year study of four hundred New York City children from Negro, Puerto Rican, Chinese, and Jewish families. Each group included kids from integrated and from segregated schools. He found that in verbal and numerical ability, reasoning and space conceptualization, youngsters from more integrated schools and neighborhoods showed significantly superior performance compared to children from segregated schools and districts.

Lesser also reported that in the integrated schools children from various ethnic groups turned in similar scores in the testing. But in the schools with lopsided enrollments from one ethnic group or another, the test scores for each ethnic group were markedly different. And Deutsch, Farrel, the Public Education Association, and Wolff in studies from 1955 through 1963 reported that the inferiority of academic performance in racially imbalanced schools becomes greater as the youngsters progress through the grades.

Lesser's observations about self-concepts are incisive:

In contrast to the white child or to the Negro child educated in a desegregated setting, the Negro child from a segregated background does not know how to interpret the school situation. He cannot quite understand what the objectives of learning and teaching are, what reactions and responses are expected of him, and what the types of rewards for learning which exist in the typical school can possibly mean. His confidence in himself as a learner is stunted, and he cannot regard school as a place which has any ultimate meaning for his real life outside of school.

There is no guarantee, Lesser points out, that integrated schools will solve the problem. However,

the point is that the unbalanced school situation is structurally self-defeating; even the most dedicated teachers will encounter severe difficulties in attempting to overcome its effects. The balanced school at least has the opportunity to counteract in part the conflicting and confusing communications of the larger community to the Negro child, to offer him an opportunity to develop a more positive, realistic, and less confused image of himself.

Another prime aspect of the educational process, motivation or "will to learn" is discussed by Lesser. He cites a number of studies that show that the achievement motivation of Negro boys is lower than that of white Protestant, Greek, Jewish, Italian, and French-Canadian boys of the same age. Lesser believes this deficiency in will to learn may be because the Negro boys see no relationship between the classroom situation, their lives outside of school, and their expectations for the future.

Furthermore, he says,

the rewards for learning offered by our schools and society are not as meaningful for the segregated Negro child as for other children. Typically, the segregated Negro child does not arrive at school equipped with the crucial ideas about the importance of knowledge for its own sake and its value in self-realization. The verbal rewards provided by the teacher which are effective in motivating middle-class white children bear little relationship to the segregated child's life outside of school and consequently have little impact upon him.

Integrated schools, Dr. Lesser points out, offer Negro children a greater range of rewards. They have broader and more effective resources available to arouse interest and aspiration. And in them Negro children see other youngsters responding excitedly and with effort to school challenges. Seeing the effects of rewards for learning on other children, Negro youngsters begin to value similar rewards and aspire to them.

This cultural lag, this incentive lack, this motivational handicap that afflicts Negro children requires concentrated efforts on many fronts if we are to counteract and eradicate it. The case is extreme, in terms of numbers of children affected; their needs are massive, in the range of requirements; they are urgent, in that a month lost in the formative years cannot be reclaimed.

Extending the Schools—to the Younger

What can be done by individuals to help overcome these handicaps? Extending education to younger children is one extremely important thing. And individuals can really have some effect in this effort.

Let me bring to your attention something that knocked me off my chair when I read it: the study by the National Education Association of the public school systems in 128 of our cities of more than ninety thousand population. The report said that

three out of ten of these cities do not have free kindergarten classes for their children. (And yet Labor Secretary Wirtz says that more unemployment is created between the ages of 3 and 6 than at any other period; it is at this time that basic attitudes and skills for education are instilled.)

one out of seven of these cities do not provide textbooks free to elementary school pupils, and one out of four do not give them free to secondary school pupils. (Of course this means that those who cannot afford them are likely not to get them: since half of our Negro citizens are below the poverty line, this obviously penalizes them.)

The lack of public kindergartens is directly discriminatory. White families with fewer children and higher incomes can better afford to send youngsters to private or church-related kindergartens. And Negro youngsters in these circumstances enter public school behind their white counterparts.

Concerned citizens in cities which have slighted their youngsters by not providing free kindergartens should do something about this. Petitions are a time-honored device in our country, so are the formation of committees and holding of forums, discussions and debates on the necessity of changing the situation.

I can't believe that the enlightened citizens in Spokane, Erie, Louisville, Little Rock, Tucson, Jacksonville, Albuquerque, Chattanooga, Knoxville, Memphis, Norfolk, Roanoke,

Newport News, Greensboro, Charlotte, Winston-Salem, and St. Petersburg and major cities in Texas, Louisiana, Mississippi, Alabama, South Carolina, and Georgia will allow this to continue.

Likewise, it seems incredible to me that the good citizens of so many cities could countenance public school systems that denied free textbooks to pupils. Textbooks do not cost much per child. In South Carolina the figure comes to between $24 and $27 per child per year. But when it comes to textbooks or food, many families have to choose food. And all too many such families are Negro families.

No doubt there is a sizable number of secondhand textbooks in these cities, and concerned citizens may find it possible to collect them in their neighborhoods and redistribute them on the basis of need. This smacks of the old food-basket-at-Christmas type of charity, and will not endear donors to recipients, but it will help to fill needs.

Much better would be neighborhood drives to raise funds to purchase books, or semiannual loans of texts through the local branch libraries. Better still would be a tax-supported system of supplying books to all. School boards listen to citizens' proposals. PTAs take on projects and have even been known to influence school boards! There are many avenues, if people wish to change conditions.

Pre-School Preparation

Dr. Martin Deutsch, director of the Institute for Developmental Studies at New York Medical College, points the finger of blame for retarding youngsters (and the resulting antisocial behavior of slum children) at teachers, school administrators, and entire communities. Dr. Deutsch has pioneered preschool teaching of three- and four-year-old deprived children. He has found that some teachers set low expectation levels, anticipate failure, and thus find an increasing rate of failure.

Other teachers, he notes, blame all the shortcomings on the environment—impoverishment, economic insecurity, segregation, second-class citizenship, historical chains. And they tend to be defeatist in their attitudes toward the problems which result.

New and different educational "strategies" are advocated by this specialist to overcome the difficulties which exist. It is unfair, he says, to pin the onus on the teacher alone. Too many school systems leave disadvantaged children out of their curriculum planning. Communities pinch pennies and cannot "afford" teachers to cope with the problem. Dr. Deutsch thinks new, self-teaching devices such as teaching machines and television (which he has found to be especially effective with slum children) should be used extensively. But he is a realist, and believes that they will not be used where school systems are marked by a lack of money and of professional leadership.

The preschool period of a child's life is terribly important. At this time many of the attitudes and habit patterns which will carry through for life are set. So it is that more and more emphasis is being placed on bringing the youngster out of the confines of a narrow well of despair and broadening his perspective by exposing him to the wider world.

One small example comes to mind. In a manufacturing town in Connecticut the local librarian was talking with local women and complaining about the lack of interest in the regular weekly story hour at the library. The women agreed that something should be done and decided to "reach out" and bring the children to these story sessions.

Soon they organized informal car pools which bussed youngsters to the library on Saturday mornings for the stories. The response was so enthusiastic on the part of the kids that the women recruited more drivers as well as more youngsters.

Now the program has expanded to five mornings a week at the local YMCA, which is located near the ghetto, and every day three or four white and a couple of Negro mothers bring in more than a dozen children, many of them Negroes, most of them from ghetto homes, for an hour of wonder and enchantment.

This activity, carried out almost entirely by volunteers, may seem slight. But in the final analysis the shaping of attitudes toward reading, toward books and teachers, toward community institutions such as the Y and the library, all of these are liberating influences of great value in the meager existence of children of the poor.

Such experience is vitally important at early ages for young Negro children. We have Dr. Kenneth Clark's frightening finding that by the age of four the child associates status with being white and lack of it with being Negro. If he continues to perceive the world in this polarized fashion throughout his juvenile and adolescent years there is little hope for him— or for our society.

Scholar Aid

An extremely important area in which volunteers are increasingly important is that of aiding students and supplementing the formal education process.

In many cities volunteers are tutoring Negro youth and counseling them about their vocational and educational plans. There is the Northern Student Movement which is active in New Haven, Hartford, and other cities, the volunteer Freedom Schools in the south, the NAACP-Wesleyan Tutorial Program in Middletown, Connecticut, the Akron Tutorial Project in that Ohio city, and there are many others.

Middletown, Connecticut, presents an interesting example in the organization and conduct of a successful tutoring program. In this manufacturing and university town of 35,000, the Negro population increased by 106 per cent in the decade 1950–60, to 1700. Observant and aware citizens of the town realized that the Negro children for the most part were not achieving as they should.

The local NAACP, with the cooperation of Wesleyan University, initiated a tutorial program, drawing on the faculty members and degree candidates for voluntary effort to help Negro youngsters. They started out in 1961 with a handful of tutors and a dozen Negro youths. The children ranged from the fourth grade up and each was tutored on an individual basis in quarters on the University campus—far from the Negro sections of town.

The second year, the Goodwill Men's Club, a Negro social group, made available its clubhouse four days a week for the tutoring program. Volunteers cleaned and painted the place, and it began a dual role as the NAACP-Wesleyan University Study Center. The number of youngsters in the program tripled the second year, reached fifty the third year, and stood at more than a hundred the fourth year. The new location had the advantage of reaching into the community, rather than making it necessary for youngsters to take the awesome trek to the University campus.

The student tutors are recruited at the dining halls, at the fraternities, and via notices on all University bulletin boards during the opening days of the college term. The youngsters are recruited in the Negro community through letters sent to all the kids, posters, announcements made at Negro churches, social and civic organizations.

Edgar F. Beckham, instructor in Wesleyan's German department, heads the project. He says that the tutors are generally enthusiastic at the outset, but their enthusiasm declines and frustration increases as the year progresses. The kids, he observes, vary in their attitudes—the leadership types are enthusiastic and the responses range down to complete indif-

ference at the other end of the scale. Some of the youngsters
are suspicious, apprehensive, and all but openly hostile.

Mr. Beckham has noted some resentment on the part of
parents because of what they construed to be condescen-
sion or patronizing behavior on the part of the tutors. However, he says that the project counts on the neutrality of the
parents, if their cooperation and support cannot be won. The
tutors are, he states, acting as parent surrogates, particularly
with the youngsters who are preparing for college. In such
cases the tutor often helps complete applications, prepare bio-
graphical data, and actually send the application package to
the college. The parents of these teenagers, even if interested,
are largely incapable of helping with the forms and required
information.

In a recent school year the Wesleyan program with its
Study Center reached about one out of every three Negro
youngsters who might be considered college potential in the
high school age group. How successful has the program been?
No accurate measure exists, but it has resulted in fewer dropouts, more Negroes applying for and going to college, and
generally better achievement in academic work.

Motivation

A severe and continuing problem is that of motivating Negro
youths to learn. Not only are they handicapped by their
environment when they come to school. They have several
other fetters: the good jobs have always gone to whites, the
poor jobs (what Whitney Young calls the "handle" jobs—
broom, mop, and brush handles) were the most that a Negro
could hope for. Furthermore, the League's 1966 study *Education and Race* revealed that the national unemployment rate
for Negro high school dropouts (aged sixteen to twenty-one)
was 20.5 per cent; for Negro high school graduates (same

ages) the rate was 21.1 per cent—*actually higher than for dropouts!* No wonder youngsters see no sense in finishing their education when they have a *better* chance of landing a job if they drop out of school. This situation obviously and understandably has discouraged Negro children from preparing for better jobs.

Unfortunately, many guidance and counseling people believed (and even today some still do) that there was no use in directing Negro youths into career preparation when (from the counselor's point of view) they would only wind up in those handle jobs anyway.

Obviously, children are greatly influenced by parental attitudes. So, when the parents and grandparents have been victimized by a two-class society and have never experienced any opportunities but those for menial jobs, the children often carry a heavy freight of preconceived notions about the work world. They observe their parents and relatives and friends either out of work or in the toughest, dirtiest, lowest-status jobs with low pay and few benefits, and they conclude that this is what the "system" has in store for them. Not an inspiring prospect. The parents, having never experienced anything better, usually are bitter or resigned.

Finally, most Negro youngsters today, even with the emphasis on new opportunities, do not know the extent of the jobs open to them. There is a catch, of course, and it is "if they have the training or qualifications."

We know the jobs are there, because the Urban League Skills Bank in just one year receives thousands of "job orders" from employers. And though the Bank does a phenomenal job in placing as many as forty thousand people a year, there are still tens of thousands of jobs open and unfilled because the skilled and trained Negro citizens to step into them have not been found.

Well, what can we do as individuals to educate Negro youngsters and help them qualify for these available jobs?

We can help motivate them. We can see to it that they get solid up-to-date guidance and counseling. We can make sure that they know about opportunities for training and apprenticeship, that they see the Skills Bank literature. We can encourage youths to enter the Job Corps, the Neighborhood Youth Corps, and other programs designed to prepare them for careers—programs of the antipoverty war, the Office of Economic Opportunity, the Departments of Labor and Health, Education and Welfare, and many others. We can make sure that vocational training in our public schools is reaching Negro youngsters and that it is training them for jobs which will not disappear as technology and automation advance.

What about specifics?

Take the matter of inspiring youngsters. There are a few highly visible examples of exceptional Negro men and women such as Ralph Bunche and Marian Anderson. The dilemma for the youngster is that he realizes that he has scant chance of duplicating such extraordinary achievement. For the most part, he receives little or no information about the successful Negro career men and women who have succeeded in virtually every conceivable type of occupation—careers for which he can expect to qualify.

It makes good sense to give youngsters a chance to meet, talk to, and hear from some of these Negro citizens who are moving along in their careers. Their achievements can be perceived by the youngsters as within the realm of possibility. Thus, these adults—particularly the men—can serve as role models. These are crucially needed in the many cases where such models are absent from the family or neighborhood.

What can an individual do to bring together Negro youngsters and these positive role models? I know a woman in one medium-sized city who asked herself this question and decided that one good possibility was the public school assembly program. In her city the public schools have assemblies of all students once a week for programs of various sorts, from entertainment to serious debate on foreign policy. Why not, she mused, see whether Negroes were included in the current school assembly programs? It turned out that almost never had any Negroes been included, and those who had were almost always musicians or entertainers.

She went to the guidance counselor at a nearby high school and discussed the need for role models with him. He enthusiastically endorsed her views and suggested that Negroes be included in the vocational assembly programs in which students are briefed about recent developments and career futures in various occupations. The counselor took it up with the other counselors in the system and they adopted the principle. The committee assigned to prepare the programs successfully located a chemist, a data processing specialist, a lab technician, and an insurance man, all successful Negro citizens, all glad to talk to school children. They participated in a series of ten vocational presentations at various schools, thanks to the initiative of this one woman.

What was the result? Encouraging. Each of the Negro citizens who participated received letters or telephone calls from several youngsters. The kids wanted to know more. And in half a dozen instances the youths were invited by these role models to visit their work places and see what kind of activity was included in their jobs. Obviously, something must have gotten across to some of the youngsters.

Another activity spurred on by an individual in one of our League cities is plant visits. It seemed to her that youngsters were too far removed from what was really going on in her city. So she arranged with some of the leading manufacturing, processing, retail, and clerical-job firms to bring in groups of junior high school boys and girls. She rounded up a half-dozen other mothers who volunteered to help out and they took the kids to see the kinds of jobs being done in their city.

Fortunately, there were appreciable numbers of Negro

workers at each place, so the object lesson was valid. In some of the places the youngsters could talk to the workers. From them the kids learned how the workers had prepared for the jobs, what education was needed, how long it took to arrive at such and such a position, and so on. And, of course, they also learned that some of these workers had started out in much the same way and come from backgrounds similar to their own.

In another case, I know a man in one of our major cities who has a deep concern for opening job opportunities to Negro youths. His special interest is to see that youngsters receive up-to-date, thoroughly practical vocational training in the public schools. He began, alone, to review the vocational training curricula in his city. They were good in some areas, he found, such as auto mechanics, but sadly out of date in others, such as metalworking and fabrication. He also found that relatively few Negro youngsters were either taking or completing the vocational courses.

He sought out businessmen who were major employers in the city and discussed his findings and the businessmen's actual needs in the way of trained employees. Soon he had a committee of interested people who were willing to review the curricula, the equipment, the teaching procedures, and to make recommendations for improvements.

But bringing more Negro youths into the vocational courses turned out to be a very complex matter. He found that guidance counselors at the schools usually advised Negro youths to enroll for the least exciting, least rewarding, traditionally "Negro job" training courses. The rationale was, "Why train them for jobs they cannot get?"

The other side of the coin was that the youngsters had no urge to train for "Negro jobs"—particularly since they observed plenty of experienced workers who were jobless.

My friend discussed these matters with church leaders in the Negro community, the leaders of the local NAACP chapter, and some of the fraternal organizations. The result was intense interest and a campaign which still is rolling along to change the counseling techniques and to inspire Negro youths to enroll in vocational training that will lead to jobs of real consequence.

These are just a few of the positive efforts that individuals can undertake to give Negro youths a fair shake in preparing for careers. There are many others, of course, and they are limited only by the imaginativeness and initiative of the individual.

Some persons may want to borrow the films and slide-films that are available to help counsel and motivate Negro youths. The Urban League has several which it has produced: *A Morning for Jimmy; You Can Be There; Charm by Choice; Plan and Prepare.* Some companies have produced excellent films for this purpose also: New York Telephone Company, for instance, brought out an excellent one designed to show dropouts why they should complete their education.

Reaching Out

Perhaps one of the greatest challenges lies in involving the parents of slum kids in this whole process of education, motivation, advice and counseling. Too often the parents of youngsters in the ghetto are unsympathetic, apathetic, or antagonistic to their children's education. This is understandable. If you have been crushed by "the system," you are not likely to believe it holds much promise for your children, and will not encourage them to cooperate with it. But the effort to gain their understanding and support for the education of their children must be made. Such efforts require great skill and tact and present the most challenging opportunities for voluntary efforts.

Volunteers play an effective role in helping newcomer

families and slum families shake loose from apathy and avoid pitfalls. In Washington, D.C., the local Urban League serves as a focal point for a program called familiarly FAN. This stands for "Friends and Neighbors" and it "ties" a newcomer family, or a family that needs counsel, to a resident family that "knows the ropes."

The children of the newcomer family are brought together with the kids of the experienced family; the wives get together; the husbands socialize and chat about common problems and interests. In short order the newcomers are introduced to supermarkets, the best places to shop for bargains, the most convenient playgrounds, the libraries that offer programs, the Y's and children-serving agencies, other voluntary and public agencies and the clinics in the area. They visit the churches, are brought into the peer groups in the schools and the afterschool activities. The parents go to PTA meetings together and enter into community life together. Thus the "acculturation" process is speeded and the police blotters and social service rolls are spared additional statistics of failure.

I never will forget the report of one of our FAN volunteer families from Pittsburgh. This family was put in touch by the local Urban League with a family of six that had lived in the city for years, but because of its isolation in the ghetto was as alien to Pittsburgh and city life as if it had just arrived from the red hills of Georgia.

Through the FAN program the children were taken once a month to a music concert or dance or theater performance, things they had never known of before. At other times the FAN family took all the children to a museum, nature center, or on a hike, or visited a library story hour program—things which were free. And perhaps once a week the "newcomer" children would eat lunch or dinner with the FAN family.

Not only were the horizons broadened for these youngsters, but the most unexpected benefits resulted. For instance, when the children first had a meal with the FAN family they were acutely embarrassed and inhibited. After a few minutes the reason became clear: they did not know what to do with all the implements because they had never eaten with knives and forks before. Another result was that these children learned the importance of cleanliness and took back to their own home the habit of washing before meals, even bringing their parents to this custom. And in occasionally helping prepare meals the youngsters learned fundamentals of both nutrition and sanitation which they likewise transmitted to their parents and their own home.

The FAN family served as an "information center" for the other family and put the mother in touch with a clinic when she had an appendicitis attack, arranging for a visiting nurse during recovery. And the father learned about the Skills Bank through the FAN family. He registered and found another and better-paying job. More important, though, he learned about adult education courses available to help him gain new, more marketable skills.

But the change in the kids was phenomenal. From sullen, suspicious, and diffident they evolved, over a period of several months, to alert, curious, intensely interested little chatterboxes. If this had been all, perhaps the change might not have been so spectacular. But the youngsters had developed new attitudes toward school, toward their city (they knew so much more about it after traveling to many of its features), toward the arts (they had thought that all music originated in a TV or radio before), and toward adults.

Where before they had sloughed off their school homework, by the end of a couple of months they were asking if they could join the FAN kids to study together. (An important factor in this was their crowded home—all four youngsters shared one room with one light, one table, and plenty of confusion. The FAN home served as a convenient study hall, among other things.)

And in the transition the children had become enthusiastic about some of their school subjects, and related them to careers that they thought they wanted to follow. One of the boys was fascinated with an outer space exhibit and decided he wanted to be an astronomer. He tackled his math and science with renewed vigor as a result.

Of course, these few examples merely begin to scratch the surface so far as the possibilities for voluntary action at the neighborhood level are concerned.

Extending Education—to the Older

There is another area of education that deserves urgent attention. It is economic or consumer education for Negro adults and it is crucial.

These citizens who can least afford to be careless with their spending need to be taught how to get the most for their money. They need to be shown how to avoid frauds, how to "shop for money" for loans, mortgages, or auto purchases.

In the ghetto, ignorance makes the deprived slum dwellers fair game for every possible legal and illegal fleecing and trimming imaginable. In East Harlem, for instance, the residents of a building will awaken one morning to find that furniture movers are placing "new" refrigerators in their apartments to replace the broken and dismal equipment they have been using. They sign a receipt for the new unit and the movers take away the old one to the junk heap. "What's this?" they think. "Is the landlord really human, replacing that forlorn thing with a refrig that really works?"

No, the landlord hasn't suddenly seen the light and installed new equipment. Sharp appliance dealers, operating just within the law, have covered the building, installing cheap, rebuilt, repainted refrigerators. Those "receipts" are really contracts, by which the tenants have committed themselves to pay for refrigerators at inflated prices and exorbitant interest rates.

The same thing, or a variation of this technique, is used to sell stoves, heaters, furniture, and TV sets. Another method is the "free trial period" come-on, in which a living room furniture set or a new rug is brought in and installed with assurances that if the family doesn't like it there is no obligation for the first seven days. Of course, if and when the family tries to locate the seller to have the furniture taken back they cannot get him on the telephone and they discover that the receipt turns out to be an iron-clad contract. By the time they finish paying for the furniture, it has long since broken down and before the final payments the seller sends his delivery wagon with a load of some other expensive wares to be forced on the family.

Ghetto families usually stick close to home and this, too, works against them. The supermarkets and discount stores, the chain drug stores and cleaners and banks generally do not locate in the slums. This automatically puts the slum dwellers in the position of trading with the little neighborhood grocery, corner drug store, local cleaner, and commercial loan or pawn shop, each of which generally charges more for the same goods or services that may be available at the big volume outlets elsewhere in the city.

It may seem absolutely impossible to you, as it did to me when I first learned of it, but many citizens of the ghetto literally do not know enough about their city to find a discount house, for instance. Nor would they think of going there, generally, because they are unfamiliar with its workings and therefore suspicious of it. Likewise the bank rather than the loan shark, and ditto the chain drug store.

It is true that the poor often have so little money coming

in that they must deal with those who extend credit rather than those who work on a cash and carry basis. But surely they and those who are somewhat better off can benefit from information about where and how to buy to stretch the money the farthest.

In some slum areas tenant groups are taking on programs of economic education. They invite in experts from the city, county, or state and in some cases the federal Department of Agriculture or Commerce to tell them about ways to figure best buys in canned goods, produce, clothing, furniture, appliances, and services. They are shown the pamphlets that are available, told about the Consumers Reports and Consumers Union publications, the Better Business Bureau and its functions and the city agencies and laws dealing with unscrupulous merchants.

Shopping for money is an exciting, tiring, and difficult thing, particularly if you never have done it before. Too often the citizen who most needs to get the best deal on his auto loan or mortgage or personal loan is the one who, because of ignorance, stress, or anxiety, makes the poorest bargain.

Here is an area in which the legitimate merchants and money lenders are definitely interested in helping. If you want to help your neighbors understand better how to avoid financial pitfalls and get the most mileage out of their money, you will find that you have willing allies in your local banks, saving and loan institutions, chambers of commerce and Better Business Bureaus and city departments of commerce and markets.

Anyone who wants to do so will find that he can put together a series of meetings on economic ABC's with relative ease. A few telephone calls to the agencies mentioned above will usually produce speakers on everything from budgeting to how to figure the true interest rate on a loan and where to shop for one. Other speakers can be found to tell how to buy a house and what the prevailing mortgage rates are and the types of financing available under different down payments and conditions. Better Business Bureau people will advise how to avoid shady merchants and shoddy goods and what recourse, if any, the buyer has. They will gladly tell the inside story of the maneuvering that goes on when you shop for a car—"high balling" and "low balling" a customer, or the "unhorsing" gambit and many of the psychological tricks of the trade that ensnare the unwary or unknowing.

Perhaps part of any such series should be devoted to the legal rights and responsibilities of a citizen. Legal clinics are sorely needed by the poor. The Legal Aid Society is a magnificent organization and the thousands of lawyers who volunteer to work with it are truly generous and accomplish much. However, their activity is focused on the individual who needs but cannot afford legal help for a specific problem.

There are many scores of thousands of citizens in the slums who need counsel of a fundamental nature to prevent falling into financial traps or signing crippling contracts, or being burdened unnecessarily, if not illegally, because of ignorance. Much of this kind of counseling could be done by law students. Some of it now is done by political clubhouses and by the local offices of national and state level politicians.

Certainly some help in understanding contracts, wills, and mortgages would be of great service. So, too, would information on where to turn in case of emergency. Also needed are basic facts about the rights of a person at a time of arrest, the laws preventing illegal search and seizure and the workings of the small claims court. Such information is fundamental, and there must be many who would be willing to share it.

In New Haven, Connecticut, the city-wide Community Progress, Inc., organization has fostered a legal adviser service available to residents in the ghetto through "community schools." This is a full-time service. The coordinator of these community schools, Robert J. Pleasure, says "people were signing their lives away in credit contracts. After the lawyer was here for a while, we found these exploiters diminishing. They were coming into the community far less frequently."

This persistent problem of the poor—signing credit contracts at exorbitant interest rates—was reduced by having a lawyer available in the same community school where mother was learning sewing and cooking, sister was taking ballet, brother was on a basketball team, and dad was enrolled in courses to increase his literacy—reading speed and understanding. In this setting, basic legal counsel is offered and is helping improve the standard of living of ghetto families.

Education for All

One of the outstanding examples of revolutionizing the school to meet the needs of the community is Winchester School in New Haven, Connecticut. Set in the heart of the Dixwell ghetto, Winchester in 1950 was eighty years old. Principal of Winchester at the time was Isadore Wexler, who had the novel idea that the school should serve the people of the area beyond the basic education of their children during the formal school day. Wexler surveyed the problems of the people of Dixwell and found a high ratio of families on relief, high unemployment, high rate of youthful lawbreakers, and general social disorganization.

Wexler was convinced that the school could help improve some of the conditions. And he was convinced that the people must help themselves. "You must do *with* the poor, not for them," he says. "And you can involve the poor. We proved it in Dixwell."

There was no lunchroom at Winchester School, and one of Wexler's first projects was to survey the eating habits of the children enrolled. "Soda pop and potato chips—that was

breakfast. Lunch: cupcakes and soda." Wexler called a conference of mothers of school children. The women showed
up and he put the matter before them. They were interested
and concerned, but lacked leadership. The meeting decided
that a community-wide effort would be launched to make sure
that every child in the school ate a hot lunch each day.

The mothers took on the task of raising the money needed
for the lunches. They conducted benefits and campaigns and
managed to ante up the needed $1400. A nearby housing
project donated space for a kitchen and dining room. Finally,
three hundred youngsters were enabled to eat a hot lunch
each day, a lunch which gave them two-thirds of their needed
daily calories.

That was the beginning. The next effort centered around
the city's plans to replace Winchester with a new building.
Wexler and his mothers' committee called a conference involving the whole Dixwell neighborhood. They discussed the
needs of the community and came up with recommendations
for inclusion in the new school building. They requested that
the new school meet "the needs of neighborhood age groups,
including children of pre-school age, teenagers and adults."
They also asked for "discussion rooms, facilities for education
in family life, home nursing, industrial arts, hobbies, and
possibly a swimming pool."

The New Haven school board tabled all of the suggestions
and threatened to fire Wexler for "insubordination." "You can
fire me," Wexler told the board, "but you can't fire the
conditions in Dixwell." Dixwell's leaders went everywhere in
the city calling on all the organizations in New Haven, from
service clubs to social groups, from Boy Scouts to veterans'
organizations, to explain why they needed a community
school.

The school board held a public hearing on the matter and
seventy-five city-wide agencies and organizations stepped up
and endorsed Dixwell's requests. Dixwell got its community

school, complete with a thousand-seat auditorium, a stage adequate for major orchestras, a small film theater, a cafeteria, library, and meeting rooms for community activities. The new plant now serves as a source of community replenishment in three basic ways:

It is an educational center for children and adults.

It is a center for community activities, where young and old may participate in sports, physical fitness programs, informal recreation, classes in arts and crafts, civic meetings, and other leisure time pursuits.

It is a center of community and neighborhood life twelve months of the year, from morning until 10 P.M.

Today there are more than fifty programs designed to extend the school into the community and bring the people of the area into the school.

Today the path that Winchester pioneered is being followed in six other New Haven schools in extensive activities financed in part by the Ford Foundation, various federal grants, and the city itself. In each of the seven schools there is a team consisting of a program coordinator appointed by the Board of Education, a recreation supervisor from the Park and Recreation Department, a group work agency person, and a neighborhood coordinator from Community Progress, Inc.

In a recent count there were 660 volunteers helping round out the programs of the community schools. They came from local colleges and universities, high schools, and prep schools —both faculty and students—from business, labor, churches, Jaycees, Junior League, and homes (represented by housewives) all over the city. More than five hundred of the volunteers are working in educational programs which enrich the curriculum offerings or help remedy problems uncovered in the normal school process. More than eighty are in the group work programs and fifty in leisure time activities.

Every effort is made to develop programs tailored to the

needs of the school neighborhood and the people it serves. There is a definite correlation between after-school programs and what goes on in the classrooms. For example, a number of Yale student volunteers who have language specialties are helping children whose first language is not English. Many of these youngsters have difficulty with their studies because of their limited knowledge of English and now those of them with Spanish, German, Italian, and Portuguese backgrounds are beginning to receive adequate attention.

The "bill of fare" at these community school "cafeterias" is extraordinary; it ranges from help with the subjects taught to athletics and aesthetics. Mrs. Edith Rosenberg, a housewife, heard about the community schools, volunteered and now heads a group of volunteers who teach cooking and sewing. Lloyd Radcliffe and Jerome Mitchell teach tennis to youngsters from twelve years up. Ruth Crego, studying for her doctorate in Russian literature, teaches that language to kids in the fourth to seventh grades. Russian is offered in the senior high schools in New Haven. Youngsters are taking creative writing, choral speaking, journalism (and publishing a newspaper). Mrs. Fenno Heath arranged to bring orchestral instruments into classrooms for inspection by the kids prior to concerts of the New Haven Symphony, which the youngsters attended.

Yale faculty members' wives help twice a week at Winchester in remedial reading programs. However, they each have completed a four-week training program before they begin. Some Southern Connecticut State College students fill certain requirements for teaching degrees by working with the youngsters on a regular basis. And members of the Future Teachers of America Club at the city's high schools are learning the ropes by tutoring and conducting reading and math games, helping with homework and showing kids how to use the library at their school. Volunteers also supervise tots in arts and crafts, games and storytelling sessions.

A valuable program called "Link" helps kids eight to twelve relate to the outside community. Yale student volunteers are the leaders, and there is a group of four kids to each leader. The small group permits each youngster to experience some of the attention he needs to develop self-confidence and to try new interests in a permissive setting. The Link leader acts as "big brother" or older friend. He is kept hopping, trying to find activities that fulfill the needs and interests of the individual youngsters in the group. So you may find these groups of five on weekends at libraries, camping out, taking hikes, playing ball, or visiting a museum or art gallery.

Amateur thespians have been encouraged and at two schools have staged productions—one of them was Pirandello's *The Jar.* An electronics club at one school built transistor radios, Geiger counters, and a hi-fi amplifier for an electronic guitar. An eight-year-old who lives with her great-grandmother takes piano lessons from a volunteer. She is so thrilled with her accomplishments that between lessons she telephones her teacher and plays new pieces on the battered family piano so that she can share the experience with the volunteer. This is but one example of awakening dormant interests through voluntary activity.

The community schools of New Haven have enlarged the lives of literally thousands (both volunteers and students) in a brief span of time. The potential in communities throughout the land is tremendous and the opportunities for individuals to participate in these exciting programs are limitless.

Chapter 5 ☞ ☜

Economics and Integration

After the 1964 Civil Rights Act went into effect compliance
and attitudes varied from place to place in the nation. One
of the stories making the rounds is about the beauty-shop
operator in a southern city who decided to discourage Negro
business by charging fantastically inflated prices. From the
first Negro woman who came in and had a permanent wave
he requested $125—and he got it. The following day, he
was seen putting a sign in his window: "No White Trash
Served Here."

Accurate or apocryphal, the story has a reasonably clear-
cut moral. As Mrs. Ruby Hurley, southeastern regional director for the NAACP puts it, "There are only two languages
the white folks understand—the ballot and the buck. When
the cash registers keep quiet, they react." The other side
of the coin also is true: when the cash register rings, they
react.

We need have no reluctance to play upon this Pavlovian
response to the cash register bell to forward civil rights and
integration. From the legal standpoint, the federal law and
many state laws now require that public money not be used
to continue, maintain, or extend segregation and discrimination.

From the moral standpoint, public money, coming from
all segments of the population, must not be used to cripple

any segment of the citizenry. Private citizens and organizations in our free society may use their money as they wish, of course. Enlightened use of purchasing power and investment may forward civil rights and hasten the end of Jim Crow in all his forms.

"Nothing," says the civil rights officer for the U. S. Public Health Service, Robert M. Nash, "is more inefficient and costly than segregated facilities." One government spokesman has described hospitals in the South: "Those hospitals have two of everything and even when the segregation signs are removed the tendency is to go on using them as before."

Item: One southern hospital recently completed an addition with federal money as well as local. When the addition was operative, it was reserved for white patients and Negro patients were assigned to the old wards.

Item: Negro patients at another southern hospital must make a $50 deposit before admittance. When an overflow of white patients occurs the Negro patients are moved out into the halls.

The National Urban League issued a coruscating report on hospital discrimination of the type cited above. It covered the nation and listed literally scores of incidents and situations of discrimination in hospitals throughout the country. The Department of Health, Education, and Welfare has used these reports in its moves to bring such practices to a halt.

Other features of the southern landscape that will stand as monuments to blind bigotry are the many Negro schools built feverishly in towns and cities of the south in the 1950s. During that decade southerners glimpsed the inevitable and hastily began to build school buildings for Negroes. It was a rear-guard action, to justify the now-discredited "separate but equal" doctrine which they had long embraced verbally and ignored in reality.

The existing Negro schools were visible evidence of the

emptiness of this "doctrine"—they were dilapidated, poorly equipped, shockingly neglected examples of human inhumanity. The new schools were often good educational plants, with newer equipment, and better facilities than the existing white schools. The cost of these duplicate facilities ran into many scores of millions, I am sure, and had an incalculable cost in terms of diverting money from other pressing public problems in those states.

The very fact that duplicate facilities are so costly should help accelerate integration of the schools. In New Rochelle, the highly publicized hometown of *de facto* segregation in the public schools, the problem was resolved by closing the all-Negro Lincoln school and bussing children to the other schools in the town. Bussing reportedly saved New Rochelle money because it cost less than continuing to operate the outmoded, inefficient Lincoln school building. This was an unusual situation and few communities are likely to find bussing is an economy measure.

Stagnation

There is evidence that some citizens of the Deep South realize how costly segregation has been. They have seen also how much more expensive it can be if federal government aid dries up, if racial friction causes industry to bypass the south in its plant locations and investments, and if it continues to be a "talent export" area rather than "talent magnet."

In Mississippi, the state that always seems to trail its brothers in statistics of economic and social health, more and more responsible citizens recognize the basic causes for lack of growth and prosperity. One-third of the state's budget comes from the federal government. In one recent year $150,000,000 was funneled into the state treasury and used by various agencies for federally supported programs. Such dependence on the federal paymaster to finance a state is precarious, when the state is committed by tradition and inclination to segregation and the federal government is committed by law to nondiscrimination, or else. The "or else," of course, is that federal funds will be cut off if segregation continues in federally supported programs administered by the state.

Other reasons for laggard positions by southern states are numerous but related inevitably to the central fact of the segregationist tradition. One of the planners of Mississippi's current industrial development drive says "when half your population is poorly educated and nonproductive it's an awful drag on the economy. We've got to change that." A Hattiesburg merchant, fed up with the lack of progress that resistance to integration has brought to the state, says, "It's brought us nothing but trouble since 1961—that's when the first freedom rides started. A lot of us are ready to try something else."

Some manufacturers have found that informal boycotts of Mississippi products have hurt them. In McComb, an aluminum fabricator claims he lost $250,000 in sales in one year from such boycotts. A southern Mississippi manufacturer of household goods now ships his goods from across the state line in Louisiana so that he can use that state as an F.O.B. point.

Tourists, who have added to the state income considerably in the past, have found other places more attractive. The state reports that in just one recent year tourists spent between $40,000,000 and $60,000,000 less than in previous years.

Consistent with that discovery, the official sanction and financial support of the state for the notorious white Citizens' Councils have been cut off. At one time the Councils were receiving $5000 monthly from the state to finance their racist activities.

Economic Pressure

The United States Civil Rights Commission during its hearings in Mississippi took testimony from many witnesses. Several of the Negroes who had the courage to testify told of economic pressure applied to prevent them from voting.

One woman, Mrs. Mary Thomas, operated a grocery store in which she sold beer for eight years with no problems. But fifteen minutes after she tried to register to vote in December 1964 she was arrested for not having a license to sell beer. She had, she said, federal, state, and city licenses. The sheriff disputed her on this and contended she had been warned months before to renew her state license.

Mrs. Mary Welsh and Mrs. Daisy Griffin testified that the circuit clerk of Humphreys County, G. H. Hood, threatened to block their supplies of federal surplus commodities when they arrived to register to vote.

These are only a couple of examples of the economic pressures applied to Negroes in southern states to "keep them in line"—which translates to "away from ballot boxes, and away from 'white' places." The direct pressures used to intimidate include firing workers, calling loans and mortgages, cutting off supplies of groceries, gas, and oil from distributors to Negro retailers, terminating leases, and so on. So severe has this pressure become in some Negro communities that national organizations such as CORE and SNCC have for years been conducting national campaigns to secure money, food, and clothing for those who are suffering from such reprisals.

Typical of the response is the action of a political club, the Ansonia Independent Democrats, on Manhattan's West Side. The club solicited the eighty thousand residents of the west sixties and seventies to contribute food, money, and

clothing through collection points at local churches, supermarkets, and merchants. The club has "adopted" Starkville,
Mississippi. One of the club's directors, Andrew Goldman,
visited Mississippi with his wife in 1964 and organized the
project. "The economic reprisals against Starkville's Negroes,"
he says, "including employment blacklists, are due to their
participation in the voter-registration drive, among other integration efforts."

Integration of the public schools has caused any number
of difficult adjustments. One of them that is highly disturbing
is the policy adopted in many areas of firing, retiring, and
putting out to pasture Negro teachers when the formerly all-
Negro schools are closed. It was estimated in 1965 that 5500
southern Negro teachers faced loss of jobs as Negro pupils
shift to "white" schools.

There are some subtle issues involved, and the stakes are
big. The assistant field secretary of the National Education
Association says that the U. S. Supreme Court decision of
1954 "applies to the integration of faculties as well as pupils.
Federal aid therefore could be cut off to districts guilty of
firing Negro teachers." A spokesman for the Department of
Health, Education, and Welfare was quoted in the New York
Times as saying there was no legal basis for preventing dis-
missal of Negro teachers under the Civil Rights Act because
federal funds are not used to employ teachers.

In some states, such as North Carolina, teachers have been
employed under one-year contracts without tenure since
1954. Dr. S. E. Duncan, president of the North Carolina
Teachers Association describes it: as Negro students made
clear their intention to transfer to white schools the communities in the state told their Negro teachers they wouldn't
be rehired. "The Negro teachers were dismissed," he says,
"and in some instances white teachers were hired to replace
them." It was not a matter of qualifications, he states, for

whites with no greater qualifications were hired to replace Negro teachers dismissed.

In Oklahoma, 396 Negro teachers lost their jobs as a result of integrating education. Most were dismissed in the years 1955 and 1956. At this writing there are only fifty-six Negro teachers on integrated faculties in the entire state.

This is what is happening at this time according to the education experts:

Some counties are dismissing all Negro teachers outright.

Some prevent Negro teachers from teaching white pupils and are putting them to work as librarians, attendance officers, custodians, or counselors for Negro pupils. In this way they have practically no contact with white pupils.

In some cases supervisors of Negro school districts are being kept on as roving "consultants" who spend an hour or two at each integrated school. Thus, some systems are reporting they have an "integrated" staff in ten schools by counting the consultant ten times.

White officials are replacing able Negro administrators to prevent Negroes from obtaining good-paying jobs and authority over schools with white pupils.

Some counties have a neat formula worked out: for every thirty Negro pupils moved into a white school under so-called "freedom of choice" plans, one Negro teacher is fired. This kind of economic reprisal has an obvious dampening effect on Negro leaders and parents who want pupil integration.

In some cases Negro teachers have been asked to submit their resignations in return for a "good recommendation" for future jobs. Others have been warned that these will be withheld if they protest their dismissals.

The only glimmer of light in the picture is the concerted opposition to this wholesale injustice by such organizations as the N.E.A., NAACP, American Friends Service Committee, American Teachers Association, National Urban League, Southern Regional Council, and state teachers associations. The NAACP Legal Defense and Educational Fund brought suits in North Carolina to block scheduled dismissals there.

Is there something pathological in southern mentality that simply rules out any possibility of qualified Negro educators instructing both white and Negro pupils? Is southern vision so narrow that it refuses to recognize qualified Negro teachers and administrators when it sees them? If the answer is yes, the south is indeed profligate.

As more *de facto* school segregation cases are unraveled in the north and student bodies are integrated, the temptation to follow the south's lead on disposition of teachers and administrators may occur. Nowhere in the nation can we afford this pattern. Men of good conscience must not let it happen. Men of good sense will not let it continue.

It is understandable that Negro leaders advocate boycotts of products in order to bring additional economic weight to bear on civil rights targets.

In recent years more and more citizen organizations have not hesitated to tell businessmen what they thought of a company's hiring policy, its services to the public, its promotion and management training programs, even its investment policies, particularly when these reflected discriminatory practices by either design or default.

The confrontation in Pittsburgh of Negro ministers and one of the world's giant oil companies is now history. In this case, after surveying the local hiring practices of the company, the ministers called on the management and requested a reversal of the policy which excluded Negroes from service station and truck driver sales positions. The company denied the allegation, demurred and procrastinated until the ministers called again with a request that specified numbers of Negroes be hired by a certain date or a boycott would be called. The company did nothing. The ministers, on the appointed date, called on their flocks to bypass all products of the oil company until the requested hiring had been accomplished.

For several weeks the company held out. And if it had been a sheer matter of a boycott in Pittsburgh alone by only one segment of the population, the company undoubtedly could have resisted indefinitely. However, the news of the boycott was flashed to Negro citizens in other cities and through newspapers, radios, and TV to the whole nation, as well as overseas. The boycott spread to other cities, to sympathetic whites as well as Negroes, and the unfavorable publicity was something less than fragrant. The company, wishing it had never thumped this particular hornets' nest, capitulated. In fact, it thoroughly reviewed its policies and is today one of the leaders in the nation in hiring and promotion based on merit rather than myopic, moss-backed policies.

Picketing has been used against companies which have lagged in equal treatment and opportunities for Negroes. One demonstration was mounted against the world's largest bank for discrimination in hiring. Citizens were urged "Don't Save Where You Can't Earn." Demonstrations were launched also against the nation's largest manufacturing concern to emphasize the need for it to open up more supervisory jobs to Negroes in technical, professional, and managerial positions.

Business Must Act

Even today the great blank spots—the companies which still lag in hiring Negroes, the unions which still persist in freezing out qualified Negro applicants—still mar the general picture of limited progress.

But it is not enough to say, "Our company hires Negroes."

How many? Who? Are they "instant Negroes"—the recep-
tionist who looks like Leslie Uggams and types 130 words a
minute; the clerk who talks like Ralph Bunche and has a
graduate degree?

Unless Negroes are represented in every department and
in all job classifications, including management levels, your
company is not doing what it could and should be doing.

Business must face up to the problems involved. Too often
the top management of a company issues the order to hire
Negroes only to have that order find its way into a middle-
management desk and disappear. Without follow-through
from the top, progress cannot be made. Procedures have to
be set up to insure that progress reports are forthcoming and
steps are taken to enforce company policy at all levels.

I know that some quarters will object to this approach.
The dreaded words "special treatment" are brought up and
somehow the impression is given that it is bad or undemocratic to go out of our way to hire people because of their
race. But isn't that what has been done in the past? Weren't
people turned down on the basis of being Negro? In other
words, whites were hired specifically because of their race.
No wonder Negroes now demand "equal time" or, to
coin a paradox, "equal preference."

The time has come to right past wrongs. Past discrimination has cost all of us, incalculable trouble and money. It
just isn't worth it. The President's Council of Economic Ad-
visers has said: "It is estimated that society loses up to $20
billion per year of potential production as a result of employment discrimination and poorer education opportunities
for nonwhites."

Add to that total of lost production the amount spent on
welfare.

Harry Truman, when he was President, had a sign on his
desk: "The buck stops here." All of us should take that to
heart, because in many ways we live in a buck-passing society.

People are all too willing to say, "It's his responsibility, not mine." The temptation is especially strong for business to point the long finger at the schools and say that the schools are not educating and training young men and women well enough to hold down jobs in today's ever more complex industry.

That may be true, but it remains an excuse for inaction. No one would dream of closing down a business because of problems in some other area; ways are found to conquer difficulties. So, too, business must teach what the schools have failed to teach. And business must use its creativity and ingenuity to reclaim from lives of frustration and poverty those young people "pushed out" or left out of our schools.

Economics and Higher Education

The "almighty dollar" has great influence in the academic field these days, as it always has had, of course. I think of four news items that illustrate this.

The first piece reported that my alma mater, Princeton, received gifts totaling $49,500,000 in one eleven-month period. This is a sizable hunk of change, in any man's reckoning. It was a record amount for Princeton; perhaps it equals or even surpasses what Harvard, Yale, or MIT may have collected in a single year, I do not know. The Ivy League schools are extremely successful in raising money from alumni, friends, business, and foundations.

The second article concerned the total annual income of the United Negro College Fund, the collective fund-raising effort that aids in the support of predominantly Negro schools in eleven southern states. To be shared among the thirty-three colleges, the Fund has raised $5,174,000 in this same banner year. This would come to $153,757 per institution, if it were divided evenly, which it is not. The colleges included have a total enrollment of approximately 30,000. The enrollment of Princeton is about one-sixth of that: 5387.

The third and fourth articles are closely related. The third quoted the late Dr. Rufus Clement, distinguished president of Atlanta University, one of the member institutions of the United Negro College Fund. Dr. Clement told a conference sponsored by the National Conference of Churches that white northern universities were raiding the faculties and the student bodies of predominantly Negro colleges. They do so, said Dr. Clement, because they "need a Negro as a symbol of liberalism."

"If they take the cream of our student crop," he said, "they leave us poor indeed. We're left with few leaders for our student bodies." What remedy? Dr. Clement suggested that money should be given to help Negro colleges compete with northern institutions.

A few days later the New York *Times* carried an article headed:

Ivy League Gains Made By Negroes

The article went on: "Negro students are beginning to feel welcome in predominantly white high-prestige colleges, according to reports of admissions officers at the Ivy League institutions.

"The admissions picture at these eight colleges is beginning to show the results of the civil rights movement, the growth and effectiveness of special pre-college tutoring programs, recruiting efforts by the colleges themselves, and increasing referrals from the National Scholarship Service and Fund for Negro students." The Dean of Admissions at Pennsylvania "guessed" that he had received about one hundred applications from "the disadvantaged category, most of them Negroes." About forty would be accepted and given scholarships, he said.

Now, judging from these rudimentary reports, I would suggest that there is more than a kernel of corroboration for Dr. Clement's position. One might conclude not only that "them as has, gits," but that "them as has, can—and do—outbid."

Certainly I do not wish to suggest that Negro students stick to the southern schools, regardless. But it seems to me apparent that the vast majority of Negro college students in the south are likely to go to the so-called Negro colleges located there for a number of years to come. The situation would seem to call for additional support, on a massive scale, of these institutions so that they can upgrade faculty and facilities and do a better job of educating these youngsters. Inevitably some of my readers are going to raise the specter of "supporting and maintaining segregated institutions by giving to the Negro colleges." This I would deny, on three counts:

1. None of the colleges generally called "Negro colleges" in the UNCF has any discriminatory policies or practices. They do not exclude on artificial grounds. They welcome students and faculty of all races and faiths.
2. Knowing that these colleges will continue to be a mainstay in the education of Negro students for years to come, it does not make sense to starve them financially.
3. The goal of the so-called Negro colleges is to become first-rate institutions of learning which will attract members of other races by the preeminence of their faculties and curricula. It takes money to reach this goal and, therefore, the United Negro College Fund deserves more support, not less.

So, when the question of contributions comes up around the dinner table of the "advantaged" American family, at the desk of the corporate contributions officer or the foundation staff men, I would hope that the United Negro College Fund would receive serious and understanding attention. Further, I would urge that it be looked at in perspective. One should consider the tremendous need for trained, well-educated Negro youths today, when one looks at the institutions that are now training them (and are likely to continue to do so for decades) and measures these factors against their needs and the needs of the institutions that traditionally have received the contribution dollars.

What would happen, I wonder, if the institutional contributors took the revolutionary step of writing all those Ivy League and Class A private colleges that now receive the bulk of their education contributions a letter such as this:

Dear President————:

You, better than I, know the current problems faced in educating the young Negro men and women of our nation for the careers they should and must have. You know the urgency of the need. You know the demand for such youngsters by business and industry. And, I am sure, you recognize that one of the most expeditious ways to upgrade the training of these young people is to improve the faculties and facilities of the institutions where the majority of them are now (and in the near future will continue to be).

You will agree, I know, that such programs require money—and lots of it. You will agree, I believe, that the need is so great that it constitutes an emergency. And you will therefore understand why our contributions committee has decided that all of our traditional education grants will, because of this emergency, be channeled immediately, and for five years, into support of selected institutions that bear heavy responsibility for training large numbers of our Negro young men and women . . .

I would like to recommend a similar approach to the support of other institutions that sorely need the money and are pressed increasingly for responsible leadership. I am thinking particularly about the major civil rights agencies, such as the NAACP, the NAACP Legal Defense & Educational Fund, the Southern Christian Leadership Conference, the Urban League—at both the national and local level—and others of proven value.

The League has finally become "respectable." By this I mean that the contrast between the attitude of the power structure, the business community and its leaders, when I became president of the National Urban League in 1960 and the attitude as of 1968, for instance, is simply unbelievable.

Since we are talking at this point about economics, let me cite as one indication of the change, the simple fact that in 1960 business support of the Urban League totaled less than $50,000 and it all came from fewer than three dozen companies. In 1967, business contributions totaled $1,056,000 and came from 370 companies whose names read like the roster of the Dow-Jones industrial index. Foundation support has blossomed also, and reached the healthy figure of $905,000 in 1967.

Top business leaders know that the League has spent nearly sixty years of dedicated effort to help upgrade Negro life in every way. They know that the League has been increasingly successful at this. And they also have the facts to corroborate Walter W. Heller's estimate that lifting the income of Negro workers to that of their white counterparts would boost our national rate of economic growth. This "equal pay" would give Negroes the money to spend an additional

> $3,600,000,000 on food
> $1,700,000,000 on clothing
> $1,500,000,000 on housing

$1,300,000,000 on household operation
$1,200,000,000 on cars and transportation
$1,200,000,000 on recreation and amusement
$ 500,000,000 more on utilities
$ 800,000,000 more on miscellaneous items

The League has consistently and ever more effectively worked to bring about "the millennium" described in those dollar projections above. It has scored untold successes, but the overwhelming dimensions of the need—literally millions of newly urban Negroes—and the very real limitations of League budget and staff have meant that today there are still hundreds of thousands of Negro Americans who have not yet been assimilated into the life of the city in productive, positive ways.

Dollar Discrimination

Discrimination, bigotry, prejudice, callousness, and fear have kept many Negroes down. Even their own tax dollars often have been used against them:

In seven states, over 40 per cent of all federal Atomic Energy Commission grants went to public universities and research centers that were Jim Crow.

State employment offices are financed wholly by federal dollars. Many of them give preferred treatment to whites, force Negroes to use separate offices, facilities, and refer them to "Negro" jobs—those "handle" jobs we spoke of earlier—particularly in southern cities.

In cities such as Atlanta, retraining programs financed by federal money place Negroes in courses for lower-paid occupations while whites receive training in subjects such as pharmaceutical and medical technology.

Of $4,000,000 paid to southern colleges recently by the National Science Foundation, two-thirds went to segregated institutions.

From 1960 to 1962, Negro pupils in Greenwood, Mississippi received only one-fifth of the federally sponsored free lunches even though they were half of the school enrollment. Greenwood is not unique.

Title VI of the Civil Rights Law is intended to change such practices by cutting off the flow of funds from the U. S. Treasury, via various government agencies, to institutions that discriminate.

It takes great personal courage and/or people who are not dependent on the local power structure for their economic livelihood to register complaints and bring about the changes that the Law is supposed to guarantee. That is one place that the League makes itself felt. The reports on the workings of the new Law during its first years showed the need for alert testing and reporting of violations:

In Perry, Georgia, the main theater in town, the Muse, has been converted into a private club to avoid admitting Negroes. Its marquee reads in foot-high letters "COMMITTEE OF 1,000, PRIVATE."

In Carthage, Mississippi, A. J. Lewis sent his daughter to a school that had previously been all-white. He was fired from his job. Other Negroes, considering sending their children to the school, "got the message."

Negroes report that those who participate in Civil Rights demonstrations as well as testing of the Civil Rights Act often become "poor credit risks" overnight. They discover this when they next apply for loans or charge accounts.

In Anniston, Alabama, Negroes are refused service at one gasoline station.

In Bessemer, Alabama, a Negro school teacher who went

to the main library for a book was directed to the branch in the Negro neighborhood. In these two cities, reports the New York Times, "local Negroes have been afraid to make wide tests of public accommodations."

The price of goods or services at formerly all-white places is often doubled for the Negro customer.

The Urban League is one important channel for bringing complaints to the attention of the appropriate federal agency in such cases.

Concerned citizens, it seems to me, have a responsibility to be alert to discrimination, particularly in its economic forms, and to report such discrimination to the agencies that can deal effectively with it. The League and the NAACP are such agencies. They have both the experience and the broad, community-wide contacts to follow through on situations requiring change.

Individuals who really want to put their principles into practice can advance civil rights by their buying pattern. The concerned individual will seek out places that hire on an obviously open basis. He will buy his clothes, drug store needs, groceries, gasoline, automobiles, and appliances from such retailers. The products are standardized and their quality is identical from one retailer to another, so why not endorse the personnel policies of the businessman who operates on a democratic basis?

Why not extend this philosophy to the purchase of all types of goods? Now I am not demanding that people boycott all merchandise produced in an area where segregation may be prevalent. But I am suggesting that where there is a choice of products of similar quality the buyer seriously consider purchasing the brands manufactured by companies that hire and promote workers without regard to color. I know that the 1965 Civil Rights Law made it illegal for most large companies to discriminate in hiring. But there are companies that have frankly and willingly embraced the equal opportunity concept—such as the Plans for Progress corporations—as contrasted with those that have been shoved into the present era dragging their heels and waving the Stars and Bars.

The concerned individual does not hide his light under a bushel. Without sanctimony, he willingly tells his friends and those who ask him what his economic policies are concerning race. And he explains why he has decided to pursue them. Furthermore, he extends his influence through his business, club, voluntary agency, and service organization activity. In each case he presents the case for selective buying—as well as enlightened hiring, upgrading, and training—as a means of furthering the economic well-being of the community.

Concerned citizens ask questions when they come across obvious cases of discrimination. When they see all-white work forces, teams, drivers or staffs in businesses, as well as schools and government, they ask questions. And if the answers seem to call for further investigation or action, they take the next step. These citizens cooperate with the local NAACP or Urban League to investigate and correct situations that require change. Such citizens may volunteer their time to aid the local civil rights agencies in these efforts, or the local fair housing committee in finding decent housing for minority citizens.

The concerned individual does not endorse bigotry with his dollars. He makes an effort to spend his money in recreational places and restaurants that welcome Negro citizens also. In his investment policies he is consistent. He buys stock in companies that have sound, integrated personnel policies. He keeps his savings and checking accounts at banks that hire and promote according to merit, not race. He does his banking and applies for loans and mortgages in the same manner.

Furthermore, he encourages his business or union and the

organizations he can influence—church, voluntary, service—
to invest and bank similarly.

If he is an officer of an organization and that organization
is imaginative and has the resources, he may suggest that it
do as the International Ladies Garment Workers Union has
done—build low- and middle-income housing for hundreds
of families. Union pension funds, business, church, university
retirement plan funds—these must be invested. Why not put
these funds to work in a socially useful role that will earn a
substantial return on investment? The goal might be the
underwriting of sound, integrated living conditions. There
are many ways in which investment toward this end can be
made.

I have spoken about individual effort. But it should be
clear that the larger and more complex the economic unit involved (family, club, church, union, business, etc.) the more
weight can be brought to bear to advance the economic well-
being of Negro Americans. Every organization that has funds
to disburse could make choices that would favorably influence or advance integration. This applies even more to
public agencies charged with responsibility for money paid
in taxes by all the people. State and local antidiscrimination
laws plus the Civil Rights Law require that public expenditures end rather than extend integration. Right-minded citizens
in public offices will see that funds are so used; alert private
citizens and organizations will monitor public expenditures to
verify that public funds have been so spent.

What else can citizens do? Those who have the power of
direction of public and quasipublic institutions such as hospitals, private schools and colleges, can review the wage and
hour policies of their organizations. There is little excuse in
the 1960s, in a seller's market and in a time of increased
awareness of the worth of the individual, for a continuance of
economic peonage in the United States. Yet, to our shame, it
is not uncommon.

Take Westchester, New York. It is perhaps the wealthiest county in the nation. There, in one of its most prosperous cities, Bronxville, the median family income is above $22,000 annually. And there the police broke up a picket line in 1965 with all the viciousness characteristic of notorious southern demonstrations. Beating sit-in demonstrators with nightsticks, the police knocked them flat, dragged and carried them screaming and bleeding into police vans. What was the cause?

Some eighty-two workers were striking against Lawrence Hospital for the right to organize, for grievance procedures, and in protest against the $1.39 hourly wage they were receiving. Civil rights leaders reported that nearly all the strikers were Negroes. They were orderlies, nurses' helpers, domestics, and kitchen help, stuck at the bottom of the job and pay scales. Their fifty-six dollars weekly for forty hours of work put their families well within the poverty-stricken category in America. And surely no one could accuse them of loafing on "cushy" jobs—hospitals just don't have that kind of work available.

I would suggest that Lawrence Hospital is not unique, that its counterpart may well exist in nearly every community. I would recommend that men and women who have the power also show concern for their fellow men and make sure all hospital employees receive a living wage. I have some sympathy but little patience with the argument that hospital costs today are high and that living wages to those who need them most will boost costs still further. Subsidizing our hospitals by working the hides off their lowest-paid, least-skilled workers is not the way to keep costs in line. In so doing we have simply moved the sweatshop from the garment district to the hospital.

I have spoken of hospitals specifically, but there are instances in education, welfare, and religion where these conditions prevail. In none of these, dedicated as they are to the liberation of the human spirit, can there be any justification for chaining men with medieval economic policies. The same holds true for all other sectors of American life today.

Chapter 6 ☛ ☚ *Jobs, Our Number One Problem*

More than anything else, the number one need today in our nation is for jobs.

In the past twenty years, four million farm jobs have been plowed under by new techniques, by mechanization, by advanced agricultural technology. Those former farm hands left the farms for the towns and cities, seeking work. Of every two Negroes in the major cities of the north and west, one is there because he was pushed off the farm by the technological progress of which we boast. But to him it was simply "no work for you here any more."

Unfortunately, there is precious little agricultural work in the city and these migrants have neither skills nor experience suitable for jobs other than day labor. They are severely handicapped because they just don't have the education needed for other jobs. As recently as 1965, only two out of five Negroes had completed high school—and some of those high schools were pretty bad. Even today half of our Negro youngsters try to find jobs without a high school diploma. For them and their elders who lack high school education the future is bleak if they do not somehow get more training. As Harvard economist Professor Otto Eckstein sees it, this— "the tragically low rate of completion of high school"—is the biggest single roadblock to economic equality for Negroes. Professor Eckstein's statement suggests the remedy—educate and train the unemployed. But the task is monumental. And it is a complex and thorny problem.

Just consider. In the fifties, advanced technology or automation hit the factories in the United States. Industrial production raced ahead in efficiency and capacity. But not without cost. The price was a general washout of unskilled and semiskilled work—the industrial jobs held by Negroes, Puerto Ricans, and poorly educated whites. These people just weren't needed any more to do the things that the machines could do so much more reliably and cheaply (machines don't require holidays, workmen's compensation, sick leave, vacation, and retirement benefits). In New York alone, 200,000 factory jobs were wiped out during the decade. In the same period across the nation a million new workers came on the labor market from the postwar baby boom. Most of them found no takers for their limited skills. This was a period in which we suffered two substantial recessions, you may recall.

But with the booming economy of the sixties we have grown industrially—just since 1950 this nation has added production capacity equal to the entire American industrial complex that existed two decades ago. In this process many new jobs have been required, many new industries have been created. In the three years 1963 through 1966 we developed 4,348,000 new jobs—equal to the population of Missouri.

In this fantastic achievement there were two jokers: Most of these jobs required skills and/or education; many of them were in new plants located in suburbs or in sections of the city remote from the ghettos. New York City, for example, added 71,800 jobs during this time, but three out of four of them were white-collar jobs and the better positions were nowhere near Bedford-Stuyvesant or Harlem. It was a similar story in city after city. So it is clear that Professor Eckstein is right about lack of education being a key factor in unemployment of Negroes.

The second most important factor is less readily apparent. It is health—or rather lack of it. Literally thousands of slum dwellers are in what the U. S. Bureau of Labor Statistics calls the "subemployment" class because of health problems or physical deficiencies. As one expert puts it, in the rural south health care is minimal and the defective or crippled are neglected.

The impact on employment is seen when we look at New York City again. In 1964 Harlem contained 25 per cent of Manhattan's population. But 40 per cent of its tuberculosis deaths and one-third of its infant deaths occurred there. Bedford-Stuyvesant, the crumbling, stinking ghetto in Brooklyn, held 9 per cent of that borough's people but claimed 24 per cent of its TB deaths and 22 per cent of its infant mortality. And when the draft boards called up youths from these two ghettos 52 per cent of those from Harlem and 47 per cent of those from Bedford-Stuyvesant washed out as a result of the military physical examinations.

There is a third factor that disqualifies many for employment. It is a police record. In the past, many, if not all, companies automatically eliminated all job applicants who had police records. This is understandable, given the desire to hire only the best workers and assuming that a police record is meaningful. However, that is just the point: What may be adjudged a "prank" perpetrated by high-spirited white children of prosperous, substantial suburban citizens who are willing to restore damage or "borrowed goods" may be virtually identical to the "crime" that lands a ghetto youth in jail. The factor of race is another element in the picture: In many parts of the nation there is definitely a dual system of justice, with white law officers and courts treating Negro youths severely. It is true also that diverting a delinquent from police formal judiciary treatment to less formal resources such as schools, clinics, and other community agencies is usually characteristic of "affluent" areas and far less so of the ghetto.

My purpose here is to suggest that police records be viewed with a tolerant eye to the circumstances involved. And further, that the man be allowed the benefit of a doubt and an opportunity to prove himself. Today some of our most respected corporations are doing just this and their results have been very good. Information about such programs is available through the National Industrial Conference Board.

So, summing up, we find that Negro slum dwellers have three strikes against them when it comes to qualifying for jobs: lack of skills, health deficiencies, and arrest records. To help them qualify for jobs we have to tackle those three major problems. Most of these people want help. And more than half of the unemployed in these ghettos said they would be willing to take vocational courses or even go back to school if it would lead to work.

The shocking fact is that unemployment and underemployment rates in the ghetto are murderously high. (The Bureau of Labor Statistics uses the term "sub-employment." This consists of the regular unemployed who are willing to work and looking for work; the jobless who have given up in despair and dropped out of the labor market; those who have low-paying part-time jobs and still are trying to find full-time jobs; and "society's dropouts"—people known to be living in the slums who do not show up on the employment/ unemployment counts.) In the ghettos of New Orleans the sub-employment rate was 45.3 per cent in 1967; in Phoenix, Arizona, it was 41.7 per cent; in St. Louis, 38.9 per cent; San Antonio, 47.4 per cent; Philadelphia, 34.2 per cent; Boston's Roxbury section, 24.2 per cent; San Francisco, 24.6 per cent; New York's East Harlem, 33 per cent; Central Harlem, 28.6 per cent; and Bedford-Stuyvesant, 27.6 per cent.

It takes no genius to see that when you have more than

one out of every four able-bodied workers standing around the ghetto with no real income you have tremendous potential for trouble. Businessmen see this too, and it has caused them to act in contradictory ways. Some of our most enlightened corporations have moved their operations out of the central cities to the suburbs, thus removing them from the potential trouble spots. At the same time, they have, in effect, put them off-limits to slum dwellers who might want to work at the new plants. The Bureau of Labor statistics tells us that in recent years more than half of all new industry has located in the suburbs rather than the central cities.

Some of these same businessmen have been active in programs to train and upgrade underskilled workers. They have focused on Negroes and Puerto Ricans and, though the numbers helped have been limited, the results have been excellent. Examples:

Carson Pirie Scott, the large Chicago department store, initiated an education/training program for potential high school dropouts. Trainees go to school two days a week and work three. This program was so successful that now two dozen Chicago companies are doing it.

Prudential Insurance Company launched two programs for high school dropouts. In one, boys learned typing; in the other, machine shop skills.

Aetna Life and Casualty has been teaching steno and typing skills to girls from the slums. The course includes educational and social skills and prepares the trainees for placement in white-collar jobs.

Xerox went after unemployed men and with the union recruited 133 who could read and do simple arithmetic, but had strikes against them, such as police records or bad credit and employment histories. For nineteen weeks the sixteen who were selected received instruction, counseling, and experience in industrial processes. Fifteen were hired.

Nautilus Industries put a new plant in Freeland, Pennsylvania, and hired unskilled men and trained them on the job. Many were former coal miners who had been chronically unemployed.

The National Association of Manufacturers has a program called STEP—an acronym for Solution to Employment Problems—that keeps its members alerted to new developments in training and hiring unemployed.

The National Industrial Conference Board has published a valuable study called *Company Experience with Negro Employment*, Studies in Personnel Policy No. 201. It gives chapter and verse on what companies have accomplished and tells in detail how they did so.

There are many government publications that are helpful in this same subject area. Since new ones are published periodically I suggest that you check with your regional office of the Departments of Commerce; Health, Education, and Welfare; and Labor for late information.

Almost all of these programs are commendable and vitally needed. The dimensions of the need, however, are overwhelming. Just look:

Forty-two per cent of Negroes who have jobs are laborers or service workers (1966 figures).

Each week 40,000 unskilled and semiskilled jobs such as these are being wiped out by technological progress.

About 38 per cent of Negro workers never completed the eighth grade. In other words, more than one out of three are what the personnel specialists call "functional illiterates," meaning they cannot qualify for jobs requiring basic educational skills. (It is appalling to look back and observe that ten years ago only 47,000 adults were enrolled in literacy programs in the entire United States!)

In addition to these factors, one million teenage dropouts have come on the job market each year of this decade. Few of them have been prepared to do more than begin to learn a skill.

Staggering!

Absolutely. There is no other term for the tremendous task that faces us. With all the War on Poverty activity, the vast majority of those who really need help have not yet been touched. When the Job Corps centers were set up, they were scheduled to open in June and planned to help about 60,000 youngsters. But by the mid-April preceding, OEO had received more than 250,000 applications! Note that these came from literate, motivated youngsters, not the hard-core unemployed. And unfortunately, at this writing it appears that many solid programs of the War on Poverty are being dropped, casualties of the war in Vietnam.

All of this adds up to imminent disaster for more and more of our cities and slow starvation of the souls, bodies, and minds of literally millions of what the Chicago Urban League calls our "urban peasantry."

What can we do about it? Let's not kid ourselves, a massive problem of such urgency requires a massive response, a crash program. We have been spending billions annually for five years so that Americans can walk on the moon by 1970. We should spend billions *now* so that all Americans capable of work can walk freely and proudly on United States soil—not have to prowl around, confined to the ghetto.

All of our citizens should be self-sufficient, contributing members of society. Our goal should be to help them achieve this. But we'll never make it until we harness the all-out efforts of government (at all levels), labor, industry and business, education, religion and the voluntary agencies. The problems are just too big, too widespread, too deep-rooted, and too costly in terms of time and money for two or three of these groups to make any considerable dent. It will take all of them, and it will require a dedicated, astutely led crusade to win this one. The dimensions of the attack must be such that the so-called "War on Poverty" will look like a minor scuffle by comparison. The Office of Economic Opportunity and its efforts will have served us well if it has provided us with a cadre of experienced, dedicated people who can supervise the larger onslaught. It is to be hoped that the Urban Coalition will play a significant role in this effort.

As a citizen, you should recognize that tackling these problems is going to cost you, your children, and your children's children a lot of tax dollars. This is inevitable, for so many of the problems can be moved off center only by the kind of concentrated widespread, coordinated effort that only government can swing. And the alternative to such action is unspeakable—the terror and torment of seeing our cities torn apart by our disinherited slum dwellers.

And while these people work, they must be made literate and skilled. Government must create emergency jobs now. Government must plan and create long-term public service jobs to rebuild our cities, to staff our parks, hospitals, schools, and other public institutions. We can use hundreds of thousands of aides—nurses, teachers, conservation, public health—all kinds. These people can, with the ingenuity of which we are capable, be trained on the job. A study by the National Commission on Technology, Automation, and Economic Progress estimated that five million jobs could be created in public services from urban development to rural conservation.

This kind of program, at all government levels, requires widespread public understanding and approval. You can help in that process. Keep informed. Participate in discussions of the employment needs of ghetto dwellers, and the needs of your community for public services, construction, modern transportation and needed facilities. Move your community to initiate programs and projects that will train, equip, and put to work the hard-core unemployed in your area.

Business Can Innovate

American business, the most creative in the world, is just beginning to apply its ingenuity to these problems. You may have more opportunity to move through business concerns than through other avenues. Let me point out a few directions that industry has taken with some success.

One company, Pitney-Bowes, Inc., the mailing machine manufacturer, has been outspoken and outstanding in its efforts to hire and upgrade Negroes.

Pitney-Bowes began equal opportunity hiring in the mid-forties and has found it entirely successful, but insufficient for today's needs. Therefore, it has gone a step further and actively recruits Negroes for jobs and says so. John O. Nicklis, president of the company, has explained this policy:

Equal opportunity is a fine principle. But it should recognize the inability of many Negroes to compete equally in applying for jobs, because of past discrimination in employment and education. Pitney-Bowes, therefore, proposes to reach out and seek Negroes with the desire and potential to learn and to train them for some of the new jobs we have available. We will continue to employ qualified white people, of course, and if white persons who have similarly been held back by circumstances also apply, we will give them equal consideration for on-the-job training. Promotions, as always in the past, will be based solely on merit.

We don't believe our policy is discrimination in reverse. For years, in common with many other businesses and industries, we have employed and trained physically handicapped workers. No one considers this discrimination. It is just good citizenship. The

Negro has been handicapped by color. If he is to compete equally, he needs special consideration, at least for a time.

About five per cent of Pitney-Bowes's work force consists of Negroes, the same ratio of Negroes to whites as in its hometown of Stamford, Connecticut. Significantly, the Negro workers are in all types of work at the company, from the lowest-rated jobs to assistant managers and supervisors as well as engineers and executive secretaries.

Some other "preferential" techniques have been adopted by business (even though many businessmen have publicly disowned "preferential treatment"). Some of the nation's largest corporations have recognized that their tests, administered to all job applicants, just do not measure accurately the abilities and potential of Negro job seekers. Therefore, these companies give a certain number of "compensatory" points on the test scores, just as GI veterans of World War II received additional points on their civil service test scores to "compensate" for their being removed from the mainstream of American life by the war.

"One of the problems," points out Mahlon Puryear, former Associate Executive Director of the National Urban League, "is the difficulty Negro youngsters have with written examinations. They fail in alarming numbers to pass written and oral screening examinations. Admittedly, many Negroes have not had a great deal of experience with tests and examinations, and the major problem has only indirectly to do with skills or abilities. It is a matter of attitudes toward tests and the belief that they will not be hired no matter how well they do the tests. There is also evidence to show that even if the written portion is passed, they will be eliminated in the oral or personal interview, where the process is personal and an opportunity for bias and prejudice can enter."

The Motorola Corporation found itself in the midst of a rhubarb not long ago concerning "ability" or "intelligence" tests. A young Negro, Leon Myart, applied for a job with Motorola, passed a twenty-eight-question written test but was turned down for employment because, said the company, he did not score high enough. Myart, who had been a high school dropout, had studied electronics in the Army and afterwards and was applying for a job analyzing flaws in television sets coming off the assembly line.

He complained to the Illinois Fair Employment Practices Commission and the examiner ruled that Motorola should hire him and stop giving such tests to prospective employees.

Testifying about the exams, Dr. Benjamin S. Bloom, Professor of Education at the University of Chicago, said it was possible for an applicant to score low but do well on the job. The test, he said, required comprehension of concepts related to urban living and would discriminate against a person from a rural or foreign atmosphere. It would make more sense, he said, to use a test related closely to the needs of a specific job. Another specialist, Dr. Robert L. French, a Vice President of the Science Research Associates testing firm, testified that it was impossible to create a test that is fair to all cultures.

Both of these men, of course, were correct. And, as Whitney Young, Dr. Kenneth Clark, and a host of other highly qualified Negro observers have pointed out, that is just the point. The Negro job applicant is usually less skilled in test taking, is often oriented to a rural southern rather than an urban northern community, and, because of segregation and discrimination, is not likely to respond in the same fashion to questions designed by white academicians from results with northern, white, middle-class, city-dwelling respondents.

Looking again at "preferential" techniques which some companies have adopted, the one of seeking Negroes to fill job openings before broadcasting their needs to the total community. In other words, when they need turret lathe operators they go to the Negro community, its leaders, agencies such as the Urban League, YMCA, and recruiters who specialize in Negro workers. They do this for ten days, perhaps, before opening the jobs to all applicants.

Nowadays industry, the unions, federal government, and foundations are all reaching out to convince Negro citizens that they are needed.

Recently a three-day "Employment Fair" was staged in a Negro section of Chicago by thirty-one companies, government and private agencies. They told the story of job availability and spelled out the way to go after the jobs to six thousand Negro school pupils and unemployed men and women. Included on the program were personnel men from such blue chip corporations as International Harvester, Inland Steel, Commonwealth Edison, Illinois Bell Telephone, Motorola, and Zenith Radio. IBM invited likely prospects to its offices for interviews and Kroger Company tested apprentice meat cutters and other job applicants right at the "Fair."

This event was a first in Chicago. It was, said one observer, the first time that many of these companies had come out seriously into the Negro community to see and be seen. At the Fair, Negroes were shown how to go about applying for a job and their eyes were opened to what the "downtown" companies are after as well as what they offer.

The companies learned some valuable lessons, too. As one personnel man put it, "It proved there are well-qualified Negroes who don't come to the aluminum and glass towers downtown." Inland Steel for instance, reported meeting fifty Negroes it was interested in. Another company interviewed more than a hundred and planned job offers for at least twenty-five of them.

Also at the Fair, Negroes were urged to register on the spot for the Urban League's free "Skills Bank." This phenomenally successful system of matching employer needs and applicants' skills mushroomed in the short space of a year into a major clearinghouse for talent.

The Skills Bank was launched by the National Urban League in 1963 to "locate Negroes and nonwhite persons who have skills for sale and place them in rewarding jobs," as Mal Puryear describes it. Established with a Rockefeller Brothers Fund grant, the Skills Bank was initially conceived as a demonstration project. It was set up at a time when new efforts by employers, government, and the community to place more Negroes in jobs were to be seen on all sides.

With a skilled staff and the resources of the nationwide Urban League, the project was designed to locate trained men and women, clerical workers, professional and semiprofessional workers, and candidates for apprenticeship, on-the-job, and other training programs.

The original plan was to set up the activity in twenty-six Leagues as a demonstration. "We estimated that the Bank would contain from two thousand to three thousand highly qualified applicants," says Mal. But demands from industry, government, and the flood of registrants which poured into League offices changed all that.

The Bank became a full-blown, extremely efficient operation in fifty-six cities in less than a year, and during those first twelve months it screened more than 50,000 persons. Of these, 33,600 with "salable or usable skills in a wide variety of occupations" were registered. Furthermore, in its first year the Bank was able to place 5300—more than a hundred a week—of these registrants in new or better job situations. More than 10,000 job orders were developed (that means League staffers went out to industry to locate openings) or received.

The Bank then shifted its emphasis. Mal Puryear comments, "There are plenty of skills available now to fill many more jobs than we have filled. We need to concentrate on finding jobs for persons already recruited, registered, and available."

As an extension of this approach, the League is helping unskilled and underskilled workers in forty cities to qualify for jobs. Since 1965 the local Leagues have been under contract to the U. S. Department of Labor through an $8 million Manpower and Training Act program to conduct on-the-job training (OJT) in a wide range of skills needed by employers. In its first two years the project trained more than seventeen thousand people, largely in light industrial and clerical skills, some in managerial and some in basic jobs such as nurses' aides. There are many positive aspects to these programs:

The worker is paid from his first day in training.

The training is 100 per cent practical, helping the worker to qualify for existing openings using current techniques, tools, methods, etc.

The project reaches smaller companies (most of them with one hundred workers or less) that normally could not afford to conduct such training without the federal assistance supplied.

Seventy per cent of those who have completed training have been hired as full-time workers by their employers.

As an example of the impact of the OJT project, in St. Louis the combined income of 220 workers placed zoomed from a paltry $26,852 (averaging $1222 per year) to $601,284. This happened in one year. The net gain to the community was $574,431—not to mention the "invisible gains" from reduced public assistance, better health, strengthened families, and all the positive effects that occur when dependency becomes self-sufficiency.

Programs such as these have literally changed the lives of

thousands of men and women for the better. Richard E. Lindsay was one of these. After studying drafting and taking technical courses at an institute in Los Angeles and Kent State University in Cleveland, Lindsay studied further at the Cleveland Engineering Institute, until he was called into service. There he completed a course in the Army's guided missile repair school.

After his Army discharge in 1958 Lindsay made the rounds of employment offices and agencies. He was unable to find a job in industry, so he went to work parking cars in a downtown parking lot. By early 1964 he had almost abandoned hope of finding the draftsman's job for which he was qualified. That was when his registration at the Skills Bank meshed with the needs of General Electric Company. He was hired for GE's Nela Park facilities as a draftsman and the company says he has made fine progress.

Another living example of skills used instead of wasted is Robert Perkins, eighteen, who was mopping floors in a laundry even though he had made outstanding grades in high school math and science courses. The Skills Bank showed his credentials to Leonard Berman, Treasurer of Alloys & Chemicals Corporation, who was impressed and hired Robert for laboratory work. "His supervisors speak so glowingly of him," says Berman, "we hope to train him as a supervisor."

In Pittsburgh, Mrs. Janette Greer, twenty-six, a graduate home economist, got "the runaround" from employment agencies and personnel directors for several years when she tried to find a job requiring her background. While she was working below her level as a clerk or secretary, her registration at the Skills Bank resulted in her being hired by the Duquesne Light Company as one of its four home economists.

Other success stories include the nurses' aide who became a sales representative for a drug firm, college graduates who were hired as management trainees in large banks, and many cases of Negro citizens who went from relief rolls to job rolls.

A major factor in the break-through by these job pioneers has been the active support of major corporations for the Skills Bank. Puryear estimates that it costs business a minimum of one thousand dollars to find and hire an employee. "Our service is free," he says. "So industry's liaison with our Urban League affiliates and the Skills Bank makes good financial sense."

Varying devices have been used to spur worker registrations. In Chicago, League staffers man a mobile information-registration unit. In Cleveland and Washington, D.C., application forms are distributed by YMCAs, boys' clubs, churches, and branch libraries. The press, television, and radio have cooperated wholeheartedly in every city.

"One of our biggest problems," says Puryear, "is to make Negro workers realize that, because they were routinely turned down for years for racial reasons, they will not ordinarily encounter the same difficulties today. Times have changed."

Kindling Fires of Ambition

The problem of incentive and training for youngsters who may never reach college and for their older brothers who may be out of work is a knotty one. One of the most discouraging aspects of this is the reluctance of Negroes to train. They have been denied jobs and adequate training so long that when jobs and training become available they think that they are being kidded.

Mal Puryear says "these unqualified, unskilled workers are the product of discrimination by employers as well as the failure of the public school system to prepare them for to-day's challenges. Employers must go further than nondiscriminatory pledges and hiring. They must aid Negro workers to obtain retraining, scholarships, and work-study programs to make up for past policies of exclusion."

As psychologists such as Kenneth Clark so aptly point out, it is of paramount importance that youths see young men and women from their identical background, from their city, ghetto, or neighborhood, achieve success through routes which they too can follow. If, instead, Negro boys and girls witness their peers mired in the slum, beaten by lack of jobs, without helping hands except from the junkies and procurers who wish to exploit them, what we have is not motivation to achieve, but its exact opposite.

However, faced with the fact that you may not be able overnight to produce positive role models of the type that would inspire and motivate youngsters to achieve, you must do the next best thing. In many cities, business is taking the lead to bring to Negro youths a view of the bright future to which they now may realistically aspire.

In Minneapolis and St. Paul, sixteen of the Twin Cities' leading corporations along with the local Urban Leagues, the public schools systems and Augsburg College, staged an all-out "Equal Opportunity Career Day." Its objectives were to fight the dropout problem and inadequate education and training and to motivate youngsters by pointing out employment opportunities open in the area.

More than four hundred junior and senior high school students and their parents attended the event. Most of them were Negroes. They heard a member of the President's Committee on Equal Employment Opportunity outline the Plans for Progress program and its accomplishments and what it meant to those in the audience. Negro employees who held responsible positions with participating companies told about opportunities available to them. Business leaders talked about job futures and challenges, and a question and answer session with a roving microphone gave the youngsters a chance to ask pointed questions about careers and qualifications for jobs.

And, while the youngsters toured exhibits and the college campus, parents heard from business leaders. They learned what they as parents can do to encourage and help their children qualify for jobs. And they were assured repeatedly that the jobs are there—open to all who are qualified. They, too, had a chance to question the speakers. And they knew that the companies involved, the major business and industrial firms in the community, were sincere. They knew they could expect performance to match promise from companies such as Dayton's, Ford, General Mills, Honeywell, IBM, International Harvester, Minnesota Mining, Northern States Power and Northwestern Bell, Pillsbury, Prudential, Red Owl Stores, Whirlpool and Univac. The local radio, TV, and newspapers owned by the Minneapolis Star and Tribune Company carried word of the Career Day to people throughout the area and the state.

There are other problem areas at the high school level and they concern vocational and technical skills. Negroes have not had equal access to vocational and technical training in our public school systems. For decades the prevailing attitude was that they should not be trained for jobs unless there were job possibilities for them—which there were not. In fact, the Department of Health, Education, and Welfare fostered discriminatory practices in vocational training programs which it subsidized throughout the country by requiring that a student could only take a vocational course if there was a reasonable likelihood that he could find a job in that line of work later. Fortunately the Civil Rights Act of 1964 has taken care of this blind provision.

But the cutting edge of this "tradition" was that Negroes could not be employed in "new" jobs because they did not possess the necessary skills and training—which they couldn't get because they were not likely to be hired for such jobs. It

was a classical example of *Catch-22*, the closed-circuit, myth-
ical clause in Army regulations that is the central feature of the
wildly sardonic book of that title.

In recent years the apprenticeship freeze has thawed.
Apprenticeships are controlled by three factors: first, management's provision of a job opening; second, the union's willingness to accept the new worker; and third, meeting standards
of the Department of Labor. Thus business and unions have
both opportunity and responsibility to play a key role.

Unless businessmen assert themselves positively, the apprenticeship avenue remains blocked to Negro youths. We
cannot afford the kind of situation—all too typical—which is
described in this report from the Los Angeles Urban League:

Because school counselors were totally oriented to academic
fields they viewed machine trades and apprenticeship programs as
"dumping grounds" for scholastically low achievers and discipline
problem students. Parents were indifferent. The community, in
general, was unknowledgeable of the important role apprenticeship
could play in elevating youths' skill levels.

Manufacturing industries such as aircraft-electronic companies
and construction industries, which included 21 major crafts in the
building field, were closed to Negro applicants. The only apprenticeship programs known to accept Negro applicants were those
which might be classified as belonging to the service category, such
as baking, barbering, etc.

The League attack on this situation began in earnest in
1956, but it took several years and the coordinated efforts of
the local AFL-CIO, the Statewide California Conference on
Apprenticeship, the State Apprenticeship Council, the State
Employment Service and Division of Apprenticeship Standards. The League gives major credit to "the direct participation of the President's Committee on Equal Employment
Opportunity" for opening apprenticeship programs in manufacturing industries—aircraft and electronic companies.

The experience of the League in Los Angeles was similar to that of other Leagues in many cities. It developed a list of "priority concerns" from its efforts to increase the number of apprentices:

1. Special counselors in high schools and junior colleges, men who have industrial arts orientation and can give special attention to the problems of minority youth.
2. Establishment of state-operated "information centers" in major cities to help recruit and orient youths to apprenticeship opportunities.
3. A requirement that prime contractors on government jobs should institute apprenticeship programs in state-approved apprenticeable occupations. This should apply to government public works projects also.
4. Widespread publicity about the opportunities for Negro youth in apprenticeship programs.
5. With the AFL-CIO executive committees, open up the building trade crafts apprenticeships to minority group youths.

There are many set ideas about training. Historically, the people who were responsible for educating Negro youth either did not know or did not give information to Negro parents to help them counsel their children realistically on careers and on the shifting job market.

Furthermore, negative attitudes toward manual work were unwittingly instilled in educators and transmitted to parents and students. Educators, after all, generally had only limited association with workers and unions and little firsthand experience with manual or technical labor. Therefore, vocational training programs offered by the schools were often woefully inadequate or out of touch with the needs of the job market. They seldom offered sound up-to-date instruction in technical subjects. Too often the vocational schools were used as a "Siberia" for problem children.

For these reasons, among others, Negroes are today few

and far between in the skilled trades where wages more often than not exceed the wages paid to white-collar workers and teachers. Yet this is one important area of employment that promises to grow, rather than shrink, and therefore Negroes must move into it in increasing numbers. Since such jobs increasingly require more education, we have to motivate Negro youths to get the maximum education possible.

Another approach to opening apprenticeships to Negroes is the League's Labor Education Advancement Program (LEAP) aimed at cracking lily-white unions. In 1968, intensive recruitment and training of more than 8500 potential apprentices was under way in fifteen cities. The major thrust of the project is to prepare Negro workers to qualify for the apprenticeships by testing, coaching, conditioning them and putting them through "cram" seminars. After the League team prepares a worker for the union exams he usually qualifies without much difficulty. Then he may require an expensive kit of tools. The League helps him finance this. Unions purposely set initiation fees high to discourage applicants. Many are as high as $500 and for a man who has been out of work this might as well be $5000 unless he can "hit the numbers" or find a friend. In the League he has a friend: through LEAP, financing of the initiation fee can be arranged.

Chicago, where LEAP has been under way longest, has moved more than seven hundred workers through the preliminary requirements for union apprenticeship. Baltimore has been operating the program since the fall of 1967 and has qualified more than 240 workers. The other thirteen cities are making progress. Though the numbers may not seem impressive, they are tremendously significant. Each man placed in a union that has excluded Negroes (and until recently that meant all too many of them) represents a breakthrough. That is why the League is concentrating so much manpower and talent on this program to open opportunities in unions such as the mechanical trades—the electricians, steamfitters, sheetmetal workers, etc.—which have been exclusive for so long.

Mahlon Puryear notes that "parents of Negro youths still smart from the evil effects of the situations they find themselves in, and they need more information about changes in the world of work, and what one must do to be ready to make his niche therein. Of particular interest to youth should be those jobs that are being created as a result of technological change and advanced scientific processes, including automation."

Many businesses have picked up the challenge. GE, for instance, has stated "many white and Negro educators have told us that years of hopelessness about the future have produced a 'don't care' attitude toward good grades among many Negro young people. 'It isn't enough for us to tell them about good job opportunities,' we've been told. 'You have to show them.'" GE said this in the foreword to a booklet featuring photos of fifty Negroes employed by the company, with information about their backgrounds, their training, their current jobs, and, in most cases, their continuing education. The range of people in the booklet was vast—from eighteen years of age and a year or two on the job to twenty-four years at work; from billing clerks to shop steward and production crew chief in a TV tube plant to electronics engineers, managers of engineering, computer programmer, business trainee, biological lab technician, appliance serviceman, sales trainee, and many others.

With unusual candor, the company says, "this doesn't mean that GE is perfect. Even today we sometimes find the cobwebs of old worn-out antagonisms. What it means is that we have been trying for a good many years to live up to high standards of fairness in hiring and in employee progress. If we're not perfect—we're certainly not complacent. We're still trying to make progress—and complacency is the enemy of progress."

Then, with a direct appeal to Negro youngsters, GE says, "Can you find your own 'success image'? Can you put yourself on one of these pages? Do you have the desire? The willingness to bring out the best in yourself? Yes? Then we at General Electric believe that you can look forward to a career in industry—a career in which success is not based on race, but on your own ability, education, and ambition."

In stressing the need for education and training the GE publication is commendable. It would be an empty exhortation if it was not backed up—as it is—by evidence that preparation pays off with good jobs and advancement. The company knows that it must be consistent in its policies, attitudes, and actions or it will not get, nor will it keep Negro workers.

An example of GE's commitment to equal opportunity is its action in Philadelphia. There, one of its aeronautical engineers, Eugene C. Miller, tried to buy a home in a suburban area of Rosemont. Miller was refused the $34,750 house and filed suit against Radnor Valley Builders, Inc., accusing them of refusing to sell to him because of race bias. GE backed Miller 100 per cent by issuing a strong statement that Miller had a right to expect housing suitable to his $16,000-a-year salary in the residential area of his choice.

The significance of this is two-pronged: GE took a stand publicly supporting equal rights. This action was not lost on Negro employees or on the Negro community. Second, GE in this action recognized that, as Hobart Taylor puts it, "a plant located in an area which denies housing to minority citizens, for all practical purposes, denies those citizens jobs . . . the right of a man to choose the neighborhood in which he will live is much more than a question of social prestige or 'keeping up with the Joneses.' This right is inextricably tied into his ability to make a living and to provide his family with the decencies of life. To bar a man from living in a specific neighborhood does far more than cast a social stigma upon him; it also limits his capacity to do something that all men cherish—to provide their wives and children with the maximum security and comfort and hope available to them."

It is clear that this problem is not confined to the south. In 1966 Whitney Young and his associates at the Urban League went all out on a request from Eastman Kodak Company to find some top-notch Negro youngsters for specific professional level jobs. The League located a number of outstanding young people who were products of Negro colleges. The company interviewed them and was delighted. It hired twelve. But then, when these young Negroes discovered that working for Eastman in Rochester meant that they would have to live in the slums, that their families would be confined to the ghetto and their children would have to attend ghetto schools, they turned the jobs down. They had no shortage of offers and could do so without sacrifice. In their eyes, housing, educational facilities, and job were part of the same, inseparable package. If Eastman—and Rochester—did not see it before, they realized this after this incident.

The crux of the matter is the question of mobility. Are we to allow job mobility only to certain people who qualify by color or religion or some other equally irrelevant criteria? Is an employer to be denied the right to hire the best qualified men he can find for his business? If the worker is denied satisfactory living conditions in the community, because his race makes it impossible, for instance, then job mobility has already passed from actuality to theory.

Who suffers? The individual? Undoubtedly. The employer? Of course, for his outlay for recruitment will be boosted, and the salaries he must pay will have to be higher. The community? Without question, for business—leaving aside the moral considerations—is acutely sensitive to the competitive costs of doing business and will not tolerate or endure the penalty of higher costs in a community that imposes this kind of "head" or, to be more accurate, "skin" tax.

Yet it need not be so. Businessmen individually can influence company policies on such matters in the same way they help develop policy on any cost-cutting methods and procedures. By securing the facts, projecting the needs and costs, they can arrive at estimates of the economic factors involved. And, when their public relations department adds its counsel, the picture should be fairly complete. At this point policy can be drawn and action to implement can be outlined.

Today, with the Civil Rights Law on the books, with literally hundreds of major corporations moving positively, with government and voluntary agencies and with the new climate in race relations, a company's decision to tackle discriminatory practices in its own back yard is not made or executed in lonely isolation. And if, as frequently is the case, one or two companies dominate the life of a community, the responsibility is unmistakable, unavoidable, and urgent to place the company on the side of the future—for equal rights and the conditions to make them meaningful.

Some businessmen are going on record quietly, in significant and perhaps profound ways. For example, in case you had not noticed, there has been a substantial change in the advertising world in its treatment of Negro citizens.

Five years ago there was only a handful of Negroes employed in creative, sales, administrative, or supervisory jobs in American advertising. The NAACP and the Urban League of Greater New York had had meetings and conferences, presented statistics and data to leaders of the industry, CORE had picketed, and the results were discouraging. Not only were jobs not immediately forthcoming, but even more significant, the contents of the advertising industry product—the TV programs and commercials, illustrations for ads in newspapers and magazines, were almost pure, pure, 100 per cent pure lily-white. This was, perhaps, by default, by ignorance, by obtuseness—to give the most charitable benefit of a doubt. But the effects?

The effects were, first, to reinforce the concept of a "white" American society, one which completely excluded Negroes and other minority groups. This flight from reality may have soothed the white audiences and strengthened their "superiority cocoons" which insulate them from workaday, mundane thoughts.

The effects, second, were well stated by New York's Committee on Job Advancement in its campaign to get major corporations and advertising agencies to integrate their ads: "The systematic exclusion from advertising of Negroes, Puerto Ricans, and other identifiable minority groups, has created a serious impediment to job advancement and better race relations—the Negro boy or girl who is thus offered a glowing picture of a world to reach out for that is exclusively white loses the ambition and the wish to become a part of it. A white child gets a false view of the world he lives in."

Many readers will recognize in this quotation a reflection of Dr. Kenneth Clark's finding that by age four, the Negro child associates status with being white and lack of status with being Negro. Lily-white advertising, of course, with its view of a world exclusively youth-, success-, and white-oriented, reinforces this view, thus placing additional psychological burdens on the youngster.

More than five hundred companies and ad agencies were contacted by the Committee. Some of the interviews seemed like the old shell game—the ad agency said it was not responsible for ad content, that the corporation determined what would be in the ads; then when the corporation advertising official was called he replied that "the agency recommended alternatives for ad content and the corporation simply chose the most attractive," or some variation of this argument. Occasionally, when cornered, both agency and corporation pointed to marketing research which "indicated" that customers for the product would be alienated by inclusion of Negroes in the ads.

Yet, within six months of the letter quoted above, more than fifty companies—all giants in their fields—had quietly incorporated minority group citizens into their ads without fanfare or self-righteousness. Negroes or Chinese or Puerto Ricans simply appeared in normal situations in crowds, in the background, and, more and more, in the foreground and featured positions. But not exclusively or artificially. This naturalistic, unself-conscious approach has spread steadily.

Negroes in Business

Another move by businessmen to stimulate opportunities for Negro citizens has been voluntary counseling to help establish and aid Negro-owned enterprises. Such efforts are long overdue and critically needed.

Consider that in New York City, which has a Negro population of 1,300,000, only a dozen Negro-owned businesses have more than ten employees. Furthermore, in Harlem, fewer than 18 per cent of the retail stores are Negro-owned. Negro parents traditionally discourage their children from business careers, particularly those as hazardous as self-employment, retailing, or selling.

And added to the plentiful obstacles facing the entrepreneur, the Negro small businessman has several additional handicaps. He usually lacks business training and experience. He is often cut off from adequate business information and financial counseling. He may find the trade association closed to him by thinly disguised Jim Crow practices. And, most important, he has real problems in getting credit from suppliers and in securing bank loans.

One of the groups which has sprung up to help in this situation is New York's Interracial Council for Business

Opportunity, organized by the American Jewish Congress and the Urban League. Its co-chairman, Rodman Rockefeller, believes that the new group offers an avenue for white businessmen to participate in the civil rights movement in a meaningful way.

About one hundred businessmen are active in the Council; about one-third are Negro executives. The organization has three standing committees—consultants, banking and credit, and education. These meet once a month. Someone wishing help is first interviewed by one of the consultants who analyzes his needs and finds an expert in his field to advise him. This expert then visits the place of business, observes the operation and facilities, and works closely with the man.

If it is a question of finances, one of the banking and credit committee members steers the person to a source of credit. Further, he helps prepare the application for a loan.

The education committee is helping with counseling at local high schools and colleges. Leading Negro executives are speaking to student groups about the opportunities now open and developing.

The Council counts many New York corporations, big and small, among its participants. The giants include Macy's, Schenley Distillers, American Home Products, Bache and Company, McCann-Erickson, and Pepsi-Cola. This kind of participation was effective in inducing fourteen of New York's leading commercial banks to give special attention to loan applications from the businessmen being counseled. And the group also works with a Harlem-based office of the Small Business Administration.

Another fruitful avenue may be increasing the franchises open to Negro businessmen. Many major American corporations have franchise operations that extend down to the neighborhood corner, such as the gas stations, the drive-ins, the cleaning and laundry establishments, the sales and service agencies for appliances, for data processing, for office machines, food, and other products.

If this may sound like the most elementary, obvious suggestion of the week, I ask you merely to ponder that in late 1963 young Theodore Baker was able to open his own Esso filling station in St. Albans, New York. Baker is a Negro, and this was considered such an event that the president of the Borough of Queens, New York, and the president of the Urban League of Greater New York attended the opening. And Baker would not have been able to swing the franchise without the aid of the League, Frontiers International Club, and Associated Community Teams which cooperated to put together a development fund to finance the operation.

I cite this to show how unusual the opening of this not very extraordinary franchise was, and to give some indication of the long way we have to go to launch Negro businessmen in the numbers required to have some impact. Recent reports from the U. S. Department of Commerce describe pledges from a couple of dozen national corporations to increase the offerings of their franchises to Negro citizens.

Management Adapts

Management has adapted its thinking to the realities of current race relations speedily. A pair of studies conducted by Dr. Garda Bowman and reported in the *Harvard Business Review* revealed the thinking—and action—of businessmen on key aspects of equal opportunity policies.

Dr. Bowman reported that the most dramatic findings of her survey of two thousand businessmen were the shift in attitude on the practicality and the impact on profits of having Negroes in management positions in their companies. As she puts it, in 1962 the study discovered that *"fear* was the major block to upgrading qualified Negroes—fear of the effects of such action upon the firm's balance sheet . . . Racial discrimination was described as a 'regrettable but necessary concession to reality.'"

A year later, "reality" had apparently changed drastically, for the overwhelming majority of the businessmen questioned said that promoting Negroes into management would have no effect on profits. About one out of ten thought such integration would improve profits, and only 6 per cent thought —as had the majority the year before—that it would bring on the red ink.

What caused this extraordinary, almost instantaneous change-about? Dr. Bowman attributes it to a number of factors: "fear of running counter to community attitudes and behavior has been supplanted by even more intense anxieties —fear of picketing by Negroes, fear of losing Government contracts, fear of a bad public image . . . (or perhaps it) may be largely the result of practical experience with Negroes at supervisory or management levels."

The importance of this shift cannot be exaggerated. It means that the unanswerable argument—that profits will suffer if integration is accomplished—has largely been abandoned as untenable. The most-often mentioned argument now is that employee morale would suffer. About one out of three officials thought white subordinates would not take orders from a Negro supervisor, no matter how well qualified. This rationale is subject to proof as essentially baseless.

The files of the National Urban League, the President's Committee on Equal Employment Opportunity, the U. S. Civil Rights Commission, the various state fair employment practices committees and the Plans for Progress Council are stuffed full of case histories in which this has been disproved. True, in some of these case histories management began with this misconception, and in others there were initial negative reactions from workers. But in every case I know about, opposition disappeared and acceptance came as the Negro workers proved themselves capable.

In Dr. Bowman's study 60 per cent of the executives agreed with the U. S. Postmaster General that "if a Negro is qualified, other employees generally do not object to being supervised by or taking orders from him."

To dig into this point further, Dr. Bowman questioned the employees in firms which had integrated their work forces. The workers—95 per cent of them—said that "equality of opportunity was actually beneficial to profits, prestige, production, and the public image of the firm."

Executives, for the most part, agreed. Most of them said that individual officials of the company generally could interpret equal opportunity policies according to their own beliefs. Thus, the attitude of the individual in the company is of crucial importance. The study uncovered an interesting paradox: the executives saw four basic reasons why integration into industry was moving slowly, yet they—most of them—had no practical suggestions to overcome the roadblocks.

These are the reasons they cited for slow progress:

1. We promote from within, so the last man hired is the last man up—and, obviously, the last man in is likely to be a Negro.
2. Minority group citizens don't apply for jobs in some industries.
3. Few Negroes have the education required to be successful managers, even though they do have the necessary personal characteristics.
4. There is an "unwritten law" that minority group citizens can go so far and no farther (the junior executive level was the ceiling mentioned by many).

What could be done to speed and increase integration of work forces?

1. Let a clear policy of merit selection and promotion speak for itself, without any special Negro management recruitment or training programs. (Three out of five agreed with this approach.)
2. Recruit able Negroes, then let the natural management development process in the company proceed. (About one in four advocated this.)
3. Make special efforts, without lowering standards, to recruit, train, and develop able Negro managers. (Eleven per cent favored this.)
4. Seek out and develop potential Negro managers even if standards may temporarily have to be lowered. (A scant 1 per cent endorsed this.)

I daresay that if the study was repeated now, we would find that far more managers favored the third and fourth avenues suggested above and that far fewer would subscribe to the first. Furthermore, from the information collected by the Urban League it is apparent that there is a decided change under way in the thinking reflected in the reasons for slow progress listed above.

For example, the president of the world's largest bank, Rudolph A. Peterson of the Bank of America, states "management's first responsibility is to ensure the profitability of its institution. But within this framework, there are opportunities for recruitment, training, and development of Negro managers, and the effort is worth making. In fact, today's world justifies and demands special efforts along these lines."

Dr. Bowman's study points up one paramount area in which special effort is mandatory: She found that though 62 per cent of the company officials answering said that skin color should not be relevant to promotion, only 9 per cent thought it actually did not affect promotion.

Should management be asked to remake society? Does its responsibility extend to crusading for human rights? Dr. Bowman's respondents—54 per cent of them—said management does have these responsibilities; but 42 per cent rejected this view. Perhaps the view of the chief engineer of a California defense firm comes closest to the prevailing thinking among the executives: "It is in my role as a businessman that I can be most effective in furthering the principles of racial justice since I have the opportunity to hire and promote fairly. As a citizen, I have far less opportunity to affect the condition of other people." I cannot help but marvel at the contrast between his open endorsement of equal opportunity hiring and promotion and the timorous, temporizing, cautionary advice I received from my friends only a few years ago when I spoke with them about taking on the Urban League presidency. Not one of them could possibly have conceived of any leading businessman taking the stand Rudolph Peterson and so many other corporation heads have endorsed.

We have a long, long way to go before we reach the millennium, but at last we're moving on the right road!

Chapter 7 ☞ ☜

Better Health for Our Citizens

In tribal warfare in Africa, warriors took with them into battles away from home not only sword and spear, amulet and witch doctor magic, but bags of dirt. Why? Before the attack the warriors would eat the soil from the homeland to infuse themselves with strength for the onslaught.

What has this obscure custom to do with health of American citizens today? In a curious way, it demonstrates that we are still captives of the past. And it tells a good deal about some of the problems we have to overcome.

The fact is that the African warrior's custom was brought by slaves to America. Then, during slave times, many Negroes ate dirt—especially clay—not only for strength, but to kill hunger pangs. The practice of eating clay was passed on from generation to generation. But when the descendants of the African warriors arrived in the city, clay was unavailable and a substitute was found—starch, specifically laundry starch, available at every grocery store.

From the old African custom, southern folklore invented practical benefits: eating clay—or starch—supposedly aided pregnancy, prevented syphilis, nausea, and dizziness, kept the fetus properly positioned and protected it from harm. Today, in the giant cities of the most advanced nation on earth there are many women and some men who still follow this ancient practice, eating as much as three pounds of starch a day. And what does it really do for them? Taken in large doses it makes them ill and, for reasons still unclear, it is associated with—if it does not actually cause—anemia.

An obscure and probably insignificant problem, did you say? Yes, it is true that relatively few Negroes eat starch. But this whole habit pattern reflects certain basic problems that we have yet to lick.

Eating clay or starch and depending on folk remedies or ineffective patent medicine to cure what ails you are sure signs of several things: people who rely on these don't understand modern medical care. They are not being reached by the medical services or by health centers. They mistrust professional medical services and the people who administer and run them. These people are not aware of their rights under Medicare or Medicaid. They believe that doctors and drugs and clinics and hospitals are too expensive for them. And they may be right.

Ebony magazine gave this report of how one Negro mother in Watts watched her nine-month-old son die. Police asked her why she had not taken the baby to a hospital. "The onliest one I got money for is County. That's twenty miles away. It cost $2.50 to take the baby on the bus (the fare now has been reduced to $1) and it means I got to lose a whole day of work. I have to wait until my children gets $20 worth of sick before I can afford it. I didn't know my baby was that sick."

Health Gap Widening

The awful truth is that even though we have poured millions into health research, into building hospitals and medical facilities, spent huge sums educating doctors, nurses, dentists, and all kinds of public health specialists, the benefits of this incalculable investment have been distributed unequally. In a word, medical science has benefited whites far more than Negroes. In fact, the health gap between the two races is widening, not narrowing, when we look at medical statistics. Just consider:

The death rate for Negroes is more than twice as high as that for whites in the ages between 1 and 4 years and 25 to 54 years (1963 data).

Death rates from hypertension (other than heart disease) have been from three to five times greater among Negroes than whites for the past thirty years.

Influenza and pneumonia killed Negroes at a rate more than twice that affecting the white population in 1963: 55 per 100,000 Negroes; 24 per 100,000 whites.

In the same year tuberculosis killed nearly three times as many Negroes as whites (proportionately).

Heart and circulatory diseases hit Negroes harder than whites. In 1963, for every 380 whites per 100,000 who died of such ailments 522 Negroes per 100,000 died of them also. In some categories the differences were even greater—twice as many Negroes as whites (proportionately) died of vascular lesions of the central nervous system; nearly three times as many Negroes as whites (proportionately) were killed by nephritis and renal sclerosis.

Pregnant Negro women were twice as liable to die in childbirth as pregnant white women in 1930. But a generation later (in 1964) four times as many Negro mothers died as did white mothers. (The actual rates per 100,000 live births were 89.9 and 22.3, respectively.)

In 1940, fourteen times more Negro mothers than white mothers had midwives rather than doctors. By 1960 the ratio had increased to 23 times as many.

Between 1960 and 1964 the tuberculosis rate for Negroes

in New York City rose by 1 per cent; among Puerto Ricans it dropped 12 per cent and for whites it dove 28 per cent.

As recently as 1963, the infant death rate per 1000 live births was 16.7 for whites and 26.1 for nonwhites.

In 1950, 154 per cent more Negro babies died than whites in their first eleven months of life. Thirteen years later, in 1963, the infant mortality rate for nonwhites was 180 per cent greater.

These mournful comparisons are deeply discouraging, but must be faced squarely. Why are there these gaps? The easy, automatic answer is that there simply are racial differences in health. This is true, unfortunately, but not for any constitutional physical reasons—except skin color. Yes, the degree of carotene in the skin has a definite effect on availability of health facilities, information, and care. This physical "problem" with which 11 per cent of our population are born is the only fundamental factor causing a difference in health of Negroes and whites. Of course, skin color as such does not cause our Negro citizens to be less healthy—it simply is the trigger for prejudice to be unleashed. Bigotry does the rest.

The facts are these: Ill health and poverty reinforce each other. The Negro poor live in conditions that attack both physical and mental health. I mean conditions such as malnutrition, crowded, unsanitary housing, inadequate heating, poor personal health habits, and family disorganization. These conditions cause illness and prevent or handicap many poor people from using educational, training, and employment opportunities that could lift them out of poverty.

In general, the health services now being offered the poor are insufficient, inferior, impersonal, fragmentary, and inconsistent. The Urban League's Health Service Program outlines what this means:

In too many instances health services for the poor have these shortcomings:

1. Inadequate scope, bad location, and faulty organization.
2. Negative attitudes toward persons who use public health and welfare services, viewing them as less worthy and worthy of less, resulting in low-quality, impersonal, and fragmented care.
3. The poor don't know about health services and their rights to such services.
4. Confusing, complex, and irrelevant eligibility requirements.
5. Overlooking the huge health problems of mental health burdens, and social patterns caused by discrimination, the ghetto, and joblessness.
6. Powerlessness, or sense of powerlessness of the poor to overcome these problems, leading to an increased sense of dependency and low self-esteem.

Some of the health problems of the family that lives in the slum are easy to spot. One authority says the most important factor is the limited accessibility of services. What he means is that the health services available are out of reach. For instance, clinic schedules generally are arranged for the convenience of the staff, not the patients. Another major problem is the shortage of doctors, nurses, and trained technicians. Of course, this very fact provides opportunities for youngsters who want promising careers.

Well, what can be done and what is being done to tackle these problems?

To start with, action to improve the health of the poor should coordinate with action to improve housing, education, and employment because they are all interrelated. To heal the ailments of a poor, jobless person from the ghetto and thrust him back into the squalid set of conditions that caused his illness in the first place is like running on a treadmill, only worse. On a treadmill you develop leg muscles and lung power;

in the complex of ghetto conditions a person develops fatal afflictions.

One important beginning point in improving the health of the poor is to make school health services first-rate. These should give maximum possible diagnostic and remedial care to youngsters and should include strong, effective information, referral and follow-up aid for both children and parents. The youngsters should be an avenue to their families for accurate word about nutrition, hygiene, sanitation, available health counseling, family planning, and diagnostic services.

Also of fundamental importance to local health programs are federal funds and grants. Under Public Law 89-749, passed in 1966, Public Health Service money is available for planning and actually delivering health services through various types of projects. Literally millions ($135 million in 1968) were allocated under this law for such purposes as "health needs of limited geographic scope or of special regional or national significance; to stimulate new programs; or for studies, demonstrations, or training to develop new methods, etc." The grants may be made to any agency, public or private, with a qualifying project. Such financial resources should not be overlooked by citizens who seriously wish to improve the health of ghetto dwellers.

In still another action area, determined people who recognize the importance of upgrading the health of Negro Americans are striving to integrate hospitals and medical facilities from top to bottom. It is important to have Negroes on the boards of the hospital or clinic, to have Negroes as accredited physicians and medical specialists (anesthetists, pharmacists, etc.), as nurses, orderlies, technicians, and, of course, staff workers. But the hospital administrators who have an eye on the future are seeing to it that Negro and other minority group employees are brought into training programs that teach them new, vitally needed skills, giving them solid opportunities for medical careers as lab and X-ray technicians, for instance.

It goes without saying that where Negroes are on the policy-making level of a hospital many of the problems may be eliminated in short order. Few such hospitals, I am sure, have segregated waiting rooms or wards or facilities. And when Negroes have a say in direction of the hospital they are bound to open the facilities to Negro physicians. This, believe me, is crucial. For if a doctor is not attached to a hospital he cannot refer his patients there. This fact alone served for generations to keep Negro Americans from first-class hospital care. It is tied in also with the long, reactionary history of the American Medical Association and its Jim Crow policy that excluded Negro physicians. Only in recent years have Negro doctors been brought into the A.M.A. The A.M.A. also shares blame with the country's medical schools for preventing Negro youths from getting top-flight medical training.

For a generation, under the Hill-Burton act, federal money was put into hospital construction around the nation. But until the 1964 Civil Rights Act many of these facilities were frankly and without apology Jim Crow institutions. They were lily-white and didn't care who knew it. Today, Title VI of the Civil Rights Act has made this illegal and hospitals receiving any federal support are subject to a cutoff of that support for acts of segregation or prejudice.

Since federal aid is used to assist in building and renovating health facilities, in training, research, and demonstration projects, in supporting ongoing programs of health care in cities, states, and counties, this financial support can be influential in changing patterns. There are 7500 medical institutions in the nation that receive federal funds. After negotiating with and persuading administrators to open segregated facilities, federal funds may be withheld or terminated as a last resort if they

do not mend their ways. The discriminatory practices pro-
hibited under Title VI are:

*Any difference in quality, quantity, or manner in which a
benefit is provided;*

Segregation or separate treatment in any part of the program;

*Restriction in the enjoyment of any advantages, privileges,
or other benefits provided to others;*

Different standards or requirements for participation;

*Methods of administration which would defeat or substan-
tially impair the accomplishment of the program objectives;*

*Discrimination in any activity conducted in a facility built in
whole or in part with federal funds;*

*Discrimination in any employment resulting from a program
with a primary objective of providing employment.*

Now this has caused considerable change for the better,
especially where the authorities have accepted the inevitable
with good grace. However, there still are any number of foot-
dragging institutions. The devices and schemes to avoid integration are various and ingenious, ranging from the strange
to the ludicrous. For instance, federal investigating teams are
sent out by the Department of Health, Education, and Welfare
to see whether hospitals are complying with the law and
qualifying for continued aid. So, in some hospitals, administrators actually hustled Negro kitchen and laundry employees
into beds in the wards to "prove" to the investigators that
they were integrated.

Another dodge is the practice of physicians to ask white
patients if they object to being in a ward which may have a
Negro in it. If the white "objects"—and many times the seed
of objection is planted by the doctor when he asks the

question—the physician tells the staff that placing the patient in such a ward would be "injurious" to his health. The staff then may assign the patient to a lily-white ward or shuffle patients about to meet the doctor's "requirements." Usually ignored is the question of what might be "injurious" to the health of the Negro patient.

In some hospitals, wards are not segregated by color, but according to the physician who admits you. So, referrals from Dr. Zilch, who is known to have Negro patients, are all assigned to Ward B, to which all patients of Negro doctors— or other doctors who have Negro patients—are automatically sent. See how easy it can be? The devices are many and ingenious, but the result is generally the same—inferior treatment or inferior facilities for Negroes.

Action for Health

What can be done about the hospitals, clinics, and the broader problem, the health needs of Negro citizens? Plenty! But it requires facts with which to work. How to get the facts? Do the logical thing, survey the situation in your community. Conduct an audit in your neighborhood. Confine the inquiry to health. Draw the boundaries of your community. With a group of companions settle on the health questions you will tackle. Your list might include:

1. a. Does the hospital that serves your neighborhood have an integrated
    (1) administrative staff?
    (2) nursing staff?
    (3) board of directors?
    (4) staff of physicians with admission privileges?
    (5) policy on admissions and assignment to rooms and treatment?

  b. *Does the hospital have a clinic that is integrated as in* a. *above)?*

2. a. *Is the nearest clinic (if different from the hospital in* 1.) *integrated throughout? (See* 1. a.)

  b. *Is it open evenings and Saturdays so that working people can use it?*

  c. *Is it doing an educational job about*

  (1) *personal hygiene?*

  (2) *preventive medicine—X-rays, vaccinations, immunization, prenatal care, etc., where to get them, why and when?*

  (3) *family planning information—where to get it?*

  (4) *available day care centers for working mothers' children?*

  (5) *postnatal and child care programs?*

  (6) *visiting nurse availability?*

  (7) *health programs offered by public and voluntary agencies in the city?*

  (8) *nursing homes for aged and in-home services for senior citizens?*

  (9) *VD, its treatment and prevention?*

  (10) *maternity care, particularly for unwed mothers?*

  (11) *adoption procedures and agencies as well as foster care?*

3. *What public and voluntary health agencies exist in your city?*

  a. *Which of them have facilities in your community? What are these facilities and services?*

  b. *Which of them have extension services such as the TB Association's mobile X-ray unit, making the rounds of your community? Are they reaching the grass roots?*

  c. *How many Negroes are on the staffs of these agencies? How many Negroes are on the boards of these agencies?*

  d. *How do these agencies circulate information about their facilities, program, and services? By mail? By news-*

*paper, radio, TV, posters, etc.? Do they come into the
community and meet the people face to face? (You
know yourself how much more persuasive it is to have
information presented in person.)*

4. *Do the local health institutions carry on intergroup or
human relations programs for their staff members? Have
all staff members gone through such training?*

Now you have one side of the picture. Using the list you
have developed in items 1, 2, and 3,

5. *How many Negro citizens in the community have used
one or more of the facilities or services on your list in the
past six months? How many could or should have used
them? How many knew about half or more of them?*

Other questions and guidelines are spelled out in the U. S.
Public Health Report for December 1967.

If there are Negroes living in your neighborhood and there
are health facilities somewhere in the immediate vicinity, you
probably will come up with a mixed picture: the hospitals
and clinics may offer some of the services and may have gone
part way in integrating; the Negro citizens may use these
services and know about some but not all of them.

If you check the ghetto on the same basis, you are likely
to find an even greater disparity. It is almost axiomatic that
those who have greatest need of services are most ignorant
of them or reluctant to use them.

Hospitals

Now if you have made your audit conscientiously you will
have found, inevitably, certain areas that require improvement. It may be that the local hospital pays lip service to a
policy of integration but has yet to put it into practice.

In some hospitals the admitting clerks have had instructions to assign "compatible" patients to the same room. "Compatibility," however, has been defined from the clerk's viewpoint, usually a white viewpoint, so that all patients in a room are either white or Negro. Often such a policy is "justified" on the basis of solicitude for the "feelings" of the white patient. The Negro patient presumably has sturdier "feelings" and a hardier constitution, for when it comes to a choice, and the Negro must be either turned away or placed in a room with whites, there have been too many instances of refusing admittance.

As late as the end of May 1965, the Assistant Secretary of Health, Education, and Welfare, James Quigley, reported that his department was investigating 98 hospitals cited by the NAACP Legal Defense and Educational Fund. "In none of the hospitals we checked," he said, "did we fail to find some elements of noncompliance (with Title VI of the Civil Rights Act of 1964, barring discrimination in programs receiving federal aid)."

In hospitals checked up to that date, Mr. Quigley reported a general pattern of segregation. It encompassed, he said, separate floors, wards, or wings for Negro patients and separate delivery rooms and dining facilities. The hospitals often have all-white staffs of physicians and, in rare instances, separate operating rooms, he said.

Discrimination of the crudest kind is diminishing in the health field. Overt discrimination undoubtedly will decline more rapidly, with the pressure of the Civil Rights Act steadily visible and its provisions on tap to cut off funds of many hospitals and health programs in case they don't toe the line. Gross discrimination has gone out of fashion with most thinking people, particularly those on the firing line in the health field—the visiting nurse, the family doctor, and usually but not always the health department clinic and general hospital. Yet there still remain many holdouts—medical specialists, dentists, nursing homes, sanitariums, and other specialized facilities and health personnel who will not treat Negroes.

The Clinics

What about the clinic serving your community? If you have a sizable Negro population in your community this may be the most crucial health agency affecting it. Negroes are hospitalized at a rate about one-fifth less than the entire population. However, they use hospital outpatient clinics at a rate twice that of whites. With medical care as expensive as it is, it is understandable that they must use the facilities they can best afford.

But all too often the clinic is so overburdened that it cannot serve as the major community health resource that it might and should be. Furthermore, the working man who must take off from his job to visit the clinic loses part of a day's wages. He usually finds that the physician who sees him is terrifically rushed and can spare him only a few moments. If a return visit is scheduled, it will be by mere happenstance that he may see the same doctor. Usually it will be a different doctor. Thus there is little continutiy to his treatment, for each physician at the clinic is, in large measure, starting "cold" with the case.

The clinic can be a place for dissemination of information about how to prevent illness and maintain good health. It can be a clearinghouse directing patients to public and voluntary agency programs intended to serve them. There may be an agency organized to aid unwed mothers, for instance. But its clientele may come from a certain geographical area and be largely, if not entirely, white. Information about such services is little known among ghetto dwellers, generally. In fact, the lack of understanding among Negro women about the importance and availability of prenatal and postnatal care as well as experienced—if not hospital—maternity care, is one of the major tragedies of our day in the field of health.

Most Negro mothers do not receive basic prenatal care today. And women without such care are three times as likely to give birth prematurely as those who receive proper care. Small premature babies are ten times as likely to be mentally retarded as full-term children. Furthermore, the odds against a Negro baby born today being alive on this day next year are twice as high as those against the white baby.

As an example that sums up this situation, consider Selma, Alabama, where in 1960 there were just as many white as Negro families with incomes below $3000. In 1963 there were 1600 babies born to women who lived in this county. Only *four* of the 600 white babies were born *outside* of hospitals without attending physicians. But of the 1000 Negro babies, only 300 were delivered *in* hospitals *with* doctor care. The other 700 were born outside hospitals and most of these births were attended by midwives. (In the entire state of Alabama, 10,000 out of 11,000 Negro births outside of hospitals were attended by midwives.) And the infant mortality rate there was 13.2 per thousand for whites and 32 per thousand for Negroes.

Little wonder that the Urban League has placed top priority in its health programs on stimulating efforts to cut infant and maternal mortality rates. We need imaginative demonstration projects, using federal and local resources. Clinics, as major dispensaries of medical attention and health information, can play a vital role in such efforts.

Too many of our citizens receive medical care on an emergency, stop-gap basis when they cannot manage to drag themselves through another day's work without some aid, after they have exhausted all of the popular folk and patent medicine remedies they can afford. Then in desperation they turn to the clinic.

All too often Negroes have experienced the rankest, crudest kind of discrimination in their treatment at clinics. It is to prevent such treatment that human relations courses are now given staff members by leading hospitals and health institutions in the country. You might talk with your Negro neighbors who have used local clinics to see what they would recommend: if they have experienced discrimination at the health facility you can be sure that they will favor human relations courses for the staff.

The health audit will uncover plenty of opportunities for helping improve services to citizens of the community.

It may be that instituting evening hours at the clinic would be a great boon to many who are now unable to use it.

It is likely that a systematic, truly effective program of getting information to people is urgently needed.

Be a Town Crier

People in general are less likely to act upon information contained in a piece of literature than in a face-to-face situation such as a forum, panel discussion, or institute in which they are urged to bring up health questions that bother them. In such gatherings some basic health and hygiene facts can be conveyed, but most important, people can be informed about the health facilities in their community—where to go for immunization and X-rays, for cancer and heart checkups, for visiting nurse services and help for senior citizens. Family planning clinics may be operating in your city without the general knowledge of many who could use their services. The need for maternity care, prenatal and postnatal care is so urgent that a block-by-block campaign should be carried on to bring the word of available facilities to those who need them.

You might organize an information clinic, with the aid of the health organizations in your city, in which the basic facts about preventing disease would be presented. Or it might be organized around the major diseases and focused on diagnosing the most prevalent killers and cripplers. Or it might be concerned with infant and child care: there are some excellent films available, with little or no rental cost, from health agencies, social service organizations such as the League, departments of health, film libraries such as Association Films, certain pharmaceutical companies, and some university extension services.

The approaches may vary, but the important thing is to get the information to the people who need it. No doubt methods better adapted for your community will come to mind. Perhaps existing programs, such as library extension offerings, can be expanded for this purpose. Perhaps local women's clubs can include such meetings in their programs. And service and social clubs can take on projects to spread the word.

Often the person who needs health aid does not take advantage of what is available. The reason may be a trivial one, from the broad, long-range standpoint of his future. The health facility may be difficult to reach, it may be located in territory unfamiliar to the person, and taxi fare may be out of the question. The individual may have heard nothing positive about the health facility and may, because of fear, pain, suspicion of authority, anxiety about the cost, and belief that discrimination will be visited on him again, decide to "wait it out."

Some of these factors can be alleviated through better communication on the part of these facilities. Some can be minimized by simple expedients—car pools, for instance. And some require concerted efforts—such as human relations training for staff members of the agencies—and feedback from those who have been helped to those who need help.

Studies have revealed that those who live in the slums appreciate and understand best the services that are offered them where and when they need them, i.e., in their neighborhood, and *now*. The visiting nurse service is a first-rate example of this. It reaches those who need it when they need it, and in their own homes. The visiting nurses are respected, appreciated, and welcomed, in contrast to other health and welfare activities, which do not extend themselves to reach the people and whose motives are less clearly understood by the people they are there to help.

The Oldsters

Another area of health care that demands attention is the care and feeding of our senior citizens. This tidy label that is so frequently applied to our older Americans conjures up visions of retired businessmen, robust and ruddy-cheeked, playing golf in St. Augustine with their smiling, zestful wives. For every one of these there must be scores of thousands who exist on the outer rim of public assistance, barely managing to survive.

The picture of the lives of older Negroes has been sketched in stark outline by the Urban League in a booklet entitled, appropriately, "Double Jeopardy." The title comes from the fact that 1,500,000 Negroes who are over sixty-five are different from most whites first, by being Negro, and second, by being old. As the Detroit Urban League puts it, "age merely compounds those hardships accrued to him as a result of being a Negro."

The League's Subcommittee on the Aging put together this eloquent document. Consider these facts:

Seven out of ten elderly Negro couples exist on less than $3000 per year. The federal Bureau of Labor Statistics says that $3010 is the lowest annual income that will provide a "modest but adequate" budget for an elderly couple. The League has taken this and examined it and found that this amount will provide the couple with just short of an egg a day per person, "about half a pound of meat, fish, or poultry (barely enough for two 'modest' servings) and no provision for a special diet or the expensive kinds of medical care all too often associated with terminal illnesses that strike one in ten aged couples every year."

One out of two Negro aged couples must make do on less than $2000 per year.

One couple in ten must eke out an existence on less than $1000 per year ($19.23 per week, or $2.73 per day).

Though the BLS says $1800 is needed for the elderly person who lives alone to sustain life, seven out of ten Negro women and nine of every twenty Negro men who live alone in their old age have to scrape along on less than $1000 per year.

There are three times as many Negroes as whites on old age assistance, a total of 480,000 in 1960. Each state makes its own eligibility rules and sets the amounts paid, ranging from $325 per month in Washington to $40 a month in Mississippi. State welfare department officials and legislators, therefore, hold the power of life or death over these people. (In November 1963 the penny-wise officials of the Illinois State Department of Public Aid cut the assistance to old men in that state from $41 to $33 a month, and trimmed aid to aged blind men from $47 to $33—$396 per year, a sum that makes Mississippi's $480 a year seem princely by comparison.)

The majority of those 480,000 Negroes on Old Age Assistance are managing to squeak through by living without telephones, hot and cold running water, inside flush toilets, and central heating. Most of us certainly don't consider these to be luxuries. Think what the lack of them would be like after age sixty-five!

Of all the men and women in the nation who are in homes for the aged, only 3 per cent are Negroes.

Of all the Negro oldsters, more than half live in houses that are dangerously dilapidated or lacking in essential plumbing.

Aged Negroes who are ill or infirm and have no relatives or friends to care for them most often are sent to mental hospitals, the only custodial care institutions available! The League has found this pattern in state after state.

Older Negroes—as well as whites—urgently need several things: better incomes, better housing and health and medical services.

Concerned citizens can help in their neighborhoods by checking to see how many older Negroes there may be and what kind of help they specifically need. The National Council on Aging, 49 West 45 Street, New York, New York, has much helpful material on this, particularly its "The Community and Its Older Residents" and its checklist of community services and programs for older people.

The Council recommends checking to see what can be done to aid oldsters to be as independent and self-directing as possible in their own homes as long as they are able and wish to be so. Among the things which help are homemaker services (though most of the agencies doing this focus on families with children), friendly visiting, and portable meals or "meals on wheels." The Council also recommends multiservice centers which offer the aged all kinds of counseling, home finding, health, educational, and recreational services. This often includes protective services for oldsters who are unable to manage their own affairs.

It should be kept in mind that in the aged Negro we find a person who probably was born and reared in the south, and educated in inferior schools which he left at an early age. If he is literate he is one of the fortunates. Many do not read. For them, recreational and educational aid could and should start with basic reading. Assistance to help oldsters master reading can be a genuine service to them, for reading can open new worlds.

The Recruiter

There is another concrete action that the individual can take in his neighborhood: he can act as unofficial scout and recruiter for youngsters to enroll in medical careers. The shortage is so great and the medical schools so eager to find bright young Negroes that scholarships are going begging. And these are to the finest schools in the country. The same thing is true to a lesser degree of nursing.

But not all of the medical careers are confined to these two professions; medicine is increasingly complex and demands scores of specialties that were rare or nonexistent twenty years ago. There are few career areas as promising as those in the health field. For the youth who has a penchant for biology, chemistry, or science there are fine futures in the laboratory, pharmacy, X-ray, physical therapy, and many health-related fields.

In his special Message on Health and Education in 1967, President Johnson pointed out that the United States will need one million more health workers in the next decade. He called for new training programs to develop these skills. For Negro citizens this field can provide tremendous opportunities.

Few Negroes are entering medicine and its subsidiary specialties. The lure of other professions has attracted more of them. And, let's face it, the Jim Crow attitudes and practices of the medical profession, its schools and training institutions—the teaching hospitals—did a magnificent job of convincing Negro youngsters that they were not welcome for decades. So they looked elsewhere.

That is why today there is only one Negro physician to every 4000 Negro citizens. Not that we want to confine Negro doctors to Negro patients or rule out Negro patients for white doctors. On the contrary, white doctors, with only 640 white persons to make demands on their time, obviously are practically at loose ends—by comparison—and can spare time for Negro patients, if they will. And if they won't, the nearly impossible health problems of the Negro will exacerbate.

Whitney Young estimates that it would take 23,000 additional Negro doctors to equalize the medical care load. The medical schools seem to be making extra efforts to attract Negro youths and their scholarship offers are genuine and attractive for those who can qualify.

Today concerned individuals can help others to maintain health. Stimulating and aiding youths to take up medical careers is one long-range way to promote better health. Encouraging and assisting ghetto families to use available health services are valuable steps. For those who are truly interested in helping, there are innumerable ways to aid our citizens to gain and maintain better health—and keep them out of the starch box!

Chapter 8 👉 👈

Wake Up Your Neighborhood!

Maybe you remember the headlines back in mid-1957 when a laboratory technician named William E. Myers, Jr., and his family moved into the Dogwood Hollow section of Levittown, Pennsylvania.

In this 15,500-home community, the Myers' were the first Negroes to settle. They were greeted with a rain of rocks, eggs, garbage, picketing, and near-rioting for nearly ten days. State troopers were called out to protect them and had to disperse crowds with riot clubs. The disorder reached a climax when one trooper was knocked out by a rock and further gatherings were banned. The family was subjected to nasty phone calls at all hours of the day and night. Some neighbors formed a group to "restore our entire white community." The harassment was so bad that the court issued an injunction against seven Levittown residents prohibiting them from any further antagonistic action.

Though the bigots and unthinking or unknowing citizens had a thoroughly self-degrading, spleen-venting time, there were a number of neighbors who stood firm and aided the Myers family. The obnoxious activity soon dwindled and fizzled out completely in a few weeks.

Seven years later an exceptional change had taken place in Dogwood Hollow: James E. Newell, chairman of the group formed to "repel the invaders" back in 1957, said in

1964 "integration has worked out far better than we antic-ipated." Furthermore, the community chose as its Outstand-ing Young Man of 1964 and gave its eleventh Distinguished Service Award to Mr. Henry Ford, a math teacher at Trenton Junior High School. Mr. Ford is a Negro and he lives in the house which was the target of the mob in 1957. He has directed and coordinated the Community Center in the Bristol Township section of Levittown. Some 250 youngsters partic-ipate in sports, arts and crafts, modern dancing, library and music activities at the Center.

Says Mr. Newell: "Mr. Ford is a fine fellow and is doing a wonderful job for the children. If all the colored people, in fact the people of every race, were of his caliber, they would be a credit to any community."

More than twenty Negro families live in Levittown now, and, as the president of the local Junior Chamber of Com-merce puts it, "The integration we have in Levittown has worked out just fine." The scaremongers were wrong—there was no mass exodus of whites from Levittown; there were no more demonstrations; there was no drop in property values.

This is just one story of interracial housing with a happy ending. There are many, many others. There is, for instance, the half-century-old Brooklyn, New York, community in which hundreds of Negroes of all occupational levels in-cluding professional and businessmen live side by side with whites in attached and semidetached brick and frame houses. The area was originally settled by dozens of Negro stable-boys at the old Sheepshead Bay race track. Today the kids fill the streets after school, playing stickball and touch foot-ball, black and white together, inseparably, unself-consciously. The families shop for groceries together, have their hair cut and set at the same beauty parlor, and patronize the same local tavern. They visit back and forth in one another's homes. And the property values are at record highs—$20,000 up for one-family homes, $35,000 plus for two-family homes.

Here is a neighborhood of long-term integration. It is stable; the integration is successful.

There are today many neighborhoods where integration is a fact and a matter of choice. They are found in Denver, Washington, Chicago, Long Island, Philadelphia, and elsewhere. But, there are all too many places in our great country where timidity, superstition, avarice, and fear prevent Negroes from securing decent housing.

Paget Alves, the Urban League's former associate director for housing, points out that in spite of some gains, housing has become more segregated in the past ten years. Negroes who try to buy or rent better housing outside "Negro areas" still are too often met with abuse or filth—physical or verbal —if not actual explosives, and with threats and harassment. Too often they face inflated prices when they seek to buy. Then they find panic-stricken white neighbors when they move in. Segregation and discrimination, says Pat Alves, confine the Negro's search for housing to a limited area which becomes more and more crowded, the housing deteriorates progressively, and the ghetto becomes a slum.

What about the need, the desire, the artificially pent-up demand for decent housing for Negro citizens? There are more than five million Negro families in the nation today. Half of these families have to manage shoes, shelter, and meat on the table for less than $75 per week—less than $20 per person. The rule of thumb on rental is that you should spend no more than one-fourth of your income on housing. Show me, if you can, the city that has decent, clean four-room apartments available for $75 a month these days. There just aren't any, except in public housing projects—and those have long waiting lists.

The Urban League estimates that one out of every five Negro families needs low-rent public housing because it can't afford decent quarters otherwise. The fact is there is an extreme shortage of low-rent housing. The real estate interests are delighted to stunt and blunt programs designed to provide low-cost housing. And actually, they don't have to do too much to prevent such construction. The apathy of the rest of us usually is sufficient to let public housing programs die a-borning.

What we could do, of course, is write and call on our representatives in the state and federal legislatures and urge them to support public housing programs. We could study the needs in our own bailiwicks and bring these needs to the attention of other organizations and agencies, the radio, TV, and newspapers, and our neighbors and press for action. We could get together with other interested citizens and look into the plans for urban renewal in our cities and see what proposals are included for public housing, if any. And we might also examine existing public housing occupancy in our cities to find out just how well it is serving the needs of the community.

The honored maxim that a man's home is his castle is still only verbiage to six out of every ten Negroes. Only about 38 per cent of our Negro residents are homeowners, though two out of every three whites own their own homes. But beyond this, the significant matter is the quality of housing. Here we find that more than half the Negroes in the nation —56 per cent—live in substandard houses or apartments. Nearly half of these dwellings were found by census takers to be unsound or requiring plumbing facilities. And, because of the squeeze to confine Negroes to ghettos, they are jammed into apartments and houses more than *three times* as densely as whites, the 1960 census reveals. This represents real progress in reverse: in 1950 the census found that Negroes were crammed into their dwellings only *two and a half times* as densely as whites.

Another sobering fact is that the number of houses and apartments which were overcrowded *increased by one-third* for Negroes and decreased for whites by a fraction of 1 per cent during the decade. There were 44,000 more overcrowded Negro dwellings in 1960 than in 1950, while in the same decade 41,000 white families managed to escape from overcrowded houses into "standard" housing.

Now if you have any doubt about the reality of the ghetto, the fact that Negroes cannot buy the same housing with their dollars that whites are able to purchase, the census for Los Angeles, as a case in point, neatly comes up with the facts.

The figures in 1960 showed that when both whites and Negroes were paying the same rent for their dwellings (i.e., between $60 and $70 per month) *one of every four Negroes* was living in a dilapidated and deteriorated house. But of the whites paying the same amount per month, only *one of every fifteen* was found in dilapidated or deteriorated housing! It is stretching belief beyond the breaking point to assume that Negroes voluntarily pay such rates for jampacked, stinking, unsanitary, dark, drafty, cold, damp, and unheated, vermin- and rat-infested places with inadequate plumbing and few if any lights when the same dollars could purchase decent housing—if it was available.

Again, look at the forced concentration which discrimination clamps on the metropolis: in 1960 there were 335,000 Negroes in Los Angeles and 95 per cent of them lived in the central district. In fact, the Negro population virtually doubled in ten years, from 162,000 in 1950 to 314,000 in 1960. And yet, only 21,000 Negroes in that city live *outside* the central district. But 11,000 of these live in ghettos in San Pedro, Venice, and Pacoima, which leaves 10,000 scattered among the 2,140,000 Angelenos who are not Negro— hardly an example of integration!

The picture is similar, if not identical, for too many other cities in our land. In some cities it is worse: in Manhattan's Harlem, for instance, there was and is ferocious crowding of human beings in absolutely inhuman conditions. Picture, if you can imagine it, the entire Negro population of Atlanta—232,000—jammed into three and a half square miles of Harlem. And for the privilege of living in this dehumanizing jungle a Negro citizen pays from $50 to $74 per month for a one-room flat. His white counterpart may rent an identical flat in a white slum for from $30 to $49 per month.

It is a tough problem to work with, this matter of increasing housing opportunities for Negroes. It is tough because of the huge number of people who require better housing and the staggering sums of money needed to refurbish and renovate dwellings for them and the persistent obstacle of prejudice against our Negro citizens on the part of builders, lenders, realtors, and the citizen who puts his house on the market as well as the people in a neighborhood where a Negro might conceivably buy or rent.

The Problem

Rapidly, here are the needs:

About two million Negro families need low-rent public housing because they cannot afford any other decent housing. However, if we consider as a priority only those families living in dilapidated houses, i.e., places that are actually unfit or dangerous for humans to live in, the figure is 860,000 families. Adding those families who are overcrowded in deteriorating housing—and leaving out those families that are living in deteriorating places but are not "overcrowded"—we have another 200,000 families. Rounding this off, we come up with an estimated 1,000,000 families that need public housing at low rentals *today*.

The Urban League estimates we will have enough such housing for these families if we continue at the current rate of construction for another *thirty years*. Of course, the birth rate will have outrun the remedy by then.

Middle-income housing is needed by Negro families in the $4000 to $6000 range. These people find that they cannot escape from the ghetto because of color, and they cannot qualify for public housing because their income is too high. They are squeezed, therefore, into the only alternative: some overpriced, undersized, superannuated dwelling within the confines of the ghetto.

If this "middle-income" family vaults over the invisible ghetto wall into a "white" neighborhood, it is taking a calculated risk: it is paying more down payment, a higher price, and higher interest charges for a mortgage (if it can get one—even from conventional lenders). It knows that the odds are great that colored citizens will suffer embarrassment, insult, harassment, perhaps vindictive persecution and even property damage or injury for their temerity in buying freedom from the slum at a premium for the "privilege" of living among enlightened, cultured, religious white citizens who thus have an opportunity to show what the advantages of superior education and jobs can produce in the way of upstanding, friendly neighbors.

This "middle-income" Negro family group is not large. However, the census found that in twenty-one metropolitan areas around the nation there were nearly 190,000 Negro families with incomes of $6000 or more. Thus there were then and must be now scores of thousands of Negro families desperately seeking chances to leapfrog out of the slums into decent housing—perhaps in your neighborhood?

Face Reality and Act

Let's be realistic about housing. Millions of our citizens live in the ghettos in decaying houses or apartments today. This will be the case ten years from today and, unless our sluggish housing industry is revolutionized by a massive federal program of low- and moderate-cost housing construction, it will be so twenty years or thirty years from now.

We just cannot stand by and allow these people and succeeding generations of our citizens to be subjected to such living conditions. If we have any of the decency we profess, we must, at the very least, try to improve their lives by bringing their housing up to standards of sanitation and safety. How? By insisting that landlords meet the standards, without exception or excuse.

In Washington, D.C., Sherwood Ross, former news director for the National Urban League, has achieved amazing results in getting landlords to toe the mark. Sherwood is a dynamo, and he organized interested, socially conscious young adults into teams to canvass ghetto neighborhoods. Their purpose was to get the facts on housing violations. The teams fanned out throughout the city's worst ghettos and within a month Sherwood had piles of information about the misery in which thousands were forced to live.

Now Ross and his associates used this information very effectively. They spent hours poring over the property records at City Hall to find out the names of owners of the buildings. In many cases they found fictitious names or "blinds." But to each they sent notices about the existing problems. Copies went also to the appropriate city department—Health, Sanitation, Water, Public Works. Then the committee did check-backs, to see what, if any, action had been taken.

At this point, Ross trained his guns on those who had done nothing to correct the situations. Among his many talents, Ross is an accomplished newswriter, interviewer, and broadcaster. He has a radio program on a local station in Washington, and on this he broadcast reports and interviews with tenants.

The teams used a simple questionnaire form. It looked like this:

No. _____   Date: _____

Name of tenant: _____

Address: _____   Apartment No.: _____

Phone: _____   Rent: $ _____ /month

What's Wrong

	Living Rm	Dining Rm	Bedrm	Kitchen	Bathrm	Other
Windows						
Lights						
Heat						
Plumbing (specify)						
Stove						
Roof or Ceiling						
Other						

Last painted: _____

" repaired: _____

" complained to landlord: _____ or city health dept. _____

He would, for example, interview John Williams, of 224 E Street, S.E., asking him about his home. The man would tell how long he'd lived there and about existing conditions—two broken windows, no heat until mid-November, holes in the floor, and rats. Ross would reinforce this with a reading of the report from his committeeman who visited the place.

At first, there was little result from this, but in a few weeks the tide turned completely. The city began to act as soon as it heard from the committee, sending out its own inspectors to check and post violations to the owners. The owners began to listen and take heed. In fact, it has been interesting to note how quickly some of the landlords get on the job after they hear Sherwood's broadcasts about the charms of their properties. He will cite a particular address (to avoid legal repercussions, he does not name the landlord) and describe how and where the roof leaks. Sometimes within a day a roofing crew will be climbing all over the building, repairing a condition that has existed for years.

We need more crusading of this type to give our fellow citizens at least the minimum in decent housing. We need more people like Sherwood Ross to take the leadership in keeping city bureaus and landlords alike "honest."

Urban Renewal

What about urban renewal as an answer to our housing problems? By 1970 eight out of ten Americans will be living in metropolitan areas. The urban renewal programs have done much and will do more to renovate our cities. The highway programs have made central cities more accessible via safer routes. But both have been accused (with ample justification in all too many instances) of manipulating Negroes out of locations needed for projects and failing to relocate them in decent housing. Hence the old saw, "urban renewal means Negro removal."

Urban renewal projects are controlled and directed at the local level, by men and women who are your neighbors and your elected officials or their appointed representatives. So, when the authorities in your city blithely pass over the problems of the low-income or minority families who may be displaced by urban renewal, the responsibility is not theirs alone: it is in part yours and mine and those being displaced. None of us is voiceless.

Another persistent weakness of urban renewal and highway programs has been their blindness to the capabilities of Negro citizens. Few Negroes have been hired for redevelopment phases of renewal in technical or professional capacities, such as architects, contractors, or appraisers. Lacking the resources of such experienced members of the Negro community, the projects have often stumbled when they should have moved boldly to meet the needs of nonwhites who are displaced.

Ghettos don't just happen. It takes the active cooperation of many individuals to create a ghetto or extend a slum—just as the active participation of dedicated individuals can prevent ghetto conditions.

Fighting Back

Many people have vested interests in slums—the blockbuster wants to cause panic sales so that he can buy cheap and sell dear to Negro families hungry for housing. And he sells so dear that these families often must take in roomers to meet payments on the house. Thus, overburdened with debt, barely able to meet the carrying charges, the family finds it difficult if not impossible to maintain and repair the place and the inevitable decay is accelerated. Those who can afford to move out, do so, leaving the least financially able in the deteriorating houses. And when these poor people find they are having trouble keeping up their payments, they take the easiest way out: hire out more rooms in the already crowded house.

In many cities neighborhood groups organize to "stabilize"

their areas, to fight the blockbuster and to keep their community attractive. One of these groups, in northwest Washington, D.C., is called Neighbors, Inc. It is interracial, and is trying to keep its section a vital, integrated, stable neighborhood in an increasingly Negro section of the city.

Neighbors, Inc., knows that when a community will not accept people of different colors, nationalities, or religions, that area is ripe for panic selling and the stampede call of the ghetto-makers. Characteristically, the panic-monger is a real estate broker who plants the four fears in owners of houses in neighborhoods into which a Negro family may have moved:

1. Property values will drop.
2. Crime will increase.
3. Neighborhood standards—including the schools—will deteriorate.
4. Older residents will be pushed out.

Neighbors, Inc., has vigorously combatted these four fears through block meetings to promote and build a sense of togetherness. It has also traced down rumors, secured the facts and presented them, thus spiking scare-waves. And it has encouraged property owners to put up signs saying, "Not for Sale—We Believe in Democracy." Visitation committees have been formed to call on residents who may be wavering or may have specific problems.

The group also circulates pledge cards which list the reasons for staying in the community. Members call on community leaders to ask them to discuss the situation in their organizations. And responsible real estate agencies are encouraged to show homes in the area to members of all groups.

Neighbors, Inc., keeps people in the area informed about real estate practices and values, about current moving costs, about methods of squelching panic and about ways and means of keeping the neighborhood attractive. Its kit of techniques includes newsletters, block organizations, neighborhood receptions, membership meetings, consultations with key people, negotiations with real estate men and others. Further, it has sponsored clinics for real estate salesmen, programs to help local schools, neighborhood cleanup campaigns, receptions for residents and volunteer help to new residents moving in.

The heart of the Neighbors program, however, is its effort to buck the psychological and commercial currents that hustle a neighborhood onto that downhill slide. Neighbors refutes the fears of residents. It rebuts fears of declining property values with statistics developed by the Commission on Race and Housing. It points out the high achievement records of youngsters in the local schools to answer fears of deterioration of schools. It does not, however, deny the cultural disadvantages of many Negroes. The Neighbors program is designed to prevent "inundation" by Negroes, to bring in white families and to make it clear that there is little danger of being "the last white family in the block."

Neighbors has found that at this point in time, some whites feel they will be looked on as residents of a "colored neighborhood" and have feelings that they have "lost status." While not giving an inch to this spurious reasoning, Neighbors takes the positive approach of building neighborhood *esprit* and personal pride and self-respect by spreading word of the superior education, experience, jobs, and achievements of Negroes who live in the area.

As for the fear that crime will increase with the increase of Negro residents in an area, this is highly unlikely.

The Urban League reports that all of the evidence it can gather shows crime and social disorganization to be as low (if not lower) among middle-class Negroes as among middle-class whites. It is the middle-class Negro family that has the wherewithal and the drive to make the jump from a segregated neighborhood to an "all-white" area. And, as experience has shown, such families generally try to outdo their neighbors in upholding the mores and standards of the community. The danger to any neighborhood is not from Negroes or from whites *per se*, but from poverty, blunted opportunity, ignorance, and despair.

What can you as an individual do about housing needs of minority citizens?

You can work for fair housing laws in your state or city if they do not now exist. And you can keep in mind that such laws are only as good as the breadth of their coverage, the machinery and the teeth they have to do the job. The National Committee Against Discrimination in Housing, 323 Lexington Avenue, New York, N.Y., has a fount of material for you if you are interested in this area of activity.

If your city or state has a fair housing law, you and like-minded friends can make the law work to achieve its objectives by organizing to see that it operates as it should and by getting information about the law to those who need it.

Join hands and forces with others in your community to seek homes for Negro families who wish to move into decent housing and decent neighborhoods. There are more than 500 such groups in the country today. You can find out more about them by writing NCADH (see address above).

As Whitney Young says, "Northerners habitually heap scorn on Mississippi and Georgia for the fiery crosses that light up the night sky in those uncivilized backwoods regions and conveniently overlook the charred bodies of families taken out of slum housing—people who die because suburbia says, 'Keep out!' and because, to some banks, the slum is a profitable business. They overlook the slum schools and the inferior jobs and the discrimination in the trade unions and all the quiet men and women—'the gentle people of prejudice'—who toil night and day behind the scenes to keep their block or their union hall all-white. They vote down bond issues for public housing. And they cheer the demagogues and hate-peddlers who mask their hostilities in bills to 'cut taxes' by cutting welfare allotments and medical care."

In many cities around the nation fair housing committees, Urban Leagues, NAACP Chapters, YWCA, American Friends Service Committee, and other groups are cooperating to locate housing opportunities for Negro families. In eight metropolitan areas* the League operates a program called "Operation Equality." It is essentially a clearing house for information, bringing together Negroes seeking decent dwellings and property owners interested in selling or renting to stable, responsible families.

In the New York metropolitan area the League issued a sixty-three-page report which listed available housing opportunities when the project was announced. At that time some 276 apartment buildings and home sites incorporating tens of thousands of dwellings were included. In launching the effort, Pat Alves appealed to Americans of conscience and decency to open their communities and neighborhoods to Negro families. This would, he said, improve property values in previously all-white areas.

Property Values

Now this statement is directly contrary to the usual story about Negroes moving into a neighborhood, stories that are whispered or shouted hoarsely, depending on the audience and bias of the speaker. But Alves is backed by facts. A Federal

* Seattle, Cleveland, Pittsburgh, Philadelphia, Rochester, Miami, St. Louis, and the New York metropolitan area.

Housing and Home Finance Agency report states that the value of homes owned by Negroes rose 123 per cent between 1950 and 1960. This was at a time when the value of homes owned by whites increased by a mere 59 per cent!

Perhaps the outstanding study in this area was a five-year investigation of ten thousand house sales. It was conducted by the Commission on Race and Housing with a $350,000 grant from the Ford Foundation. Professional economists and social scientists carried it out. They learned that in 85 per cent of the neighborhoods where Negroes bought houses for the first time, property values remained the same or rose above similar neighborhoods that remained all-white. In 15 per cent of newly "integrated" neighborhoods values declined from 5 to 9 per cent. However—and this is the part the hate-mongers always neglect to mention—the declines were usually *short run* and were followed by *rises* to or above previous prices.

This exhaustive, extra-cautious study has been corroborated time and again by similar research in San Francisco, Baltimore, New York City, Portland, Oregon, New Haven, and other places. Furthermore, the census data on home values also substantiate this.

Sherwood Ross spent two years on a mammoth study of 1,323,762 homes in forty-seven major American cities over a ten-year period. The cities ranged from Akron, Atlanta, and Austin to Trenton, Utica, and Wichita. Did home values drop when Negroes moved into neighborhoods? Far from it. "In fact," says Ross, "home values are soaring all over the nation, in white, Negro, and changing census tracts. Trying to find a neighborhood that declined is like looking for a needle in a haystack."

Ross's study covered 1810 census tracts and found that of these, 1793 had large increases in value of their houses; two tracts remained the same and only fifteen declined. Values in tracts of Negro homes zoomed an average of 61 per cent over the decade, compared to 35 per cent for white communities.

Integrated neighborhoods jumped 45 per cent and changing neighborhoods 42 per cent.

For instance, in Syracuse, New York, Negroes moved into several all-white neighborhoods during the decade. Yet the census reveals that there was no census tract in the entire city in which home values dropped. And this included areas where Negroes moved in for the first time. Comparing the 1950 and 1960 values in each integrated area, the census shows that all values increased and the smallest increase was $2200.

One neighborhood had 603 white families and one Negro homeowner in 1950. Ten years later there were twenty Negro families and 537 white homes. Meanwhile, property values rose $3500 to $14,200—up by 33 per cent. Such increases were the rule, rather than the exception, in cities around the nation. Evidently those who integrate their neighborhoods do themselves an unexpected financial favor.

Housing Committees

If you seriously want to help Negro citizens there is nothing more basic or more immediately effective than aiding human beings to secure decent housing. Fair housing committees are formed by citizens who want to help Negro families find such places to live without regard to race. Generally the committees carry on either educational programs or direct action to secure housing, or both.

In northern New Jersey there are forty town-wide committees and these are loosely federated through a clearing house operation sponsored by the American Friends Service Committee and the Urban League of Essex County. The clearing house helps coordinate the activities of the fair housing committees and also spreads word in the Negro community that housing is available on an open-occupancy basis.

This program is run largely by eight volunteers working with a coordinator and consultants from the League and AFSC.

Members of the local fair housing committees constantly watch for houses for sale in their neighborhoods. They seek out the sellers and persuade them to sell to qualified applicants. Such houses are referred to the clearing house, which scans its records to see if a Negro family is on file as wanting a house in that area. Sometimes Negro families are referred to brokers known to be cooperative.

Another part of the program, and an essential part, is an educational effort directed at the Negro community. Because membership in the fair housing committees tends to be 80 per cent white, there is danger that information about housing opportunities will not get to those who can use it and act on it in the Negro community. So the Jersey committees have organized a speakers bureau which tells the story to church and civic groups, and social clubs. Speakers go out as an interracial team and tell the facts about their community, about the need for open occupancy and housing opportunities for Negro families and the fair housing movement in other urban areas.

Many fair housing committees have volunteers who specialize in teaming up with Negro couples who want a place out of the ghetto. The technique is simple. A Negro couple sees a selling agent about an apartment or house. Afterward, the volunteer "checker," a white, calls on the agent for the same dwelling. The information given the Negro couple and the checker is then compared, and acted on accordingly.

For example, in New York City a Negro couple looked at an apartment, liked it, and wanted to rent it. The superintendent of the building claimed that there was a deposit on the place from a prospective lessee. The couple called the housing secretary of the Committee on Civil Rights in Metropolitan New York, who called a volunteer to check on this. The checker looked at the apartment, talked to the superintendent and asked to rent the place. The superintendent agreed and they set a time to sign the lease. The checker and the Negro couple confronted the super at that time and he agreed to rent the place to the Negro couple without further argument. They had caught him in the act of discrimination.

In states and cities where there are antidiscrimination agencies, the fair housing committee helps file complaints against landlords and renting agents for evasive behavior of this type, or for setting the rent arbitrarily high to exclude Negro applicants.

Fred Barbaro, formerly of the Urban League of Essex County, New Jersey, suggests that people who wish to form a fair housing committee consider these four points:

1. Know the provisions of your state's real estate laws thoroughly; make certain that the activities you wish to conduct in your fair housing committee are legal.
2. Continue to work with local real estate boards, but be aware that you are a threat to their operation. Be sure to impress them with the fact that you will disband your program when they prove that they will deal with all potential buyers equally.
3. Don't forget the Negro brokers. They will benefit from the open market. Open occupancy encourages people to seek the best housing available for the price instead of settling for less, as when the choice is restricted to ghetto dwellings.
4. Set realistic goals for your program. The activities of a fair housing committee and clearing house cannot meet the housing needs of 90 per cent of the Negroes in most urban areas, even if they are outstandingly successful. The majority of Negro families just do not have the money.

Fair housing committees need volunteers to man their offices, to serve as checkers in teaming up with couples seeking housing and apartments. Also, when the activity of a fair housing committee becomes as widespread and demanding as that of the Committee on Civil Rights in Metropolitan New York, it requires volunteers to handle telephone calls and correspondence on a continuing basis.

Fear

Unfortunately, the job is not always complete when a sale or rental is transacted. Too often there is apprehension by the whites in the neighborhood and not a little fear on the part of the Negro family. If you were to read the Negro press each week you would understand this fear, for in every issue there is at least one article which has a headline like this: "Moves Into White Neighborhood, Windows Broken, Family Threatened," or worse. Back in 1964, the head of the Warren, Ohio, Urban League, W. Robert Smalls, moved into an all-white neighborhood. Bob Smalls is a fine citizen with years of service to Warren and to the League. Bob and his family had been in their home scarcely a month when two fire bombs were tossed through a window one evening, presumably to usher in Brotherhood Week, which began the following day.

The point here is that when this kind of attack happens to the most prominent, responsible, and respected Negro in a city, what can those who are less well known expect if they attempt to move to all-white areas? It's like the old business of the neighborhood bully deliberately bloodying the nose of the new boy in the neighborhood with the statement "That's for nothing"; the warning is implicit—don't get out of line or you'll *really* get hurt.

Community effort is needed before and after move-in. Mr. and Mrs. Ralph Watkins moved into an $18,000 home in Kings Park, New York. A year and a half later Mrs. Watkins reported "the most devastating thing is the neighborhood declaring war on our youngest son (a six-year-old). We had to restrain our eighteen-year-old son from starting trouble and finally signed him into the Marine Corps. The older boy would become violent when he saw the six-year-old scrubbing himself raw in the bathtub, crying that God hated him and made him black.

"Any child who plays with ours is ostracized, and mothers report to each other if their children are seen talking to him. We've been subjected to constant crank phone calls and hate mail, and bags of garbage are left on our doorstep at night."

This certainly seems to be an extreme case, and for every one like it there may well be dozens such as the experience of Dr. Thomas H. Bembry, in Greenville, New York. "If anything," he says, "our neighbors here are more congenial than the neighbors we had at our old home." And Mr. Neal Hemachandra who moved into a modern ranch house in Searingtown, Long Island, reports, "The neighbors have been just fine. We visit back and forth and we talk about our lawn problems and children and things in the community. You couldn't ask for better neighbors."

This kind of reception may not be automatic. Mr. Irving Winters moved into Oakdale, Long Island, and neighborhood acceptance of his family was immediate and friendly. "It wasn't until months after we had moved in," he says, "that I found that a meeting had been called to discuss our purchase of the house and that the residents had agreed to adopt a wait-and-see policy."

Perhaps it is better for neighbors to get together beforehand than to allow the misguided or the unbalanced to have an outlet for their aggressions. It is better to welcome change than to be an obstacle to progress. Certainly the advent of a Negro family to a new neighborhood calls for men of good will to plan with their neighbors to welcome and aid the new "settlers."

Developing Neighborhoods

In the cities this becomes even more urgent than in the suburbs. James Banks, formerly executive director of the United Planning Organization, sees the whole housing picture as an area for new breakthroughs. His agency is sponsoring neighborhood development movements, in which the people to be helped participate actively. The Citizens for Better Housing committee of UPO is active in securing new housing for moderate income families and in rehabilitating existing dwellings. It enlists the cooperation of nonprofit and church organizations in buying up, rehabilitating, and then renting houses to minority group members.

The committee also conducts schools for tenants and owners—those responsible for maintaining the buildings. It teaches them to get the regulations from the appropriate city authorities, it helps them understand their rights and responsibilities under the city codes. Further, the "students" go through the whole grievance procedure as it must be followed with city agencies. And the committee sponsors neighborhood legal centers that help tenants and owners to understand the law.

The Urban League recommends that volunteers visit local housing authorities or write federal agencies to find out what possibilities there are for the ill-housed. Then the push must be to follow through and aid the needy in entering better shelters that may be available or under construction.

The League also suggests action to relieve the existing problems insofar as possible. For instance, ghetto dwellers need information and instruction in sanitation and home care. Pest control is important, and it is dimly understood by many that lights and bits of food attract insects, for example. Further, food care, cleaning and preservation, child care, nutrition, and home maintenance can be taught in housing projects or citizens' homes.

There are methods of improving existing living quarters, and these techniques need not be costly. The League suggests bringing in community resources such as local builders and construction unions in programs of this kind. Further, home demonstration agents of the Department of Agriculture and consumer education consultants of the Health, Education, and Welfare Department and the Food and Drug Administration may have ideas and information that can be used.

The National Board of the YWCA has put out an excellent housing handbook, "Neighbors and Neighborhoods," that really tells you how you can help. It includes a listing of sources of information and help from the federal government to voluntary agencies and includes a useful bibliography of the best publications on the subject of housing for minorities. Other sources are the NAACP, the Urban League, the National Council of Churches, and the Anti-Defamation League of B'nai B'rith (which has some hard-hitting publications in this field).

For those who really want to dig in and help, there are limitless possibilities. I like to recall the successful projects that have been executed by Negroes and whites working together at the community level. And one of these which accomplished a great deal in a short time was that of the Cranbury, New Jersey, Housing Associates.

Cranbury is a town of two thousand near Trenton, New Jersey, and the project I'm thinking of probably should have been named Phoenix. It all started with a fire which gutted Cranbury's approximation of a tenement house . . . the only multiple-family dwelling in town that contained Negro families.

The next morning Cranbury awoke to the fact that these Negro citizens, all long-time residents of the town, had no place to go. Though local church groups came through with emergency clothing, there was no housing available. Only then did the white residents of the town realize what the two hundred Negroes in Cranbury had lived with for years: inadequate and limited quarters. In fact, almost simultaneously with the fire the town's newly constituted Board of Health declared four houses "unfit for human habitation"—all four were occupied by Negro families. These families faced imminent eviction and had no place to go.

So one of the local housewives got on the phone and rounded up a group of Negroes and whites who met at the school principal's house to figure out how they could cope with this housing emergency. Some of the fire refugees had huddled together in an old barracks-type building used in the past by migrant workers during harvest season. The group's first order of business was to make this temporary shelter livable. They worked evenings and weekends putting in windows, insulating the walls, liming the outdoor privies. They begged and borrowed old furniture from friends and had the well tested and purified.

As this rescue operation proceeded the volunteers continued to think about the long-range needs, and decided to incorporate as the Cranbury Housing Associates to tackle the other problems. They sold eight hundred shares of stock at ten dollars per share for capital. Then they bought a lot, contracted to buy a house to rent to one of the evicted families, located a vacant trailer for a second, and voted to help Alphonso Henderson, a local truck driver, complete a prefab shell house he had bought and could not afford to finish. They renegotiated Henderson's contract with the house company, to bring payments down to a rate he could carry. They also pitched in as volunteer carpenters, bricklayers, painters, glaziers, and roofers on weekends and in the evenings to complete the Henderson house.

Next they jumped in and built a house from the foundation to the roof-pole and even helped furnish it for the

Calvin Doggetts, a family of eight. The project was more like an old-fashioned barn-raising than anything else, with a dozen or more suburbanites going at it hammer and nails every spare evening and weekend until the building was complete, painted, furnished, and the family was moved in. They continued building and refurbishing until all the dispossessed were decently housed.

The project had unexpected ramifications. In the first place, the CHA brought together a diverse assortment of interested people who had valuable skills. It included five Negroes and ten whites, five women and ten men as directors of the Associates. David McCall was president of a New York advertising firm; Louis Spence was a writer; Jane Bos a secretary and housewife; Edna Merrill, a domestic; John Owen, deacon of the First Baptist Church; "Skeet" Trowbridge, wife of the local elementary school principal; Stan Tarr, insurance claims adjuster; Don Armstrong, a master builder; and Jim Conover, retired social welfare worker.

Jim Freer, a Negro, distrusted the CHA at first. "They were talking at one of the meetings about people who were housing problems," he says, "and I told them, 'I'm no housing problem. I can buy a house tomorrow in Ewing Township.' And they said, 'Sure, you can go to Ewing Township if you want to, but we don't want to lose you.' Well, that's the first time I ever heard of anybody wanting to keep anybody around here. I decided then, if I think I'm a fighter, I'll stay right here and show people I can do something besides shoot off my mouth."

Rudy Conover at eighteen had dropped out of high school in his freshman year and spent his time sitting around home sketching. A friend thought he had talent and brought his drawings to a meeting of the Housing Associates and passed them around. The group was impressed with the boy's ability to design women's clothes. One of the directors took the drawings to the Traphagen School of Design in New York.

On the basis of the drawings Rudy was admitted, a tuition scholarship was donated to him, and Rudy was hired by the advertising firm of one of the CHA directors.

Rudy's friend says, "They saved that boy—he just didn't know what to do with that talent of his."

But perhaps the most significant outgrowth of this CHA activity is the understanding and warmth that now exists between Negroes and whites in the community. Jim Conover, an elder statesman of the Negro community, says, "It's changed my attitude entirely, and I've been working with whites for thirty years. I never thought we could work this closely together."

The wife of Cranbury's school principal says, "It's made it possible for us to communicate. For the first time here, Negroes and whites are friends. Each time we get together, more things come to the surface. We're all on the same level, all working on the same problem."

Would to God this was so in all the communities of our great nation.

Chapter 9

Progress Through Politics

"It is in our states and local communities where we must wage the war against America's shame—slumism." The words were Hubert Humphrey's as he addressed the White House Conference on Civil Rights in 1966. I could not agree more. Mr. Humphrey did not sidestep federal responsibility for progress, but made the point that the major battles of the next phase of the civil rights struggle will be waged in city halls and state capitols.

This point must rally men of conscience to action. It is too easy to slough off individual responsibility and, with a shrug of the shoulders, say, "It's a national problem; what can I do?" You can do something. Each of us can. It is all-important that concerned citizens exercise their political power to make government—at all levels—fulfill its purposes without bias. It is essential that we each become political activists and use our political rights to the fullest to advance equality of opportunity and thereby heal our sick cities.

Let's not kid ourselves. The lasting effects of the current civil rights revolution will be determined by the responsible exercise of political power by Americans who have been excluded. Temporary concessions of one kind or another by those currently in power are not going to suffice. The only long-range basis for peaceful progress is to give citizens a voice and share in their own government. This is the fundamental reason for enfranchising Americans without restrictions of race. What justice is there in a system that, as Dr. Martin Luther King noted, "would take at least 103 years to register the 14,873 Negroes presently over twenty-one in Dallas County (Selma), Alabama?"

Responsible Government

How responsive is government to its constituents? How well does it meet their needs? These are two pressing questions in every community in the country. Different cities take different approaches.

In St. Louis one-third of the population of about 900,000 is Negro. It has integrated sports, entertainment, and public services in the city and desegregation of schools and housing is moving forward. Rehabilitation projects are under way to rebuild neighborhoods rather than raze them. And one of the most extensive urban renewal projects in the nation is wiping out slums on four hundred acres. The city was the first to establish a fair employment practices program and has the strongest public accommodations and fair housing laws in the country.

A considerable factor in all of this is the fact that at this writing the twenty-eight-member board of aldermen has eight Negro members—the highest ratio for a city council in the nation. Negro participation in the administration of the city is considerable: the welfare director is a Negro, three of the twelve members of the school board are Negroes. Five assistant superintendents of schools, forty school principals, four fire captains, three police captains, three judges, three assistant city attorneys, two assistant U.S. attorneys, four state representatives and one state senator—all are Negroes.

Of course this is not to say that St. Louis is a bed of roses. And no one can insure that just because you have all groups

of the population represented in government—for a change—
that the quality of government will automatically improve.
But you can be more confident that you are meeting the needs
and wishes of more of the people when you have such a cross
section.

The Urban League has been carrying on a pioneering
leadership development program in ten cities. This effort
brings nearly two thousand Negroes into training for greater
civic responsibility. It is so vital in its purpose and its im-
plications for the future that I want you to know more about
it. As representative of the approach, consider the way the
program has developed in Springfield, Ohio.

In this midwestern city of 130,000—12,500 of them Negro
citizens—four seminars were held, each of them two and a
half months in duration. Enrolled were Negroes who were
identified by the Urban League and other observers as having
leadership potential. Fully 150 people went through the seminars. In the groups were housewives, post office workers,
teachers, industrial engineers, clerical assistants and sales
clerks, a management trainee, minister, product control supervisor, and accounting technicians. How's that for diversity?

The seminars were bedrock practical. They covered these
topics:

1. Responsibilities of leadership.
2. Political structure of Springfield and Clark County.
3. The role of the Negro in Springfield.
4. Urban planning.
5. Process of change.
6. Mock board meetings.
7. Group dynamics.
8. Political education.
9. Group mechanics.

Now in a ten-week period, starting from practically zero,
these people came through some pretty sophisticated territory.

But the programs generated so much ferment and enthusiasm that each seminar group continued to meet informally when the series was over. By early 1966, these 150 trainees had organized into the Springfield Information Council.

So what? Well, the Council assigns members to attend all public hearings of the local board of education, hearings of various commissions (parks, public safety, etc.) and city council meetings. The Council then spreads the word to the community about pertinent matters. For instance, the Council took a position on a pending bond levy for education and made sure Negro citizens got the pros and cons of that issue straight. Furthermore, in taking a stand, the Council let the total community know just what well-informed Negro citizens thought of the proposal. This action was a "first."

The Council keeps on top of political events in the whole city and is a transmission device that sends information both directions, to the grass roots and to the top. As the Council demonstrated in its bond levy action, it articulated concern and galvanized support for an issue that was important to Negroes and to the whole city. This fills a void in the Negro community, multiplying the numbers of people willing to move out of their compartmentalized lives and become active, potent participants in the decision-making process.

That is how the leadership program has developed group action. But it has succeeded not only in Springfield: in Miami, under the auspices of the program, a group of young men have formed a panel that might be called a "political alert." They keep abreast of all issues and feed back information to the community. Two members of the panel are on the superintendent of education's quasi-official advisory committee.

In Cleveland, when charter review came up for consideration, members of the leadership "Caucus" (as it is called there) presented recommendations and observations. It was the only presentation from the Negro community. This grew out of experience the participants had in the program. They had visited Toronto and Nashville to observe different approaches to city problems.

Beyond such group action, however, the development program has scored with individual action. In one city a mother on welfare became a board member of one of the poverty programs. In another case a postal clerk who had gone through the training was elected mayor of his village. One department store sales clerk is now a member of a parks commission in his town.

Small achievements? By no means. These are light-year leaps up from the lethargy and political ignorance that prevailed in these towns and cities before. In their way, these advances are as significant for the local future as the election of Senator Edward Brooke from Massachusetts is for the national future. And just as salutory.

Votes for Negroes

There has been much crude misinformation about what would happen as a result of the federal voting rights bill. Essentially, its impact will be to make it possible for more Negroes to be nominated and elected to office in states and cities of the south. And their accession to power should end the discrimination and brutality to which they have been subjected by local government officials. This is, of course, a conditional proposition, for no one can foresee what the actual political participation by Negroes will come to in the south.

Ever since Reconstruction days the south has raised the hoary bugaboo of Negro political domination every time attempts were made to enfranchise Negroes in that section. "We will be swamped by the votes of uneducated, bloc-voting Negroes," they have said. "The Negroes will elect unprepared candidates who will misgovern us. Look at the

Reconstruction record. We will not stand for a repetition of that." It is a hollow argument.

They need not fear any "takeover" by Negroes. The reason is simple. Though in 1930 the population statistics might have given some basis to an hypothesis based on the percentages of whites and Negroes in a state, they do not warrant any panic by southern whites today. In 1930, 63 per cent of Mississippi's citizens were Negroes. By 1960 the Negro population of the state had dropped by 800,000 and the proportion was 42 per cent. In no state of the south do Negroes make up as much as 40 per cent of the voting-age population today.

Only in certain counties are whites outnumbered, and only in one Congressional District in the entire area of the old Confederacy is there a potential majority of Negroes in the voting-age population (that district is in Mississippi). Thus the fear of being outvoted by superior numbers is groundless.

Furthermore, even where there have been few hurdles to prevent Negroes from voting—in such states as Tennessee and North Carolina—whites have registered at a much faster pace. In other words, just because registration and voting bars are eliminated does not mean that every eligible voter will flock to the polls. We have found that rural Negroes never have sought to register, even where they were free to do so. And the intensive and expensive voter education and registration drives carried on by the Urban League, CORE, NAACP, and others showed us that it is tough to stimulate people to exercise their franchise.

So, on a second count it is well nigh impossible that Negro voters could outnumber whites.

As for the likelihood of unqualified Negro citizens being elected, a review of the qualifications of Negroes now serving as legislators confirms that they are better qualified by education, experience, or training than the majority of their white counterparts.

The specter of Reconstruction legislatures is a favorite of southern defenders of the status quo. Perhaps two things should be said about this old idea. First, the Reconstruction era is still popularly misunderstood and misrepresented. The facts show that many of the Negroes in Reconstruction legislatures conducted themselves well and turned in creditable performances.

Second, a century has passed and there are thousands of times more well-educated, well-qualified Negroes with political savvy today than a century ago. Candidates for office will fight it out in the arena of public opinion and be voted in or out on the basis of their ability to convince their constituents of their superior merits.

A basic effect of increased Negro voter registration in the south will be the increasing liberation of the white man from the shackles of prejudice. I am reminded of the questioning of Governor LeRoy Collins by Senator Strom Thurmond in 1964 when Mr. Collins was named to head the Community Relations Service under the Civil Rights Act of 1964. Mr. Collins had been governor of Florida for six years. Senator Thurmond, at a committee hearing on Mr. Collins' qualifications, read from statements the former governor had made condemning school desegregation and civil rights demonstrations following the Supreme Court decision of 1954.

Mr. Collins admitted that he had opposed school desegregation in the 1950s but was now in favor of it on a sound, sensible basis. "There are some inconsistencies," he said, referring to his record. "But we all grow and change, and have to meet new responsibilities. And I will not contend that I have not changed some of my positions as a result of better understanding."

We may hope and expect that there will be similar results in the understanding by his fellow citizens of increased political power for the Negro.

Bringing Negroes In

There is a tremendous distance, of course, between enfranchisement and political power. And it is in bridging this gap that individuals of good will can be helpful. For the Negro citizen with ability should be serving on boards, committees, agencies at local, county, and state levels. He should be included in the governing process by appointment to the commissions and departments of government that determine how we live. I mean, of course, the zoning commissions that decide whether that tannery can install its drying racks next to your living room windows, or whether the laundry can have a "variance" to exhaust hot gases into your back yard, and so on. The establishment of residential areas, industrial, business, and noncommercial sections has been done without consulting the minority groups for generations. It's about time they had representation on the boards that so blithely decide the future disposition of the real estate on which Negro citizens live.

The range of committees and boards is, as anyone who reads his local paper knows, extensive. Their responsibilities vary in weight. But whether it is health or education, welfare or parks, traffic or safety or sanitation or utilities, Negro representation is needed, for the sake of the present generation and the future. For service on public commissions is often a prelude to political office.

There are also the library boards, the PTA offices, the historical society and community art and music associations. These and other cultural groups need the participation and guidance of citizens who know the Negro community because they are of it. The same goes for businessmen's clubs, sororities and fraternities of professional people, the sports associations, country and swimming clubs.

The city that does include its Negro citizens to the fullest extent in its cultural and recreational life as well as its public and official activities enriches its citizens' experiences many-fold and upgrades the texture of its total milieu. The association of citizens in these many interspersed and interlocking committees and organizations bears a direct relationship to the life of the community, both formal and informal.

In my experience I have noticed a high correlation between the membership of committees in the cultural, educational, and recreational fields and committees in the world of business, politics, and public affairs. I rather think it is no accident, but that men—and women—come to know one another's abilities by such association, and one type of service tends to lead to the other.

After all this discussion, it should come as no surprise to the reader that I believe every citizen who is in a position to help determine the inclusion of Negroes on any and every kind of representative body should make an effort to see that this is done. Sure, some will turn out to be deadwood. But others will turn out to be pillars of strength. And from my experience at the League I am willing to bet that there will be more pillars than posts.

Negroes and Political Parties

Political party clubhouses should be vying with one another to find Negroes who can be groomed for political office. Our political parties can and must do better, and all who wield political influence, from the precinct captain to the party chairman, must make efforts to seek out Negro citizens for inclusion in our political life.

The importance of this is immeasurable. Consider, for instance, the fact that the Americans who suffer most, as a group, are the rural Negroes, the farmers and sharecroppers

whose income is almost invisible. How directly is this related
to the fact that the Agriculture Department has followed
Jim Crow practices in many of its aspects? There are thirty
thousand Agriculture Department employees in Washington,
and as late as 1964 only four of these at the professional level
were Negroes who worked across the board in integrated
capacities.

The Department shunted its Negro employees on both
state and national levels into a segregated wing that did not
successfully reach Negro farmers. The Extension Service,
according to *Jet* magazine, had a segregated structure that
deprived Negro extension personnel of the opportunity to
learn and transmit modern farming practices to Negro farmers. In the Soil Conservation Service, *Jet* learned that the
Washington office of the Department appointed state directors
who hired local work units to serve given districts. There
were three Negroes employed in a professional capacity in
the entire south. In reviewing thirty-three issues of the
Department's publication *Soil Conservation*, it was found that
only one had pictures or information about Negroes.

Further, Department officials not only belonged to professional societies that exclude Negroes, they participated in
meetings that excluded Negroes and training programs were
segregated. *Jet* also charged that national conferences on agricultural outlook and the 4-H Clubs were almost totally white.
These points, according to *Jet*, are all included in a U. S.
Civil Rights Commission report.

The conclusion that Negro farmers have suffered because
of the Agriculture Department's policies is inescapable. And
it requires backing up but one more step to see that the
Department's policies are determined by the Congressional
committees concerned with agricultural legislation and with
appropriations. Southerners, because of the seniority system
that gives prime committee chairmanships to men who have

served longest in Congress, have been entrenched in both agriculture and appropriations committees for years.

And, as every political observer knows, southern Congressmen and Senators owe their seniority to the "privileged sanctuaries" from which they are elected. There, nomination in the primary is tantamount to election. Perhaps the new voting rights bill plus the reapportionment in the states will let a little air into this previously closed circuit. If so, it will relieve the pressure on Agriculture and other departments so that they can do their work as they should: with more service devoted to those who need it most.

Do Your Part

What can be done in the political sphere to insure better opportunities for Negro citizens?

Individuals can vote for the best man, nominate the best man, work for the best man. And they can take the initiative in finding out where candidates stand on issues affecting Negro citizens and the slums. In their party activities they can urge inclusion of Negro citizens and nominate candidates interested in the rights of all men. As individual citizens they can help bring the word to the ghettos about candidates and vice versa. They can form car pools and volunteer to help citizens register and vote.

Organizations can carry on programs that build political awareness. One that I have long admired is the "Boys State" activity sponsored by the American Legion around the country. At these annual sessions, Legion Posts sponsor leading high school seniors from all parts of the state. The youngsters learn how their state and county governments operate by simulating the party nominating, campaign, and election procedures. Then the kids "take over" the state government for a day and discover how the wheels of government really turn.

Other *organizations* do impressive jobs in their spheres of activity and are urged to extend their operations further. I think almost automatically of the tremendously effective League of Women Voters. Its extension to the ghetto would be invaluable. And there are activities by organizations such as the unions, the NAACP and Urban League, each of which puts in long hours and great effort to educate and register voters. More, much more, is needed. The surface has been penetrated, but as of today many thousands of citizens have not yet been reached or convinced that they can help determine their own destiny through the ballot.

Elected officials have the responsibility of appointing qualified men to governmental positions. These days, they have an added responsibility: to seek out and appoint qualified Negroes to public positions. And if they cannot locate any with the qualifications, it is incumbent on them to ask a few questions (starting with "Why aren't there any qualified Negroes?" and ending with "How can we help Negroes to qualify for these positions?") and seek concrete answers.

Public servants surely must carry out their duties impartially, but with understanding and compassion. In no sector is this more important than in the area of law enforcement. We have witnessed the hair-raising spectacle of our police in major American cities panicking in the face of rioting ghetto dwellers and reacting viciously. The point I wish to make is that human relations training should be part of the experience of every public servant and that it is particularly important for those in the sensitive sectors of interpersonal relations—the police especially.

In some cities community relations programs conducted by the police department have been extremely valuable. In Baltimore, Winston-Salem, and Atlanta such programs have successfully dampened hostility between police and ghetto citizens. As the Riot Commission reports, Atlanta achieved this by setting up a Crime Prevention Bureau that concentrates on social services. In just two years it persuaded some 600 dropouts to go back to school, found jobs and food for 250 hardship cases, made life more pleasant by sponsoring dances and turning on fire hydrants for youngsters during summer. The police have gone out of their way to work fast and closely with families reporting missing persons. In general, such programs have increased communication, understanding, and trust between community and police and have provided the police with more recruits.

The Riot Report recommends several ways to improve police-community relations. I suggest that you refer to the section on "The Police and the Community." Both the Riot Panel and the President's Commission on Law Enforcement and Administration of Justice (the so-called "Crime Commission") strongly recommended quick, fair grievance machinery so that citizens can get action on complaints. Because of deep-seated existing suspicion of the police, it is almost mandatory that there be a hearing board set up outside the jurisdiction of the police department and that it have authority from the city council to make its recommendations stick.

I have focused here on the police department, because it is so crucial. However, it is both useful and highly important that grievances against other city employees be handled in a similarly objective, expeditious way, if not by the same review board. And it must always be borne in mind that the tone, the believability of the city's concern for its citizens, the example for all city employees is set by the man at the top—the mayor, city manager, executive—and the councilmen themselves. Without the dedication and determination at the top to serve all citizens fairly and with a sense of urgency, the city's lower echelon employees may bog down in the usual civil service morass of apathy and lethargy.

There are, for *all citizens*, ways to influence political

leaders to act with imagination, courage, and speed on issues
affecting the slums. Letters, petitions, rallies, speaking out at
public hearings—all of these can be effective. The prescription
is simple: for best results, act now! Don't delay, do it today!

Chapter 10

Welfare—and Other Ways of Helping People

One of the biggest laughs of 1965 in Civil Rights was the overnight transformation of the "model" Prince Georges County (Maryland) Citizens Council.

As you know, the White Citizens Councils are reactionary, right-wing organizations, dedicated to the proposition that "white is right" and, like the Nazi philosophy, that anything but the "pure" white race is tainted and inferior. They also mix some anti-Semitism with their teachings, but their main thrust is to maintain segregation and oppose desegregation, integration, and any vestige of equal opportunity for Negroes. The Citizens Councils began in the South after the Supreme Court school decision of 1954, to prevent, insofar as possible, and often by violence, the desegregation of schools and other facilities.

The Prince Georges County Citizens Council was organized as one of the first in the north (the area is a suburb of Washington, D.C.)—a high-water mark of Council expansion. It was widely publicized as a breakthrough in new, fertile territory. The chapter included as charter members government workers, a museum curator, housewives, college professors, two reporters for the Washington, D.C., *Daily News*, and a Catholic priest.

Then, January 27, 1965, the Prince Georges Citizens

Council met and voted a resolution to merge their organization with the county chapters of CORE, the Congress of
Racial Equality.

It turned out that eighteen of twenty members of the
Council were "double agents"—in fact, one of them was a
Negro (who avoided detection by simply not showing up at
Council meetings). Even the man who organized the chapter
admitted "the liberals' ruse was almost the funniest thing I've
heard in months."

The whole episode was revealing in several ways. It indicated the emptiness of the Councils' appeal, the ludicrous
method of recruitment, and it provided a flash of further
insight into the man who organized the local chapter, Joseph
McD. Mitchell, and into the national furor he fomented back
in 1961.

Mitchell at that time was city manager of Newburgh, New
York. It was he who announced on June 20, 1961, "The
Newburgh Plan" in public welfare. And the nationwide publicity that resulted made both the "Plan" and Mitchell major
topics of discussion across the land.

Mitchell told the country that his town (31,000) was being
flooded with indigent families who were coming to Newburgh
because it was a "soft touch," not because they wanted work.
The town, he said, was going broke trying to keep up relief
payments. These amounted to an "intolerable" one-third of its
$3,000,000 annual budget. Not only that, but families on relief
were pictured as shiftless and thriftless and delighted to remain on welfare. The official report also spoke of a "serious
problem of illegitimacy" and said it was unfair for unmarried
mothers to have additional children as a means of increasing
their support through federal ADC allowances.

The Newburgh situation was investigated by the New
York State Board of Social Welfare and was reported in the
newspapers some weeks later. The findings made Mitchell and

the town look foolish. They revealed that Newburgh had no problem of people flooding in for easy money:

During 1960 the city had spent only $205 on relief for newcomer families, of which every cent came from the state of New York, not from the town.

Able-bodied workers were not relaxing on relief instead of working; after two weeks of review under its new code, Newburgh had managed to find only one employable welfare recipient to put to work on a city job. All others were too old, too young (children), ill, or tied down with taking care of helpless family members.

Newburgh's welfare burden was not unusually big. Its relief bill totaled $983,000, but state and federal governments paid $559,000, leaving $424,000 as Newburgh's share. The average welfare family received $93 a month. And the proportion of families on relief was well below the state average.

Unmarried mothers could not get rich by having additional children to secure ADC payments. In fact, they could barely clothe and feed the kids on the $11 to $30 per month per child allotted.

The Urban League examined the Newburgh picture and City Manager Mitchell's statements at the time. Because of the widespread publicity and the interest of Goldwaterites, Birchites, and other far-right groups, Mitchell and his ideas were widely trumpeted and Mitchell was invited to address audiences all over the country. Therefore the League considered the Newburgh situation of extraordinary importance.

The League found that the population of Newburgh had changed and that the increases had been primarily from Puerto Ricans and Negroes who had become 16 per cent of the total population and 38 per cent of the city's relief load. Mitchell's Newburgh supporters referred repeatedly to "undesirable types of newcomers" in their defense of the New-

burgh Plan. There was considerable suspicion that the Plan
was aimed at nonwhites. This was denied at the time, of
course, but Mitchell's subsequent activity as organizer for the
Citizens Councils tends to confirm the earlier belief.

Mitchell and others implied strongly that these people
flocked to Newburgh as a haven for mockers who wanted
an easy life lounging around without having to work. In
fact, most of them were migrant seasonal farm workers from
the south and Puerto Rico, attracted to the important farm
area just outside Newburgh. At the end of each harvest a
few of the workers stayed in the town to put down roots
and escape migrancy. These people, far from being thriftless
and chronically indigent or lazy as pictured in the Newburgh Plan, were the more ambitious of the migrant workers
—people seeking a better life for their families. But, as in
most parts of America, the unemployment and welfare rates
for black workers were double those for whites.

I bring up this Newburgh case because it is timeless. It is
as current today as it was in 1961, for there are still communities where welfare is an emotional and political football, subject to uninformed, ill-intentioned, and bigoted direction.

There are ways of being responsive to the needs of constituents. The Newburgh Plan is one way of dealing with welfare problems. The approach of the city authorities in Chicago is another. In the Windy City the welfare picture is
monumental. At this writing there are nearly 300,000 persons
on relief in Cook County, 85 per cent of them Negroes. The
monthly payout for welfare is $15,600,000. Staggering as this
is, it represents an improvement. Chicago is the only large city
that has successfully reduced its relief rolls. In one two-year
period it trimmed the monthly cost by $2,000,000.

Yet it has done this by projects that help welfare recipients
break out of the ghetto. There are thousands of people taking
vocational training courses. They range from such elementary

topics as household techniques (how to wrap garbage; how to wax floors) in order to be a better maid, to fine cabinet work and wood finishing. A course in food preparation helps people qualify for restaurant jobs. A sequence in driver training has been extremely successful. The Yellow Cab Company hires everyone who finishes the course satisfactorily.

Many companies farm out rush work at seasonal peaks. Welfare recipients are assigned to these, and are tested and trained in the process. They sometimes find a job with the company as a result. The department runs a rehabilitation center that processes several hundred people a day and places about one hundred a month. Five hundred are in testing or training at all times. And the department has programs in which it teaches people to read and write, or to improve these skills. Chicago is a city which looks at welfare for its able-bodied citizens not as a permanent dole, but as a temporary setback. It is doing its best to rehabilitate and train them so they can become self-supporting.

In theory, that is what welfare is for: to help the individual get back on his feet so that he can become self-sufficient if at all possible. (In every community, however, there are Americans who are too old, too young or handicapped who cannot survive without assistance.) Yet we find that usually rehabilitation and training have played too small a part in welfare, and the stupendous caseloads have all but made it impossible for the welfare worker to do more than determine eligibility and make hasty, periodic rechecks to verify continuance of need.

The process of obtaining public assistance is one guaranteed to crush self-respect. Do you know what it entails? If you had no place to turn, how would you find money for your family—ruling out begging or lawbreaking—if you had exhausted all possible job potentials or were, because of age or physical condition, unable to hold a job? This was the process of applying for public assistance in the progressive, enlightened state of New York in 1963:

An applicant becomes eligible for assistance when he exhausts his money, gives a lien on his property to the welfare department, turns in the license plates of his car and takes legal action against his legally responsible relatives. When he is stripped of all material resources, when he "proves" his dependency, then and only then is he eligible.

As the Moreland Commission Report[1] (from which that paragraph was taken) notes, "Welfare policies tend to cast the recipient in the role of the property-less, shiftless pauper. This implies that he is incompetent and inadequate to meet the demands of competitive life. He is then regarded as if he had little or no feelings, aspirations, or normal sensibilities. This process of proving and maintaining eligibility in combination with the literal adherence to regulations and procedures tends to produce a self-perpetuating system of dependency and dehumanization."

The Welfare Picture

The nub of the situation concerning welfare is that nobody is really happy about it—not those who receive it, not those who deal with it, and certainly not those who pay for it. And yet, since this nation decided during the Depression of the thirties that no American should be forced to beg, public assistance has been the major alternative.

In our nation of 200,000,000 souls more than 7,350,000 received federally supported public welfare payments in 1967. Of these, 4.4 million were children, 2.1 million were oldsters,

[1] State of New York, Moreland Commission on Welfare. *Public Welfare in the State of New York.* Albany, N.Y., Executive Chamber, State Capitol, 1963.

more than 700,000 were blind or handicapped. There were some 150,000 fathers receiving aid, of whom 100,000 were incapacitated or unemployable. Total: 7,350,00 persons. About half, or 3¾ million of those on assistance are non-whites. Furthermore, the Urban League's experts tell me that for every person currently receiving public assistance benefits there is at least one more who is eligible but not getting them.

There are some 32 million Americans who are poor. Our welfare programs are, presumably, reaching and aiding only the most needy of our citizens. Certainly our laws are designed to make welfare benefits as small as possible to as few as possible. It is a fact that each of the fifty states sets the figure for minimum dollars needed to subsist. Believe it or not, the U. S. Department of Health, Education, and Welfare reported in 1967 that thirty-three states actually gave less support for needy children than these minimum figures they had established themselves!

Many states have residence requirements. Some have ceilings on grants to penalize large families and keep the birth rate down among the poor (there is no evidence that this is an effective contraceptive). Others demand that more fortunate relatives of the poor be required to aid their kin even though they have paid income taxes that finance social welfare programs. In Florida the legislature squeezed out mothers by demanding they surrender their illegitimate children for placement or be taken off welfare. Thousands sacrificed welfare payments in order to keep their children. The state of Michigan went this one better, however. Mothers who turned their backs on welfare in order to keep their youngsters found no refuge. The state, in Kafkaesque pursuit of these unfortunates, let them exist in total poverty for a few months then hauled them into court on charges of neglecting their children. The youngsters then were taken from their mothers.

It should be evident from these brief citations that those on welfare are extremely vulnerable. They are fair game for ex-

ploitation and intimidation. Because this is so, the National
Advisory Council on Public Welfare has urged sweeping
changes in programs aided by federal funds (that means most
of them).

The Council has drawn up a "bill of rights" for welfare
applicants. It is a positive program and calls for making sure
recipients and applicants know that these are their legal
rights:

1. The right to *apply* and to receive prompt determination of
   eligibility.
2. The right to *equal treatment* and to have needs and resources
   judged by the same standards in all parts of a state.
3. The right to *cash payments* and to spend the cash as the individual sees fit, without dictation by the welfare worker or
   department.
4. The right to *service on a nondiscriminatory basis*.
5. The right of *appeal* and to have a lawyer to help in this
   process.

Exercise of these rights by welfare recipients could make
a vast difference in the welfare picture—for the better.

Perhaps the public assistance measures and results will
continue to be unsatisfactory so long as we use the current
approach to them. In the near future we are bound to revise
our view of support programs and conclude that our nation
is too great and too concerned about her citizens to allow
any of them to grind along in abject poverty. Many people
of every political persuasion now advocate a minimum income
for each citizen, an income floor beneath which no one should
have to exist.

We have already agreed on a rough figure of $3000 per
year as the minimum necessary for a family in this country.
Some of the proposals for making our citizens self-sufficient
advocate junking the whole welfare payment machinery and

substituting a program by which each family would be guaranteed $3000 per year. If they earned any money during the year, this would be deducted from their support payments, for the purpose would be to bring their income up to the "poverty line" of $3000. Thus as their earnings increased the cash payments would be reduced, but not withdrawn until they hit the $3000 figure. This plan has been tabbed a "negative income tax." We will hear more of it in coming years.

There are many other proposals, but one that has proved valuable in Canada and other countries is the family allowance. In Canada, all families receive cash payments, with a set amount per child. Nobody asks for proof of need—the fact that there are children is sufficient. And, since the payments are based in part on the youngsters' school attendance, truancy and dropouts are at rock bottom.

Helping Today

But until that time when our welfare arrangements shall have been revolutionized there is much to be done. At present more and more people come on welfare all the time. The number of people living in poverty is not diminishing. Their problems are not disappearing, but continuing.

To help these people requires extraordinary effort. The professionals on the firing line are the trained social workers. Their lot is not a happy one.

The social caseworker's life is taken up with the miseries of the human condition. His professional duties take him to the most dismal sections of the city, cause him to meet the most bedraggled and storm-tossed of our citizens at the absolute rock-bottom of their careers. His "clients" tolerate him, resent him, perhaps hate him, but must maintain contact with him if only to secure that necessary assistance to which he is the key.

The caseworker never has a "satisfied client"; he seldom if ever wins applause or awards for his "successes"—instead he is likely to be assigned more cases or promoted to administrative work. He never completes his work, for there are always more cases than he and his fellows can handle, and more coming along all the time, it seems. As if the lack of recognition, the excessive paperwork, and the impossible case load were not enough, he is paid less than many other workers in jobs with similar educational and training requirements. No wonder the turnover in social work positions—particularly in public welfare work—is so high.

In New York State, which has a comparatively enlightened view of social welfare, there were in one recent year fewer than one hundred graduates of social work schools employed by the state, counties, and cities. The number of cases requiring trained workers called for three thousand graduates! Yet fewer than four hundred students complete graduate training in the state each year, and only a tiny fraction of these accept jobs in public welfare.

Obviously we need and must train more social workers; we must relieve them of their excessive paper work—perhaps by streamlining the reporting, perhaps by a system of "social work aides"; we must pay them better and give them recognition if we expect to keep them for any length of time.

Innovation and energy are needed in the overall effort. The War on Poverty and the Office of Economic Opportunity had launched many programs that spotlighted the needs and reached out to the redeemable and were designed to prevent a great deal of the preventable. There were VISTA, the Job Corps, the Neighborhood Youth Corps, and various work-study programs aimed at young people. There were community action programs intended to help in the cities. And there were programs for adult education and needy children, and others to combat rural poverty and even some small business aid activities.

Unfortunately, these were at best limited programs, limited in their financing, their time spent, and in numbers of people they could reach. Worse still, most of these efforts have been seriously cut back if not eliminated—starved for funds and parceled out to various government departments. This is a disheartening shame, for many of the programs had extraordinary promise; some had achieved results that could be termed sensational.

I think automatically about Project ENABLE in this regard. ENABLE stood for Education and Neighborhood Action for Better Living Environment. This was a joint effort of the Urban League, Family Service Association, and Child Study Association in more than sixty-one cities. It had financing from the OEO. In the ghettos of these cities trained social workers were helped by nonprofessional social work "aides" drawn from the neighborhoods themselves. ENABLE's mission was to reach no-income and low-income families, to give them hope and help in meeting their problems.

ENABLE staffers were unprecedented in social work— they actually included people representative of those the program was designed to help. Thus the project began by knowing the needs of those they were to serve, not requiring lengthy surveys to determine needs. Meetings were scheduled where and when the "clients" could get to them. In Jacksonville, Florida, for example, people brought their children to the evening meetings. They came even though they worked six days a week without vacation or time off. These were people whose youngsters had a candy bar for lunch, who were afraid of going to the local clinics even though they were ill, fearing that they couldn't afford the minimum fee.

The ENABLE aides made it their business to counsel parents and families about the resources of the city, helped them find assistance, and directed them to the places where they could get results. In many cases most of the digging to get the proper information and "walking the client through" the often complicated government procedures was accomplished by the ENABLE aides. Because the ENABLE workers had been recruited from the groups they were trying to reach, the program was incredibly effective in getting through, in informing and involving those who previously had been overlooked or who, because of suspicion and distrust, had shunned assistance.

Mrs. Jean Bryant was a social work aide in the ENABLE program in Salt Lake City. She had been trained by the program's professional staff to deal with local agencies and community services. Her duty was to talk with families in group discussions. When they told about their specific problems Mrs. Bryant's job was to help them contact the agency that could assist them. Sometimes she actually escorted her "clients" to such an agency and worked with them in dealing with the organization. If the agency was unresponsive, Mrs. Bryant then called on ENABLE's professional staff to apply the necessary muscle to bring about fast action.

One of her triumphs developed from one of her first visits. A poverty-stricken family's problems were multiplied a thousandfold when the father died. "The mother," says Mrs. Bryant, "was simply unable to function. She was too overwhelmed by all that had happened. She knew she would need help to carry on but didn't know how to go about getting it." Through Mrs. Bryant's encouragement, the woman joined an ENABLE group and was guided through her problems. With the immediate difficulties under control, the woman is working to become a real estate saleswoman.

Another example of ENABLE action was a neighborhood workshop where parents built toys for their youngsters out of donated scraps and bits of wood, plastic, and cloth. This one resulted from an agonized report from one of the fathers at an ENABLE discussion meeting. The man reported how crushed he had felt at Christmas. He had depended on charity for his children and nothing materialized. "It was degrading enough not to be able to provide gifts himself," Mrs. Bryant says, "but to ask for help, be assured it would come, and then have nothing for his young children, hurt him deeply."

In the Bronx, New York, Mrs. Alease Whiteside was another ENABLE social work aide. Mother of four, Mrs. Whiteside had left school at an early age in the south. However, her work with ENABLE convinced her she needed to complete her education and she returned to school.

Meanwhile, she worked with 120 families, recruiting them for group meetings, helping them deal with dozens of agencies in the forest of organizations and bureaus active in New York City. Her work varied from helping parents secure proper clothing allotments from the city Welfare Department to interceding for her "clients" with the Housing Authority, in demanding school crossing lights, and in calling on other institutions and agencies to deliver the services or goods they were supposed to provide.

Chester H. Jones, field supervisor of Project ENABLE for the League, put his finger on the project's fundamental value: "For years professional social workers found that one of their biggest obstacles to success was their inability to win the trust and the confidence of the people they were trying to help. In addition, they couldn't always determine what the people themselves wanted and needed; too often they fell into the trap of giving them what the professionals *thought* they *should* want."

Project ENABLE changed that thinking once and for all. Says Jones: "ENABLE's social work aides . . . serve as living proof that not only can poor people improve their own lot when given the chance, but that they can also help transform their neighbors as well. Not only are these men and women indispensable to the success of ENABLE, but they are the key to any organized effort to make our slums into livable neighborhoods. . . . Why, one southern city never bothered paving the streets until ENABLE workers organized the community and forced the city to pave them."

ENABLE also helped families secure running water for the first time, counseled on establishment of credit unions, organized consumer education classes, anti-TB campaigns, and many, many other deeply needed activities.

In Little Rock, for example, the ENABLE team went to a cotton and soybean plantation and worked with the share-croppers. Here were scores of people who literally knew nothing of any public health, welfare, social security, or other resources available to them. With the people themselves, food stamps were arranged for and secured, an immunization clinic was established, visits of a public health nurse were obtained, a day care center was organized, and seventy-two people enrolled in evening adult education classes.

The plantation owner called and complained that so many meetings were going on at night his field hands were no longer working from sunup to sundown. If his workers needed medical care or welfare assistance he told them where to go, he said emphatically, and he didn't want outsiders coming in to disrupt their way of life. ENABLE board members talked to him and convinced him that healthier, better-educated workers would benefit him, too, and he withdrew his opposition.

This kind of reaching out was typical of ENABLE. Across the land it served to open new worlds to the poverty-stricken. I'll never forget the words of one mother in an ENABLE group in Chicago Heights: "Me—I didn't even know how to get on a bus alone or how to get to the hospital to see the doctor, but now I know." With thousands of successes such as these to their credit it is understandable that ENABLE teams developed real *esprit* and drive.

The ENABLE program reached more than forty thousand hard-core poor people in its first year; in its second it involved more than fifty thousand. But when Congress cut back the appropriations for the Office of Economic Opportunity this program, along with so many others, was sharply reduced. Yet we learned much from the effort and helped many so it cannot be said that it was not well worth the investment of time and toil. New programs will be shaped according to the experience gained in this—and in so many other—antipoverty projects.

Individual Action

What can an individual do in his neighborhood to help?

To begin with, call a local community group such as your Human Relations Council (if your town doesn't have one, the establishment of one should be your first goal), NAACP, Urban League, YWCA, or United Fund to see what need there may be for volunteers with your background.

If there is no group active in your town, you may want to pull together your own committee. The starting point for any such group must be a check on projects and programs going on in the community, whether they be run by city, county, state, federal, or private agencies. Your committee can really serve if it will analyze the existing programs and determine what their effects are and will be. With an overview of what is going on, you can tell where you and your group may be most effective.

You may want to define and select a number of urgent problems that you can tackle with limited manpower, modest resources, and justification of those you are trying to help. Among those might be:

Help illiterates, by accompanying them to public libraries or develop remedial reading after school at the local schools, in housing projects or in their homes. Use high school students and other volunteers for this.

Bring preschool children together regularly and teach them songs, simple spelling, and arithmetic games.

Organize a volunteer brigade to take aged and sick to the local health and welfare facilities.

Help families living in hovels to find decent housing by checking the local housing authorities or the appropriate federal agency. See if there isn't some public housing open or imminent. Then help the family apply for it.

Counsel the workless and actually make the rounds with unemployed or underemployed youths to help them gain experience in applying for jobs at places such as banks, union headquarters, retail stores, personnel offices of factories or businesses.

Of course these merely indicate a few of the possibilities. Spend time talking with the families that need help. You will be able to draw up a roster of urgent needs as long as your arm. The job of translating the needs into action programs will require your ingenuity and perseverance. And, like death and taxes, action requires money. The financing of a voluntary project, free of government or nonprofit agency support, requires a heck of a lot of work. But traditionally, efforts to collect money for community projects in America have usually been fun-raising as well as fund-raising.

Some of the time-honored methods include: dinners, dances, ice cream socials, theater parties, ball games, volunteer athletic contests, concerts, bridge tournaments, raffles, picnics, auctions, white elephant and "next-to-new" sales. Also door-to-door solicitations, tag days, membership campaigns, and appeals of a formal nature to likely donors such as individuals, foundations, corporations, unions, and the local United Fund.

The formal appeals, of course, demand a carefully prepared approach describing the project, its time span and money needs, its goals, methods, personnel, administration, and direction in pretty thorough fashion.

You may want to check at your library for one of the books that tell how to raise funds. Three that are very helpful are:

So You're Going to Raise Funds by David M. Church, published by National Public Relations Council of Health & Welfare Services, Inc., 275 Park Avenue South, New York, N.Y.

How to Raise Funds by Mail, Fellows & Koenig, McGraw-Hill, 330 West 42 Street, New York, N.Y.

Fund Raising Manual, Charles W. Gamble, New York Democratic State Committee.

Chapter 11

Churches Find a Mission

We can all learn, I believe, from observing the extraordinary efforts of organized religion in the United States. From the position of being the proverbial millstone about the neck of racial progress, the churches (using the term to cover organized religions of all types) have found their voices and their reasons for existence in the civil rights revolution. Many churchmen are to be found in the forefront of the demonstrations for rights. And for every one who is photographed facing hostility of police and bigots on Alabama streets there are scores who are working quietly and equally effectively in their own neighborhoods in the north.

I do not know how thoroughly your local newspapers cover news of religion, but in my daily newspapers not an edition goes by but what there is a report of some significant action by church groups.

"Negro Minister to Head U.S. Presbyterians," "Negro Bishop Named Methodist Church Head," "National Church Council to Help Negroes in Ghettos," "United Church of Christ Opens Campaign Against Hiring Bias," "B'nai B'rith Plans to Fight Poverty," and so on. And the reports of action by church groups at the community level are pouring in also:

The United Church of Christ has urged its members to act both as individuals and groups to advance equality of op-

portunity. Review your own employment practices, says its "Action Guide for Racial Justice Now." Use your influence to end discrimination in your community. And then it gives concrete suggestions:

Send *"thoughtful, informed, and persuasive comments and letters" to employers, commending those who "take the lead toward inclusiveness." Other letters should "inquire about the absence of non-Caucasian personnel."*

Put stickers on bills when they are paid. The stickers read, *"I am a customer who would welcome being served personally by those whose race, creed, or color may be different from my own." The Council sells these stickers at three hundred for one dollar.*

Survey the hiring and employment practices of businesses in *your community and bring "pressure" if necessary, to increase rapidly the number of nonwhite employees.*

The Guide does not balk at direct action. If the survey *develops well-documented cases of discrimination, the Guide makes it clear that it may be necessary to demonstrate and picket.*

The National Council of Churches has expanded its activities. It has carried on two programs, one to spur Negro voter registration in the south, another to work with the Council of Federated Organizations (COFO) in tutoring, teaching at Freedom Schools, distribution of food and clothing and relief programs. More than five hundred ministers and laymen participated, with several results: the Council came under unprecedented, bitter attack from church members and others for this activity, but it stuck to its guns.

The presence of the ministers, working alongside volunteers from American colleges and cities throughout the land, served not only to demonstrate the commitment of organ-

*ized religion to the civil rights movement, but also to protect
the laymen who were at work. As one of the ministers put
it, the local bigots tend to think twice before taking potshots
or tossing dynamite at civil rights workers when they may hit
a clergyman and cause repercussions such as followed the
brutal murder of the Reverend James Reeb.*

*The National Council's Commission on Religion and Race
went after the problems of ghetto life, through pilot programs
in Cleveland. The emphasis is on voter education and registration to help Negro citizens achieve the political power that
they should enjoy. Cleveland's election of a Negro mayor
stems in part from such activity.*

*In 1964 the Catholic Conference for Interracial Justice
launched a program to harness the purchasing power of the
Roman Catholic Church to eradicate job discrimination
against minority groups. Twenty bishops and more than forty
dioceses undertook "affirmative action programs."*

*The bishops appoint "compliance agents" who are trained
by the Conference. The agents then supervise contracts for
services, supplies, and construction to make sure they include
nondiscrimination clauses. The agents have supervisory duties
and must report on the degree of compliance of companies.
They also make up a list of companies with nondiscrimination
policies for reference at contract-letting times.*

*The degree to which sanctions are applied to companies
with which the church deals is up to the bishops. They could
instruct, for example, that payments are to be withheld if a
company refused to hire Negroes after promising to do so
in order to qualify for a contract. The Conference's program
is supposed to apply to all who deal with the church, including banks and suppliers. The leverage of the Catholic financial
power is enormous. Its local churches spent nearly $2 billion
in 1961 on construction alone, of schools, hospitals, and church
buildings. Imagine the impact of economic power of this*

dimension, employed in a conscious way to further equality of opportunity!

Guidelines for action by Jewish communities—individuals and organizations—to help Negroes achieve equality were outlined in June 1965. The National Community Advisory Relations Council spelled them out at its annual meeting. The Council represents eight major Jewish civic religious organizations and 76 local community relations agencies.

Its *"Joint Program Plan"* identified the *"struggle for racial equality (as) inseparable from the pursuit of equal rights for Jews and for all others in our society."* The recommendations were:

1. Jewish institutions (centers, family and child care agencies, hospitals, etc.) should admit members and accept clients *"free from racial distinctions."*
2. These institutions should buy equipment from firms that do not practice discrimination and should deal only with such contractors.
3. Organizations should invest funds in causes that help promote racial equality.
4. Meetings and other events should be held at places that observe policies free of racial prejudice.
5. Employers and realtors should practice equality of treatment and opportunity.
6. Equality of access to schools should continue to get high priority.

Aaron Goldman, chairman of the Council, states that the Jewish community must place *"its intelligence and resources equally behind the effort to convert equality of opportunity into actual equality of participation in all the benefits of our society."*

Some local churches are doing a tremendous job on several fronts at the same time. In Atlanta, the Wheat Street Baptist

Church, under the leadership of the Reverend Dr. William Holmes Borders, is really pioneering. The church has built on what used to be a 22-acre slum a 520-unit apartment development with a swimming pool and a nursery for working mothers. For years the church has operated a nursery school that employs thirty full-time teachers. It also has a credit union to help its parishioners avoid the clutches of the loan sharks.

The church has built a shopping center complex a block away from its edifice. The key element is a supermarket to provide low-cost food for residents of the development, to give employment to church members and serve as an outlet for produce of the church's farm. Also included in the center are a laundry and record, beauty, bakery, and other shops. One innovation is a "cleanup" facility that has twelve showers. Here, men and women just back from their day's work can bathe, change out of their dirty clothes, and set out for the evening in one quick, convenient stop.

Reverend Borders was a leader in the movement to desegregate buses in Atlanta and worked for the desegregation of other public facilities and schools there. He sees these far-reaching projects of his church as a logical sequel to and outgrowth of the demonstration phase of the civil rights movement.

St. Louis' Presbyterian Interracial Council has been carrying on a grass-roots fact-finding project that has real dollars-and-cents practical meaning. There have been accusations and suspicions that chain groceries in the city charged higher prices in Negro neighborhoods than in white. The Council checked twelve basic grocery items in both Negro and white areas and found that there was no consistent case to prove this. In fact, the contrary seemed to be the case: there were more instances of higher prices in grocery stores in white areas, presumably because they frequently have higher overhead.

The dedicated efforts of the Reverend Henry J. Browne

in Manhattan's Upper West Side resulted in the City of New York building a low-income housing project on a "human scale." Father Browne and the Strycker's Bay Neighborhood Council of residents of the area waged a six-year campaign to avoid the "typical, sprawling, high-rise projects that look more like prisons than apartment houses."

The project is one of seven in a $24 million program which is part of an overall urban renewal project for the area. The building contains seventy apartments in a nine-story structure of plain-faced brick. The design allows the building to blend in with its neighboring buildings and instead of some grandiose memorial title, the apartment is known simply as 120 West 94 Street.

Thus the Negro, Puerto Rican, and poor white who occupy the building live among middle-class Americans who are in the buildings in the immediate area. They will not be reghettoized in some newly completed 400-family complex of brick and steel. And their experience in pressing the city government and its departments for this project will serve them well in speaking up for their future needs. The quarterback of the campaign, as well as spiritual leader of the neighborhood, Father Browne, deserved and received recognition from the mayor and borough president of Manhattan when 120 West 94 Street was dedicated.

Two Philadelphia Methodist churches merged in response to the desegregation policy adopted in May 1965 by the Philadelphia Methodist Conference. The old Negro Delaware Methodist Conference was abolished. As a result, the all-Negro Community Methodist Church of 301 members and the 75 per cent white Sayers Memorial Church merged into one body, with a communion service to mark the occasion.

Friendship House, a Catholic laymen's center in Chicago, dedicated to improving race relations, brings white Catholic seminarians from the east and midwest to week-long workshops. Part of the experience includes living in the houses of

Chicago Negro families, seeing firsthand Negro Districts of the city, visiting various projects and taking part in discussions and programs. The education director of the Center, Thomas Cook, has designed the program to make the seminarians more aware of "the profound social problems in our society" and involve them in ways for which their formal schooling does not provide.

The "other side of the coin" was the action of St. Thomas Episcopal Church in Philadelpha. Its members voted unanimously to desegregate. Since 1796 the church operated on a charter that limited membership to "Africans and descendants of the African race."

In Long Island, New York, fraternal, civic, political, and religious organizations joined hands under the banner "We Don't Burn Churches—We Build Them."

The groups raised more than $20,000 with a round of raffles, breakfasts, dinners, theater parties, solicitations, and donations. The money was used to build a new church for the 250 Negro Baptists of Long Beach, Long Island, who have been worshiping for twelve years in a converted garage that was dingy and leaky. The drive was interracial and included the Kiwanis, Lions, Masons, Elks, B'Nai B'rith, and NAACP.

The Southern Christian Leadership Conference launched a program called VISION. Its goal was to put one hundred tutors in ten Alabama cities to help fifteen hundred youngsters. Working with kids in the high school grades, the VISION tutors aimed to help them with remedial education to prepare them for college entrance exams.

This humanitarian concern is finding echoes in many parts of the land. For instance, during a recent Christmas holiday northern students from Oberlin and Yankton colleges and the University of Massachusetts spent their respite from books with carpenters' tools in hand. They went to Ripley,

Mississippi to rebuild a church burned by bigots during the summer. Faculty members from the three colleges went also. And, to round out the picture, some $36,000 was raised by the interracial, interfaith Committee of Concern in Mississippi to help rebuild the churches burned during the summer. There were fifty-four "unsolved" church burnings in that state in one year alone, so both students and fund-raisers had their work cut out for them.

Another glimmer of light, thanks to enlightened action by the trustees of Methodist-supported Millsaps College, came when the school announced that all qualified students would be accepted regardless of race. Millsaps thus became the first all-white college in Mississippi to lower racial barriers voluntarily. It did so with this statement: "The college cannot remain unresponsive to the call of the church for an end to discrimination and for the opening of its facilities to qualified persons in a spirit of Christian concern for all men."

Just for counterpoint, at about this same time the South Carolina Baptist Convention vetoed by a vote of 905 to 575 a plan to open its three colleges to all. The schools are Furman University in Greenville, Anderson Junior College in Anderson, and North Greenville Junior College in Tigerville. The vote came about because Furman trustees decided in 1964 to admit all comers, regardless of race. The action was held up pending the Convention deliberation, which killed it. (By 1968 even this policy had changed. Furman and Anderson had admitted a combined total of twelve Negro students.)

Yet, the direction signals must be clear to those willing to see them for what they are:

The General Assembly of the United Presbyterian Church of the U.S.A. elected as its Moderator the Reverend Dr. Edler G. Hawkins, distinguished churchman who happens to be a Negro. The Moderator is the spiritual leader of the Presbyterians.

The Methodist Church in the U.S. named as president of the Council of Bishops of the Church, Bishop Prince A. Taylor, a church leader who happens to be a Negro. The Council President is titular head of the 10,300,000 member Methodist Church.

From these examples, it seems to me, we get a flavor of the kind of action the churchmen and their flocks are capable and willing to take these days, to witness for brotherhood. Many of the congregations are joining hands with other organizations to carry out valuable, energizing operations in their communities.

Religious Resources

The League in more than forty cities in the nation has religious resources committees striving to confront and involve their communities.

The emphasis is on "faith in action." It seeks to move religious groups and individuals to translate their beliefs into concrete terms. The themes that run through this activity are these:

Religious citizens are morally responsible for following the religious teachings on brotherhood, respect for individuals, and obligation to God in their daily lives.

Social patterns should be altered through planned and implemented programs.

Church, temple, and synagogue members pledge themselves to help bring about and to follow through on nonsegregated community life.

Acting on these basics, the committees ask men and women to examine the specifics of racial problems in their communities. They urge citizens to help through such activities as:

improving the books and educational aids used in the schools.

backing and working for passage of civil rights and other legislation.

speaking out publicly in favor of Supreme Court Decisions on desegregating the schools, student sit-ins, etc.

opening their congregations to all men.

writing letters to elected officials and the news media about public issues; to radio and TV stations commending constructive programs; to stores and business places, endorsing fair employment practices.

conducting and making public the findings of surveys of local problems.

helping in housing surveys, open occupancy projects, clearinghouse activities that list available housing, etc.

participating in marches of concern.

organizing home visits to elderly and ill.

operating day care centers for children of working mothers.

participating in tutoring, higher horizons, adult education programs in the community.

outreaching into the community with forums, programs, workshops and institutes. (These can be espe-

cially helpful when, for instance, pastors and parish-
ioners may both be confronted simultaneously and
publicly with actual situations that, by themselves, each
would duck by blaming the other for unreadiness to
act.)

Time after time, the League office has learned about situations in various cities where the church leaders and the civil
rights movement are not in communication. The League's
emphasis on the religious resources activity is intended to
minimize this unfortunate situation. There is so much to be
done that we must eliminate duplication and half-strength
efforts in every possible way. Coordination and cooperation
of religious and civil rights leadership activities can help to
make these efforts more effective by improving efficiency.

Raison d'Être

We might speculate about why the church has come to life
so dramatically in recent years. But basically we probably
would conclude that most denominations have been seeking
for some time ways to relate religion to life in our modern
world. The social significance of religious teaching and
preaching has been too long on the theoretical plane. It kept
warm on the back burner in men's minds through weekly—
or less frequent—rekindling by the local minister. But it was
a Sunday phenomenon, isolated and unrelated to everyday life.
Few of the clergy and all too few of their flocks were stirred
to carry the great Judeo-Christian teachings into practice.

Dean Liston Pope of the Yale Divinity School puts it this
way: "The church has lagged behind the Supreme Court
as the conscience of the nation on the question of race, and
it has fallen far behind trade unions, factories, schools, department stores, athletic gatherings and most other human as-

sociations, as far as the achievement of integration in its own life is concerned."

It was churchmen such as he who came together in 1963 at the historic National Conference on Religion and Race. This epochal meeting brought together 657 delegates from all over the country under the auspices of the National Council of Churches of Christ, the Synagogue Council of America and the National Catholic Welfare Conference.

The delegates issued "An Appeal to the Conscience of the American People" after three days of discussion. In this they described racism as the most serious evil facing the nation, and backed the Supreme Court's antisegregation decisions and nonviolent protests. They also charged Americans to "seek a reign of justice in which voting rights and equal protection of the law will be everywhere enjoyed; public facilities and private ones serving a public purpose will be accessible to all; equal education and cultural opportunities, hiring and promotion, medical and hospital care, open occupancy in housing will be available to all."

Moreover, the Appeal challenged Americans "to work, to pray, and to act courageously in the cause of human equality and dignity while there is still time, to eliminate racism permanently and decisively, to seize the historic opportunity the Lord has given us for healing an ancient rupture in the human family, to do this for the glory of God."

No doubt this ringing call to action was an important factor in the upsurge of church activity for integration. I doubt that there is a parish or congregation in the nation that has ignored the Civil Rights struggle.

Act Now

What can you and your church do? Of course the actions reviewed earlier in this chapter should spark some ideas, but just to sum up, let's consider some avenues for action.

First of all, it makes sense to talk with other members of your congregation and seek out like-minded individuals who are willing to move from talk to deeds. Surely you should be concerned about any shortage of Negro parishioners. Reaching out to find them may be required. Church socials are still very much a part of the American way of life, and inviting Negro families to them would be a logical way to introduce them to the congregation and vice versa. Surely your own ingenuity will dictate many other ways to solve this "problem."

Look at the structure of your church organization. Are Negroes represented in it? Do you have deacons, electors, elders, sextons, readers, wardens, vergers, or whatever, who are black? Is there some valid reason if the answer is no?

Isn't it possible for your congregation to take actions such as those outlined earlier:

> voter registration and education campaigns
> preschool programs
> tutoring, teaching, and vocational counseling
> adult literacy and education
> consumer education
> youth programs and recreation

Let me suggest two more projects that may lie within your grasp, projects that can mean new lives for your Negro fellow citizens. The first is sponsorship of housing units, whether new or renovated. If your church will play a part in breaking the housing logjam that corrals Negro citizens off from American life, it can work a minor miracle. And that's what religion is about, isn't it?

Second, can your congregation manage to operate a day care center where Negro women can take advantage of it? The lack of such day care facilities locks untold thousands of

Negro women into a life of dependency. Unable to leave their youngsters, they cannot work to provide for them. Day care centers can release these mothers to earn their own way and escape from relief rolls.

We spoke about economic pressure. Will your congregation take a stand and follow through? Will it see that church purchases and hiring are predicated on strictly nondiscriminatory bases? Will they endorse boycotts of merchants or products manufactured by producers who are not doing their part?

How about other major steps? Is the congregation willing to see that the bank where it keeps its funds is integrated? Will the congregation move to have the bank use its power to advance open housing by encouraging developers as well as extending mortgages to Negroes? Will it urge the bank to help Negro businessmen to get financing for new and expanding small business operations? Will it put in a good word to aid Negro youngsters to secure college loans from the bank? Or can it take up the extension of such loans as one of its own projects?

Many churches are involved in secular life in a constructive and very large way. You may wish to analyze, with fellow parishioners, just how your church is doing as an operator of things such as recreational facilities for youth and adults; preschools, schools, and colleges; housing; homes for the aged and/or indigent; summer camps; and hospitals. I don't believe at this point in our discussion it is necessary to spell out what to look for or how to tackle oversights or glaring omissions. Men of good will cannot blink the shortcomings of organizations and activities that make up the fabric of their lives, for these will determine the futures of their children and their children's children.

The fight for Negro rights has truly given religious leaders a galvanizing cause in which they and their flocks can witness to their beliefs in all those pious words that for so long were simply platitudes. Now, all over the nation, congregations and their leaders have jumped into the civil rights struggle with both feet and their actions speak louder than their platitudes ever did.

Is your congregation witnessing with its platitudes or its feet?

Chapter 12

The Joiners

America is a nation of joiners as well as doers. Has there ever been a country whose people so avidly joined organizations? Or started new ones so freely and enthusiastically?

Think about your own memberships. Most likely you belong to more organizations than you realize. Most Americans belong to a church, temple, or religious organization. And most of us belong to political parties. Many of us have memberships in social clubs or recreational groups, business associations, service clubs, women's organizations for everything from cooking to social service, from Cub Scouts and Campfire Girls to the League of Women Voters. And there are many varieties of youth-building and educational activities such as the Y's, Boys Clubs of America, Parent-Teacher Associations, local libraries, historical societies, and cultural associations.

The range is infinite. Their purposes and their power may be inconsequential, or they may be key forces in the community. They may be forces for good, as our churches, or for evil, as the notorious Ku Klux Klan and American Nazi Party.

The American who is seriously concerned about his country and making it a stronger, more healthy nation will find it a natural thing to analyze what he might do through the organizations to which he belongs. Without question much can be done through formal program activities of organizations as well as informally through their ongoing practices.

Reaching Out

The agency that today fails to reach out will probably be swept aside by new programs launched by public or other private organizations to meet the clamoring needs. Such agencies are likely to find the needy suddenly demanding their services. In many cities the Urban League and other groups are telling the deprived people what is available and urging them to make use of such resources.

As Vigdor Gross, former associate director of the St. Paul Urban League, says, "Agencies sometimes do not reach out in terms of time, place, and services to potential clients. As a result their services are underutilized or not even known." The St. Paul Urban League decided to change this pattern by involving local agencies in a "community fair." As co-sponsors they lined up the Ober Boys Club and Hallie Q. Brown Community House, located in the part of St. Paul where most Negroes live.

The goals of the fair were several:

To inform, educate, and encourage people to use the resources of the community and to urge their friends and relatives to do so.

To enlist citizens in prevention and early detection of disease and to be more responsible for their own health.

To publicize the services of many agencies that were virtually unknown to the general public (because of small budgets, for instance).

To help agencies discover unmet needs.

Gross and his associates knew only too well that Negro citizens were overlooking many community resources. One index of this is the fact that cancer of the breast and uterus is consistently the number one cause of death among Negro women. Among the reasons for this are the lack of understanding about early signs of cancer and ignorance about regular checkups. As Vigdor points out, "Many Negroes were and are hesitant about utilizing agency services because of deprivations, inequalities, and exclusions which they have suffered."

The Fair was held on a weekend in April. It was publicized widely in the press, on radio and TV, with posters in stores, churches, and schools and handbills delivered by local Boy Scouts to homes. Announcements were made in classrooms, PTA newsletters, neighborhood newspapers and churches. During the two days of the Fair a car with loudspeaker cruised through the neighborhood periodically urging people to "come on over."

One key target group was senior citizens. Social workers alerted their clients, notices were posted on bulletin boards in housing developments and included in a senior citizen newsletter. Free bus rides brought senior citizens to the Fair the first day. Nearly two hundred oldsters attended. They talked with a Social Security Administration representative, had free chest X-rays and free diabetes tests, viewed films and ate and drank free refreshments.

There was something for each of the other age groups also. Thirty-two health, adult education, and welfare agencies gave tests, made demonstrations, showed exhibits, handed out literature, and answered inquiries in twenty-six booths. In the auditorium films and entertainment alternated with demonstrations on a round-the-clock basis. There were three mobile units and a camping demonstration in the front yard of the community center. Free refreshments, door prizes, a first-aid mobile unit, and an information booth rounded out the Fair attractions.

As frosting on the cake, the Fair was opened with a ribbon-cutting ceremony by the mayor and this was televised over local TV stations and covered by local papers. Local celebrities from the Winter Carnival and professional football team also were present (one of the gridiron stars was a co-chairman of the event and publicized it widely beforehand).

What was the result? More than three thousand citizens of the community attended the Fair. Fifty agencies participated and one hundred people planned, manned, and fanned interest in the Fair. It was a break-through in two directions: the agencies, with professional and lay volunteers, had made a "beachhead" in the community on an unprecedented basis; and potential users learned about services they never dreamed existed, or feared were too expensive or too remote.

Reaching out makes all the difference. The agency that stretches out its hand in the ghetto can be a true lifesaver.

The Cost of Success

One day in June the New York *Times* ran an article headed "8 Youths Charged with Bomb-Making." It told about the arrest of eight youngsters on the roof of a deserted Harlem building. They were making Molotov Cocktails to use on the West 123 Street police station. These boys were sixteen and seventeen years old.

The Urban League of Greater New York carried on an outreaching pioneering project aimed at just such youngsters. Called "Success Center," it consisted of a street-level, storefront school for dropouts aged sixteen to eighteen. Its purpose was to return youths to school to get their high school diplomas. Where this was not possible, the Center counseled the youngster on training opportunities and career planning for jobs suited to his abilities and interests.

It was a costly project, requiring $75,000 a year from New York State and $10,000 annually from the League, because it encompassed casework interview, psychological testing, and vocational assessment to begin with. Then, depending on the youth's needs, vocational guidance, group and individual counseling (sometimes with the parents), remedial reading and math, job counseling about opportunities available and job placement were used. For some there was a work stipend or prejob training program with a weekly twenty dollars for twenty hours of work.

The remedial math and reading are so essential that for many youngsters no sensible plan could be designed until they had completed these parts of the program. And the results were sometimes phenomenal. One boy jumped from second-grade reading level to eighth-grade level. He was thereby enabled to return to school.

The pre-job training phase was a very valuable part of the activity: for twelve weeks the youngster would be assigned to serve as assistant to a regular staff member of some nonprofit organization. These ranged from the local "Y" to social agencies and community centers. In this way they learned the fundamentals of what is expected of people who work, in terms of attendance, grooming, job responsibility, and cooperation with supervisors and co-workers. They also attended weekly group meetings at the Success Center to discuss their experiences. And they were coached in the elements of filling out job applications and behavior during a job interview.

What did the community get for spending untold man hours and $255,000 over a period of three years?

More than four hundred youngsters were set on their feet and started on their way to responsible, rewarding citizenship. Most of these youths are now tax-paying rather than tax-draining members of the community.

The prognosis for careers for dropouts is so dismal that the Department of Labor estimates they are doomed to dependency, or, if that word offends you, to reliance on welfare for their subsistence. This, says the Department, costs the community $1000 per head per year and may last fifty years, or more per person. As a conservative estimate, call it forty years at $1000 per year per person. Those four hundred youngsters who cost society $255,000 as teenagers, would have cost society *$16,000,000 plus* by their sixtieth birthdays! That's a fantastic saving. And, of course, it doesn't reflect the gain from taxes on the income produced by these people as workers, or the contributions to society they may make in their vocations and extracurricular activities.

If the economic reasons for the antipoverty war were obscure to some, this kind of example should help clear away the fog. The humanitarian reasons should have been obscure to none.

Agencies Shape Lives

Many organizations have for many years done wonders with youths in helping them become productive citizens. I think our scouting, "Y's", 4-H, Future Farmers, girls and boys clubs have been absolutely marvelous in helping youth—as far as they went. The best of them have been limited only by budget and staff. I happen to be particularly proud of the Boys Clubs, for I have had a lifelong association with the Madison Square Boys' Club.

This 108-year-old agency operates in three boroughs of New York City and runs a summer camp as well. It is much more than the name might imply, however, for it is not simply a place where the kids come to have a few games and then take off. It is a place where nearly five thousand boys a year have a chance to explore avocational and vocational skills.

As my long-time friend Lawrence Weill, associate director of the Club puts it, recreation is the fundamental activity of the Club, the thing that attracts the kids. But the Club offers a "cafeteria approach" in which there are all sorts of exciting activities to sample, with the encouragement of staff and volunteer workers: photography, rifle marksmanship, stamp and coin collecting, crafts, cabinet work and carpentry, metal work and auto and aviation mechanics, debating, even preparation for College Board exams.

The transformations wrought in youngsters' lives by this agency that I know so well are similar to those achieved by other agencies. One typical success that I vividly recall was with a boy called Tommy. He was disturbed, mad at the world and himself, and so self-destructive that he literally used to gouge chunks of flesh out of his face with his fingernails when he was angry. He was a borderline juvenile delinquent—he hadn't been caught.

Tommy came to the Club at first out of curiosity. He began by deriding the place, the staff, the kids who use the facilities. But coming to the Club became a habit, and, seeing others learning photography, art, and crafts, he somehow became interested in art. He joined the painting group and really pitched in. In fact he had some talent, and painted some very competent pictures.

One day Tommy took one of his oil paintings home to his mother, who suffered from rheumatism. This was such a bombshell to the old lady that she scurried down four flights of stairs in agony with the picture under her arm to ask at the Club if Tommy had stolen it!

Tommy had been able to relate to the positive aspects of society at the club. He had had warm, sympathetic encouragement from knowledgeable, skilled instructors—both staff and volunteer—and had gained respect and approval from his peers by constructive achievement. Previously he had taken the destructive route to impress his pals and flaunt society and family.

To succeed with boys like Tommy, agencies need great patience, professional skill in depth, and a pool of dedicated, talented volunteers. If you have the time and the qualifications you can "save lives" too, by volunteering to help.

Profile of Volunteers

Larry Weill has some excellent pointers for volunteers, pointers that are valid for most youth-serving and many adult-service agencies. Volunteers, says Larry, should analyze themselves and decide what they want to do, what they have enthusiasm for, and see how this fits the needs of the agency and the people it serves. He has found that those volunteers who stay with it are getting something out of the volunteer activity—perhaps they find satisfying relationships with the individuals they are working with, for instance.

Bringing together volunteers who have usable skills is, Larry quips, like gathering nuts: finding nuts on photography, basketball, stamps, etc. These people are so wrapped up with their special interests that they can't wait to interest others in them.

Volunteers are needed to give kids a sense of their own worth by building their confidence. They don't need another person to tell them what's wrong with them—they get plenty of that at home, school, and from the denizens of their neighborhoods. Volunteers can help the youngsters discover their good points and convince them of their self-worth. All kinds of workers are needed. For instance, volunteers have to be good listeners. Too many kids have never had an adult they can respect take time to listen to them. And people who can relate to the lonely ones, the quiet kids who are withdrawn, are much needed.

Often, Larry finds, volunteers miss some of the key signals. For instance, a kid will say, "Boy, I hate to dance. Do I ever hate to dance!" Fundamentally, Larry points out, this is a signal that the boy would like to dance, if he knew how. That's the challenge to the volunteer's ingenuity.

And some of the seemingly most discouraging experiences can be real indications of progress. One that happens often enough to be common is the case where one of the youngsters will tell a worker (staff member or volunteer—it happens to both) to "go to hell." As Larry so shrewdly observes, this seeming insult is actually an indication that the worker has built up a relationship with the boy to the point that the kid expects to continue it. It is evidence that the boy knows the worker well enough to say this and still maintain the relationship.

If that experience doesn't discourage a volunteer, he must really possess missionary zeal. Such dedication is extremely valuable. Also, he must identify with the youths he's working with, in the sense, perhaps, that "there, but for the grace of God, go I." He must be confident, in addition, that in his experience or training he has learned some of the answers and can therefore help his "clients."

For instance, the volunteer must have enough confidence as well as wit and humor to cope with the kid who resists and rejects and seems deliberately to make the whole situation seem absolutely hopeless. Larry always tells about arriving with a trainload of boys at Brewster, New York, the train station for the Club's summer camp. And, as the boys start to file off one of them starts bawling and hanging on to the seat, the door, the handle, anything he can grab. And through the screeching and wailing he yowls, "I hate camp! This is the lousiest camp in New York! In the U.S.! The food's awful! I hate this camp!" And, of course, he's nine miles from even seeing the camp for the first time.

The volunteer has to find out what good attributes there

are in the youngster, in spite of how difficult he makes it for
you. And he must be prepared to work without thanks from
the kid he is trying to help. The rewards, remarks Larry, in
terms of recognition (expressed) are not likely. In fact, the
tougher the case, the less likely, for the essence of the worker's success is that the kid should believe he "made it" himself.
For if the youngster believes he achieved only with help, his
dependency is continued and his confidence is still inadequate.
After all, the volunteer serves, in many respects, as a parent
substitute, particularly in setting goals and convincing the kid
he can reach them.

Volunteers Wanted

Finding enough volunteers is like trying to fill a bucket with
a hole in it. You never really get enough to do the job as well
as you would like.

As an example, consider the possibilities at just one social
agency doing a specialized job in New York City. I am thinking about Spence-Chapin Adoption Service, which I know
reasonably well because of my wife's long association with it
as a volunteer. Just as there were times when she thought she
had been "widowed" by the National Urban League, there
have been more than a few moments when I thought home-
making was her part-time job and Spence-Chapin her full-
time activity. This kind of situation is almost unavoidable,
I am afraid, when one is a truly dedicated volunteer.

Anyway, Spence-Chapin is working in the terribly difficult, demanding, and discouraging area of adoptions, foster
home placement and services to unwed mothers.

It's amazing how many volunteers an agency needs and
can use. My wife Shirley and I sat down with Jane Edwards,
Executive Director of Spence-Chapin, and discussed this.

Here is the list of possibilities for volunteer effort at just this one agency:

Volunteers are needed for driving mothers to the agency, for taking children to outpatient clinics for examinations and care, thus relieving a trained nurse or caseworker for other duties.

Home care for pregnant, unwed mothers is needed, and volunteers could pitch in on this.

The agency itself needs volunteers to make clinical notes, dress and undress babies, etc. Nurses can do these things, of course, but taking the load off them means the agency can serve more children and adults.

One of the most unusual volunteer activities is serving as sponsor for the baptism of Catholic babies. This makes it possible for Spence-Chapin's legal secretary to continue her work typing up adoption papers rather than taking out two or three hours of the day to go to church and back. And it also relieves the adoptive parents of the task of finding sponsors.

Volunteers are needed on all of these fronts, in depth. Sound programming of agency efforts requires this, because of human fallibility and the inevitable problems of emergencies that arise in the volunteer's home making it impossible for him to do his job that particular day. When this happens, another volunteer has to be on tap.

Professional skills are in great demand, particularly among volunteers who serve on the board and committees. Men and women with skills in handling pension funds, in finance, in personnel work, social casework policy, legal and investment activities, fund-raising and benefit planning and execution—such people are urgently needed.

Agencies are always concerned, naturally, with succession

—the problem of continuity and keeping the organization functioning. Thus they want to build a pool of board members to provide for the future. One stepping stone to board membership is fund-raising activity. If you like to go out and convince people that they should support a worthy cause, fund-raising may be your cup of tea. Another aspect of fund-raising is planning and organizing benefit affairs. Perhaps this activity appeals to you—it can be of vital importance to the agency—and, of course, to those served by the agency.

The Volunteer

One primary message of this book is that volunteers can make the drive for civil rights succeed. It is pertinent to quote here Francis Kornegay's "six C's for volunteers." Mr. Kornegay, as executive director of the Detroit Urban League, is one of the most ebullient of civil rights workers, effervescing with enthusiasm and confidence. Volunteers, he says,

must have *Concern*. They must be deeply concerned about extending to others the benefits they themselves enjoy.

Concern dies quickly unless it is buttressed with *Commitment*; one must be willing to carry on the fight, regardless of the cost.

If one is concerned and committed, one will have the means for *Cooperating*. He will do things with others.

Coordination is more difficult. Ambitions and differing viewpoints often make coordination complicated, but this will become ever more important as the number of programs in progress multiplies. We must minimize overlap and waste motion as well as wasted expenditures.

Communication, the fifth item on the list, occurs at its best when volunteers have gone through the first four C's and have become so convinced and free of personal concerns that communication with others comes easily. As Kornegay says, one will find many means by which to tell his story to others and it is through such sharing of experience that what we are doing spreads and blossoms.

Criticism, positive, constructive criticism and the ability to accept it and benefit from it, is the final item on the list. "God gave us one mouth and two ears," says Kornegay. "Thus we should listen twice as much as we talk." We need to take the suggestions of others and capitalize on them.

I believe that there is a great deal of wisdom in what Kornegay says and I hope that volunteers will take it to heart. So doing, they will become even more effective and a better life for all our citizens will come about just that much faster.

As the U. S. Riot Commission concluded, time has run out for this nation to temporize about justice for Negro citizens. "Only a commitment to national action on an unprecedented scale," it stated unequivocally, "can shape a future compatible with the historic ideals of American society."

It is my hope that this small book will play a positive role in crystallizing the commitment of men of good will and in strengthening their determination to meet the inescapable, urgent needs of our country in its time of trial.

Appendix I

List of Organizations

The agencies listed below are sources of information, data, research reports, and/or assistance. Those marked with an asterisk (*) welcome volunteer help or can refer you to local organizations which do so.

A. Philip Randolph Institute, 217 West 125 Street, New York, N.Y.

ACT, 765 East Oakwood, Chicago, Ill.

AFL-CIO Department of Civil Rights, 815 16 Street N.W., Washington, D.C.

American Civil Liberties Union, 156 Fifth Avenue, New York, N.Y.

American Friends Service Committee*, 160 North 15 Street, Philadelphia, Pa.

Anti-Defamation League of B'nai B'rith, 315 Lexington Avenue, New York, N.Y.

Chamber of Commerce of the U.S., Human Resources Development Group, 1615 M Street N.W., Washington, D.C.

Congress of Racial Equality*, 200 West 135 Street, New York, N.Y.

Interracial Council for Business Opportunity*, 110 East 23 Street, New York, N.Y.

National Association for the Advancement of Colored People* (NAACP), 20 West 40 Street, New York, N.Y.

National Association of Manufacturers, 277 Park Avenue, New York, N.Y.

NAACP Legal Defense and Educational Fund, 10 Columbus Circle, New York, N.Y.

National Committee Against Discrimination in Housing*, 325 Lexington Avenue, New York, N.Y.

National Conference of Christians & Jews, 43 West 57 Street, New York, N.Y.

National Council on Aging, 49 West 45 Street, New York, N.Y.

National Council of Negro Women, 1346 Connecticut Avenue N.W., Washington, D.C.

National Council of Churches, Commission on Religion and Race*, 475 Riverside Drive, New York, N.Y.

National Industrial Conference Board, 845 Third Avenue, New York, N.Y.

National Urban League*, 55 East 52 Street, New York, N.Y.

Opportunities Industrialization Center*, 1225 North Broad Street, Philadelphia, Pa.

Southern Christian Leadership Conference*, 334 Auburn Avenue N.E., Atlanta, Ga.

Southern Regional Council, 5 Forsyth Street N.W., Atlanta, Ga.

United Church Women*, 475 Riverside Drive, New York, N.Y.

Urban Coalition*, 1815 H Street N.W., Washington, D.C. (local offices in major cities)

Young Men's Christian Association, Interracial Commission of the, National Board, 291 Broadway, New York, N.Y.

Young Men's & Young Women's Hebrew Association, 92 Street and Lexington Avenue, New York, N.Y.

Young Women's Christian Association, Office of Racial Integration, National Board, 600 Lexington Avenue, New York, N.Y.

U. S. Government Agencies

Listed below are government agencies that are active in the civil rights picture and/or have major responsibility for programs in the field. Please remember that there are counterparts of these federal agencies in many states and cities today. Be sure to check in your locality.

United States Commission on Civil Rights

Department of Commerce (particularly Bureau of the Census for Facts)

Department of Health, Education and Welfare (including Office of Education, Public Health Service, National Institutes of Health, etc.)

Department of Housing and Urban Development (including Urban Renewal Administration)

Department of Labor (many job and training programs administered by the department; also Bureau of Labor Statistics for Facts)

Equal Employment Opportunity Commission

Department of Justice (in which is the Community Relations Service)

Appendix II

Reading List

Reference Works

Adams, Russell L. *Great Negroes, Past and Present*. Chicago, Ill.: Afro-American Publishing Co., 1964.

Davis, John P., ed. *The American Negro Reference Book*. Englewood Cliffs, N.J.: Prentice-Hall, 1966.

Ebony, eds. of. *The Negro Handbook*. Chicago: Johnson Publishing Co., 1966.

Marder, Noel N. *The Negro Heritage Library*. 20 vols. Yonkers, N.Y.

National Advisory Commission on Civil Disorders (the so-called Riot Panel), *Report of*. New York: E. P. Dutton & Co., 1968.

U. S. Civil Rights Commission. Publications, especially annual reports.

General

Bernstein, Saul. *Alternatives to Violence*. New York: Association Press, 1966.

Carmichael, Stokely, and C. V. Hamilton. *Black Power*. New York: Random House, 1967.

Clark, Kenneth B. *Dark Ghetto: Dilemmas of Social Power*. New York: Harper & Row, 1967.

Commission on Un-American Activities, U. S. House of Representatives. *The Present-day Ku Klux Klan Movement*. Washington, D.C.: U. S. Government Printing Office, December 1967.

Ellison, Ralph. *The Invisible Man*. New York: Random House, 1953.

Farmer, James. *Freedom—When?* New York: Random House, 1966.

Handlin, Oscar. *Fire-bell in the Night: the Crisis in Civil Rights.* Boston: Little, Brown & Co., 1964.

King, Martin Luther, Jr. *Where Do We Go From Here: Chaos or Community?* New York: Harper & Row, 1967.

————. *Why We Can't Wait.* New York: Harper & Row, 1964.

Morgan, Charles, Jr. *A Time to Speak.* New York: Harper & Row, 1964.

Powledge, Fred. *Black Power, White Resistance.* New York: World Publishing Co., 1967.

Young, Whitney, Jr. *To Be Equal.* New York: McGraw-Hill Book Co., 1964.

Education

Bloom, Benjamin S., Allison Davis, and Robert Hess. *Compensatory Education for Cultural Deprivation.* New York: Holt, Rinehart & Winston, 1965.

Buchheimer, Naomi and Arnold. *Equality Through Integration.* New York: Anti-Defamation League, 1966(?).

Clark, Kenneth B. *Prejudice and Your Child.* New York: Beacon Press, 1963.

Keppel, Francis. *The Necessary Revolution in American Education.* New York: Harper & Row, 1966.

NAACP Education Department. *Integrated School Books: a Descriptive Bibliography* (for preschool and elementary). New York: Association Press, 1966.

Noar, Gertrude. *The Teacher and Integration.* New York: National Education Association, 1965.

U. S. Commission on Civil Rights. *Racial Isolation in the Public Schools.* Washington, D.C.: U. S. Government Printing Office, 1967.

Pamphlets from the Anti-Defamation League:
   Guidelines for Testing Minority Group Children
   Human Relations in the Classroom
   Language Learning Activities for the Disadvantaged Child
   The Treatment of Minorities in Secondary School Textbooks

Health

Haughton, James G. *The Government's Role in Health Care, Past, Present and Future*. National Medical Association, 72d Annual Convention, St. Louis, Mo., 1967.

Rainwater, Lee. *And the Poor Get Children*. New York: Quadrangle, 1966.

History

DuBois, W. E. B. *Black Folks: Then and Now*. New York: Henry Holt & Co., 1939.

———. *The World and Africa*. New York: Viking Press, 1947.

Franklin, John Hope, and Isidore Starr, eds. *The Negro in Twentieth Century America*. New York: Vintage Books, 1967.

Freedman, Leon, ed. *The Civil Rights Reader*. New York: Walker & Co., 1967.

Ginzberg, Eli, and Alfred S. Eichner. *The Troublesome Presence: American Democracy and the Negro*. New York: The Free Press of Glencoe, 1964.

Housing

The Commission on Race and Housing (series). *Residence and Race; Property Values and Race; Privately Developed Interracial Housing; Studies in Housing and Minority Groups; The Demand for Housing in Racially Mixed Areas*. Berkeley: University of California Press, 1960.

Northwood, L. K., and Ernest A. T. Barth. *Urban Desegregation: Negro Pioneers and Their White Neighbors*. Seattle: University of Washington Press, 1965.

Taeuber, Alma F., and Karl E. *Negroes in Cities: Residential Segregation and Neighborhood Change*. Chicago: Aldine Publishing Co., 1965.

260 *Reading List*

Weaver, Robert C. *Dilemmas of Urban America*. Cambridge: Harvard University Press, 1965.

Pamphlets from Anti-Defamation League, National Committee Against Discrimination in Housing and National Urban League, including:

Urban Renewal Planning for Balanced Communities
Fair Housing Handbook
Ghettos, Property Rights and Myths
Citizens Action for Housing and Renewal
Residential Integration and Property Values
The Myths of Racial Integration

Jobs

Ginzberg, Eli, ed. *The Negro Challenge to the Business Community*. New York: McGraw-Hill Book Co., 1964.

Kothe, Charles A., ed. *A Tale of 22 Cities* (report on Title VII of the Civil Rights Act of 1964, compiled from N.A.M. seminars). New York: National Association of Manufacturers, 1965.

Marshall, Ray. *The Negro and Organized Labor*. New York: John Wiley & Sons, 1964.

Ross, A. M., and Herbert Hill, eds. *Employment, Race and Poverty*. New York: Harcourt, Brace & World, 1967.

Sociology

Frazier, E. Franklin. *The Negro Family in the U. S.* (revised edition). Chicago: University of Chicago Press, 1967.

———. *Negro Youth at the Crossways*. New York: Schocken Books, 1967.

Ginzberg, Eli and Associates. *The Middle Class Negro in the White Man's World*. New York: Columbia University Press, 1967.

Johnson, Charles S. *Growing Up in the Black Belt*. New York: Schocken Books, 1967.

President's Committee on Law Enforcement and Administration of
Justice. *The Challenge of Crime in a Free Society.* Washington,
D.C.: U. S. Government Printing Office, 1967.

U. S. Department of Labor, B.L.S. Report ⚹332. *Social and
Economic Conditions of Negroes in the U. S.,* October 1967.

Welfare

Elman, Richard M. *The Poorhouse State: The American Way of
Life on Public Assistance.* New York: Pantheon Books, 1967.

Wolfgang, Marvin E. *Crime and Race: Conception and Miscon-
ceptions.* New York: Institute of Human Relations Press, 1964.

Youngdahl, Benjamin E. *Social Action and Social Work.* New
York: Association Press, 1967.

For Young Readers

Young, Margaret B. *The First Book of American Negroes.* New
York: Franklin Watts, 1966.

Fast, Howard. *Freedom Road.* New York: Crown Publishers,
1964.

Bowen, David. *The Struggle Within: Race Relations in the United
States.* New York: W. W. Norton & Co., 1965.

Emery, Anne. *The Losing Game.* Philadelphia: Westminster Press,
1965.

Katzoff, Betty and Sy. *Cathy's First School.* New York: Alfred
A. Knopf, 1964.

Keats, Ezra J. *John Henry: an American Legend.* New York:
Pantheon Books, 1965.

Miers, Earl S. *The Story of the American Negro.* New York:
Grosset & Dunlap, 1965.

McCarthy, Agnes, and Lawrence D. Reddick. *Worth Fighting
For: a History of the Negro in the U. S. During the Civil War
and Reconstruction.* New York: Doubleday & Co., 1965.

Schechter, Betty. *The Peaceable Revolution.* Boston: Houghton
Mifflin Co., 1963.

Showers, Paul. *Your Skin and Mine.* New York: Thomas Y. Crowell Co., 1965.

Wier, Ester. *Easy Does It.* New York: Vanguard Press, 1965. (A Negro family moves to an all-white street.)

Films & Filmstrips

History of the American Negro Series, filmstrips, McGraw-Hill Book Co., New York, N.Y.: *From Africa to America; Slavery in the Young American Republic; Slavery in a House Divided; The Negro in Civil War and Reconstruction; The Negro in the Gilded Age; The Negro Faces the 20th Century; The Negro Fights for the Four Freedoms; The Threshold of Equality.*

 Willie Catches On. Film; 24 min.

 High Wall. Film; 32 min.

 What About Prejudice? Film; 12 min.

 Drop Out. Film; 27 min.

National Urban League, New York, N.Y.:

 From the Outskirts of Hope. Filmstrip. 28 min.

 The Road Ahead. Filmstrip. 28 min.

 (League films are available through Association Films, Inc., 347 Madison Avenue, New York, N.Y. 10017.)

Index